For Sonny

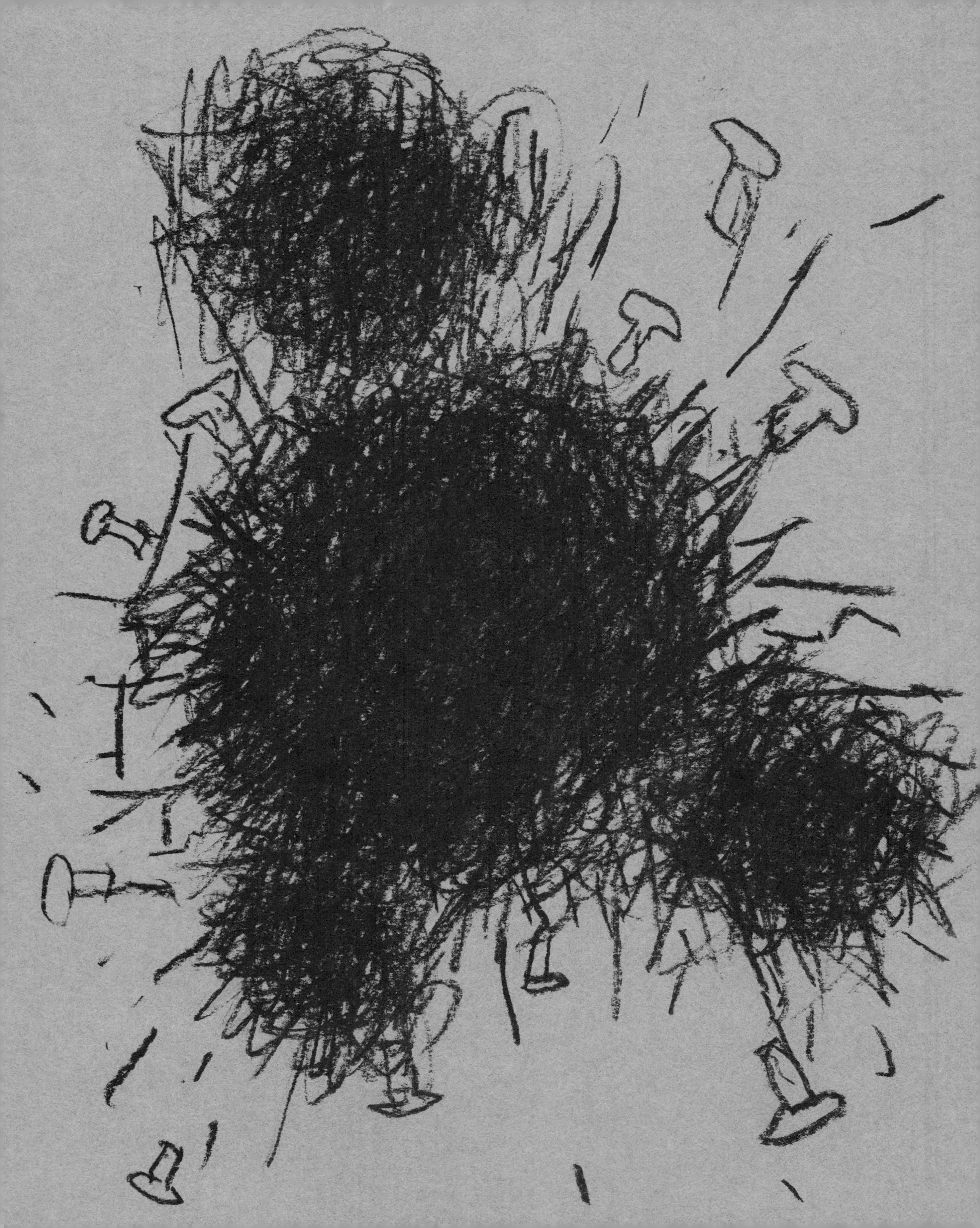

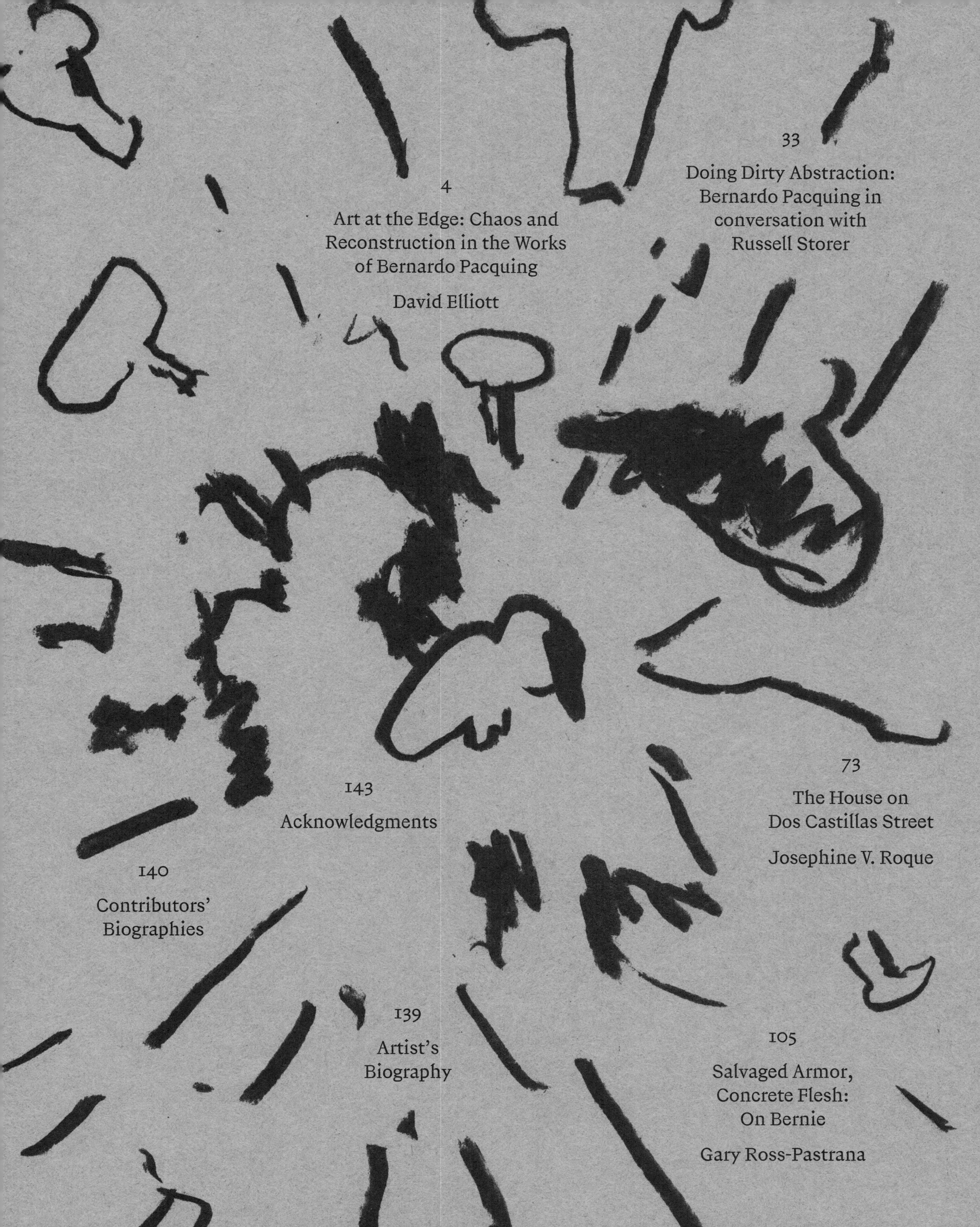

Art at the Edge: Chaos and Reconstruction in the Works of Bernardo Pacquing

David Elliott

Matrix

The sprawling collection of different islands, languages, religions, and cultures scattered across the Western Pacific that today constitute the Republic of the Philippines first grabbed the attention of the West in 1521 when Portuguese-Spanish explorer Ferdinand Magellan stopped off there during his voyage around the world. After a short break in the Kingdom of Cebu where, under the patronage of the local raja, he converted more than 2,000 of his subjects to Christianity, he moved, at the raja's suggestion, to the neighboring island of Mactan under the false impression that its leader would also embrace the new religion. Inadvertently, he had become ensnared in a bitter local feud, and the King of Mactan, along with his subjects, violently resisted his advance. After a standoff, Magellan decided to subdue them by force and was slaughtered in the ensuing battle.

Over the following decades, subsequent Spanish expeditions visited the islands, which—despite the prevalence of pirates, typhoons, and volcanic eruptions—were in 1543 named Las Islas Filipinas in honor of the future King Philip II of Spain. From 1565 on, colonization began in earnest with Mexico as a staging post for the occupation of the different islands. In 1571, the Spanish, supported by Latin American recruits and Filipino allies, attacked and occupied Maynila, then a vassal state of the Sultan of Brunei; they renamed it Manila and designated it the capital of a new grouping of colonies, the Spanish East Indies. With its territories consolidated under the administrative umbrella of the Mexico-based Viceroyalty of New Spain, the Philippines remained under Spanish rule for more than 300 years.[1] Spanish became its dominant language, alongside its many indigenous tongues, and Catholicism its state religion, in competition with Islam and local shamanistic beliefs. Today one of the world's most densely populated cities, Manila was then a fortified trading post for shipping spices, textiles, and exotic woods as well as an important conduit for trade with China.[2]

1. Mexico was the administrative "capital" of New Spain from which Spanish colonies in Latin America and Asia were governed. This entity was dissolved 1821 following the Mexican War of Independence, when Spanish rule was terminated in Mexico. The Philippines was then under direct, if more remote, Spanish rule.

2. All trade with Europe was directed back via Mexico, where land transportation westward across its narrow isthmus was considerably quicker than the longer sea route followed by the British and the Dutch.

As colonization incrementally progressed, Spanish traders, administrators, and soldiers settled in the newly fortified centers as did indigenous people attracted by work there, soon to be joined by Indios from Mexico and other Spanish Latin American colonies and by traders and settlers of Chinese origin; within this melting pot, people intermarried. Conversely, some Filipinos began to settle in Mexico, other parts of the Spanish East Indies, and Hispanic Latin America, where during the 19th century, revolutionary ideas from Europe, North America, and Mexico fostered preexisting resentment against the Spanish Empire and a growing desire for independence. In 1821, after the American Revolution, the French Revolution, the Napoleonic Wars, and eleven years of conflict and negotiation, Mexico declared its independence from Spain, and the effects began to reverberate eastward. Strong revolutionary sentiments, often supported by priests, began to proliferate within the Philippines, and in 1892, the Katipunan, a secret society devoted to the overthrow of Spanish rule, was founded in Manila. The authorities lashed back, imprisoning and executing anyone suspected of sedition.

From 1896 to 1902, Philippine independence was briefly and chaotically established against the background of Spain's war with America. What had started as a revolution against a demoralized colonial ruler intensified when the US defeated Spain and, without local consultation, demanded that its colonies—the Philippines, with Puerto Rico, Guam, and Cuba—be ceded to the US in the settlement. Outraged Filipino leaders refused to accept this, and the First Philippine Republic was born into a brutal conflict with America. After its defeat, the whole of the Philippines was effectively recolonized by the US.[3]

3. The Spanish–American War (April 21 – August 13, 1898). The US initially encouraged the Philippine Revolution in order to weaken the Spanish state; the withdrawal of this support culminated in the Philippine–American War (February 1899 – July 1902). The First Philippine (Malolos) Republic was declared between January 2, 1899, and July 4, 1902.

The United States' control of the Philippines continued until 1946, with the Japanese Imperial Army's invasion during World War II providing a brutal finale. After the end of the Pacific War, the severely ravaged Philippines became an independent democratic republic under US protection. Nearby, in Malaysia, Vietnam, and Korea, other neocolonial wars were being fought with direct US and European intervention, and the Philippines became a host for US military and naval bases with zones for the troops' "rest and recreation." At the same time, serious divisions resurfaced within Philippine society: the Maoist Communist Party, encouraged by the guerrilla resistance that had fought successfully against the Japanese, formed the New People's Army (NPA), and the newly established Moro National Liberation Front (MNLF) galvanized the long-standing grievances of the country's substantial Muslim communities, which began to agitate for an independent nation on the southern island of Mindanao.

These political tensions culminated in an escalation of violence throughout the country that in 1972 provided President Ferdinand Marcos with a perfect pretext to end democratic rule by the declaration of martial law (1972–81). Torture and extrajudicial killings became increasingly common, and many political opponents, protestors, journalists, and students were assassinated, while others disappeared or were forced into exile. All dissent was brutally stifled to be replaced by the thin oligarchic veneer of Marcos's "New Society."

Chaotic Energy

Bernardo Pacquing was born in 1967, the fifth, penultimate child of devoutly Catholic parents, in Tarlac City, capital of a powerful province on the northern island of Luzon; his former war veteran father was a government analyst, and his mother was a ballet dancer. At the time of his birth, a Communist insurgency was taking place in the province where the governor was Ninoy Aquino, a vehement critic of the Marcos regime and an opposition figurehead.[4] To extract him from this violent and chaotic situation, as well as to relieve pressure on an already large family, one-year-old Bernardo was sent 1,200 kilometers south to live with his mother's parents in the colonial town of Ozamiz on the north coast of the island of Mindanao. In this more stable, bucolic environment, surrounded by mountains and farmlands, he attended Catholic primary and secondary schools and began to take pleasure in drawing. Suddenly, in 1982, because of the increasingly violent activities of the Moro National Liberation Front, he was moved to Manila to finish his education. There, in the family's ancestral home in the downtown district of Sampaloc, he was reunited with his father and siblings.[5] Although he recalls being happy in Mindanao, Pacquing's memories of the island focus on its religious sectarianism in addition to the dangers posed by the guns and assault rifles that were readily available in the markets and streets.[6]

4. Arrested soon after the imposition of martial law, Ninoy Aquino (1932–1983) went on a hunger strike and was sentenced to death; following international pressure, his sentence was later commuted to imprisonment. After a severe heart attack in 1980, he was allowed to travel to the US for medical treatment. He stayed there and began again to criticize the Marcos regime. As the political situation deteriorated in the Philippines, he decided to return home in 1983 to face Marcos and call for democratic elections. On his return, he was immediately assassinated at Manila International Airport. This catapulted his widow, Corazon Aquino (1933–2009), into the political limelight, and in 1986, she successfully ran as the eleventh President of the Philippines for a six-year term as head of the United Nationalist Democratic Organization (UNIDO) party. In 2010, the couple's son Benigno Aquino III (1960–2021) became the fifteenth President of the Philippines (2010–16).

5. His mother was then trying to reopen the ballet school she had established in Ozamiz, but she abandoned the idea as a result of the violence that had driven Bernardo to Manila.

6. Unless stated otherwise, biographical information and quotations by Pacquing were derived from two Zoom interviews conducted on July 7 and 14, 2023, respectively, as well as subsequent clarifying emails.

The cultural shock of moving suddenly, at age fifteen, from a small, provincial town to a lower-middle-class community in the seething megalopolis of Manila, provoked a sense within him of awe and excitement. He discovered there a vast new city with its stench, mess, dark underpasses, drugs, and street gangs, and was particularly struck by the marks and textures of its constantly repainted walls, stained by human traffic: grime, graffiti, urine, and spit. All this mixed with the control, precision, balance, and grace of the performing arts that occupied so much of his family's time and energy. Three members of his family already worked professionally as classical musicians and ballet dancers, and he began to take violin lessons from his oldest brother, the beginning of his lifelong engagement with this instrument.[7] His fascination also turned back to everyday things, to the dereliction of the old buildings in his neighborhood and the "tidemarks" left on their walls by fire and floods. His interest in music now exploded to include pop, rock, and punk—also manifestations of chaotic energy.[8]

7. When talking about his paintings and three-dimensional works, Pacquing still ironically describes himself as a "frustrated violinist." His brother performed regularly with the Philippine Philharmonic Orchestra, the Philippine Symphony Orchestra, and the Manila Chamber Ensemble. His sister and an older brother were both dancers with the Ballet Philippines. Many musical analogies and subjects appear throughout Pacquing's work, and in the catalogue of his 2022 exhibition "Disquietude," at Silverlens in Manila, he provided an extensive "lockdown" playlist of different genres of classical and popular music he was listening to while making the work on view.

8. Pacquing mentions The Clash, The Cars, and The Cure as bands that he particularly appreciated at this time.

Before graduating from secondary school in 1982, Pacquing had decided that he wanted to study fine art at the nearby University of the Philippines (UP), but he realized that he would need a gap year in order to prepare for its entrance examination. He was accepted to start in 1984; however, his father insisted that he should major in the vocational study of visual communications rather than the less practical field of fine arts.[9] Accordingly, Pacquing finessed the best of both possible worlds by enrolling in the former course while also taking elective classes in the studio arts department. Here, he recalls encountering "a remediated view of chaos and confusion in terms of the divergent ideologies and diverse sensibilities that triggered discourse among free-thinking students. My awareness, curiosity, and sense of inquiry grew exponentially, and I believe that this is when my creativity awoke in earnest."[10] At the same time, he encountered conceptual artist, teacher, and curator Roberto Chabet, a professor there who became a vital and continuing source of encouragement and inspiration for his work.[11]

9. The study of visual communications in editorial design included elements of graphic design, calligraphy, illustration, and photography as well as some art history and theory.

10. See note 6.

11. Pacquing describes Roberto Chabet (1937–2013) as "a teacher and friend who gave me the inspiration to be different." Between 1995 and 2011, Pacquing's work appeared in 13 separate group exhibitions curated by Chabet in Manila and Singapore.

After completing his thesis in 1989, to make ends meet, Pacquing accepted a position as a designer at the Cultural Center of the Philippines (CCP) in Manila, a concrete "arts palace" built by the Marcoses in the 1960s. He quit this job in 1992, ostensibly to restore his family's old house in Manila, but with the real intention of establishing himself as an artist. By this time, his mother and father had emigrated to the US, settling in Los Angeles, while other family members had moved to different parts of the country. Ravaged by two fires, the family home was in a terrible state, but he regarded this as an opportunity "to hone my carpentry and woodworking skills," talents that he knew would stand him in good stead for art. That same year, he won the prestigious Grand Prize (Non-Representational Painting) at the Art Association of the Philippines Open Art Competition.[12]

12. Pacquing was again awarded this Grand Prize in 1999.

In the Philippines, as in other swaths of postcolonial Southeast Asia, the question of cultural identity has remained problematic. At the end of colonial oppression, the lack of an underlying cultural unity meant that, like before, national identity was primarily expressed in terms of politics and institutions. However, this freed artists from having to follow any prescribed style and enabled them to look for inspiration where they wished.

Since independence and even before, Philippine art had been split between the poles of figuration and abstraction in various styles that, at different times, were described as beaux arts, impressionist, modernist, folk art, socialist realist, neorealist, abstract expressionist, conceptual, and (oligarchic) kitsch. Yet all of these had originated either from the Americas or Europe. From the 1950s to the 1970s, the ideals of international abstraction had been firmly and elegantly expressed by avant-garde artists such as José Joya, Napoleon Abueva, and Lee Aguinaldo,[13] while in the background, the republic's controlling "new elites [felt that they] could treat Euramerica as an immense cultural warehouse over which they had the sovereignty of consumer choice."[14] Emerging from the Marcos dictatorship, the "non-elite" generations of the 1980s, 1990s, and aughts rejected this consumerist approach by establishing a relaxed, open cultural discourse in which the world could be remade according to their own image and open to any committed and informed artist. In this atmosphere of realism rather than optimism, the causes of chaos and violence remained, as did memories of the ever-present possibilities of natural disaster.

13. See Ahmad Mashadi, "Some Aspects of Nationalism and Internationalism in Philippine Art," in *Modernity and Beyond: Themes in Southeast Asian Art*, ed. T.K. Sabapathy (Singapore: Singapore Art Museum, 1996), 49–51.

14. John Clark, "Modern Art in Southeast Asia," *Art and Asia Pacific*, Sample Issue (1993): 36.

Manila sustained relatively few commercial galleries, and the modernist conservativism of the Marcos years had stunted art in the public sphere; similarly, traveling exhibitions of work by "superstar" foreign contemporary artists were virtually nonexistent, and local artists could not afford to go abroad themselves. Yet, despite, or, perhaps, because of this, there was lively debate among artists, teachers, students, and art afficionados about new international artworks seen from freely circulating images.[15] Pacquing recalls that the latest works by artists such as Cy Twombly, Georg Baselitz, and Julian Schnabel were being vehemently debated and evaluated by his young student friends, their teachers, and himself in coffee houses and bars. The established canon of modern and contemporary Philippine art was of relatively little interest to this younger generation. With abundant new information and a passion for art, the world was their oyster – and they were as well informed, and opinionated, as many of their Western counterparts.

15. In magazines such as *Art Forum*, *Flash Art*, and *Art in America*.

Pacquing circulated within this milieu and recalls that these discussions were "an essential part of the process of self-reflection that enabled me to establish my artistic identity… I felt in my bones the sensibility and sensitivity of the works that I saw, and my art developed by figuring out what worked and [what] didn't in them. The art that I found interesting served me as both a stepping stone and as a scaffold that could help me find my own voice and point of view. With every encounter with new work, I began to realize what was and was not necessary…. Anchored by my own gut feelings and intuitions, these different stimuli coalesced to propel me to do more—to experiment more."[16]

16. See note 6.

But this initial process of self-interrogation was a prologue for the real drama still to take place in the studio, where, confronted by blankness and uncertainty, risks could not be avoided and the artist alone had to decide whether a work was complete.

Starting out solo, Pacquing then joined up with four university friends—painters and sculptors—to create Source: Manila, a group that they used to request exhibition spaces.[17] Other than in competitions, opportunities for young artists to show their work in Manila were practically nonexistent; but together, they could make an impact exhibiting outside of the capital. In 1992, Source: Manila presented its inaugural exhibition at the Museo Iloilo in Iloilo City,[18] and the following year, they exhibited in three different provincial centers, consolidating their success.[19] Subsequent group exhibitions occurred in Iloilo in 1995 and in Manila in 2000, 2008, and 2009.[20]

17. The members of Source: Manila were Joven Alcala (painter), Juan Alcazaren (sculptor), Nubbin Beldia (painter), Felix Bacolor (painter), and Pacquing (multimedia). They exhibited together in 1992, 1993, 1995, 2000, 2008, and 2009. By the last show, only Alcazaren and Pacquing remained in the group. Pacquing describes what the group had in common as "a form of dirty abstraction" (see note 6).

18. Situated in the Western Visayas region on the island of Panay, Iloilo was the second city in the Philippines to have been colonized by the Spanish.

19. These exhibitions were held at the CAP Art Center, Cebu City (Central Visayas); the Galleria Martinez, Bacolod City (Western Visayas); Xavier University Gallery, Cagayan de Oro City (Northern Mindanao); and the Cebu Museum, Cebu City (Central Visayas). (The Cebu Museum exhibition included only works on paper.)

20. "Source Manila: Square One," Museo Iloilo, 1995; "Source Manila: For George McGuffin," West Gallery, Manila, 2000; "Source Manila: Études for More Than Two Hands," MO_Space, Manila, 2008; Alcazaren & Pacquing: Finale Art File, Manila, 2009.

In 1993, Pacquing organized his first solo exhibition, "Chasms-Saltando-Coalesce," held at West Gallery in Manila. His persona as an artist was developing on two related levels: as a flaneur experiencing the world directly, opening his emotions and intellect to random experiences and encounters, and as a researcher and exploiter of different materials, concentrating on their properties and on how they could be molded and reassembled in various ways. Catalan artist Antoni Tàpies was an important influence for this latter direction: largely self-taught, he had decided in the early 1950s to move away from Surrealism toward *pintura matèrica*, an informal, less structured approach in which non-art materials, such as clay or marble dust, rope, rags, and other incongruous objects, became crucial elements. Not linked to mimesis, symbolism, or Marcel Duchamp's objets trouvés, Tàpies's "paintings" were instead unified assemblies with their own qualities — to be constructed and deconstructed at will: burned, mutilated, or combined with other elements.

Pacquing's artistic evolution showed a similar trajectory, and he produced a number of works in response to those by Tàpies. At different times, Pacquing has also explored the work of artists such as El Lissitzky, Robert Rauschenberg, and Richard Tuttle, among others, whose approaches have either bothered or intrigued him enough to push him in new directions. He recently explained: "I have sought to present emotion in the simplest way… I am not just a painter. I'm a builder. I tell myself that I construct more than I paint…."[21] He frames his approach as a rejection of the pretentious "sectarian" spirituality of painting (a hot topic in Europe in the 1980s),[22] by embracing what Tàpies described as the "materialist and sensual conceptions of life, of things 'just as they are,' of everything that can be touched and felt, of the earthly and even the carnal."[23]

21. Pacquing, speaking in the video *Bernie on Bernie*, Manila, Silverlens, 2017. In regard to building and carpentry, the artist has studied many different forms of construction and traditional ways of making joints.

22. The exhibition "A New Spirit in Painting," held at London's Royal Academy of Arts in 1981, reacted against the materialism of Minimalism and Conceptualism by presenting different forms of transcendent figuration made by both a new generation and previously neglected artists in Europe and the US.

23. Antoni Tàpies quoted by Jonathan Olazo in *Measured by Images: Pardo de Leon, Bernardo Pacquing* (exh. cat.) (Manila: Silverlens, 8 May – 6 June, 2021).

Talking about his *Untitled: After Antoni Tàpies's Grey Paintings* (2021), made during the COVID-19 lockdown, Pacquing explains that "when I first saw Tàpies's works, I thought that some of them depicted *Muertos*, crosses, and earth…" His response — the more than eighty variants of intensities, scumbles, and memories of gray that appear in this series — "represent[s] uncertainty… I was hanging onto an undetermined time and space. I saw myself staring at a huge concrete wall! Or [at] purgatory — a transitional state — which I desired to leave but without any [further] expectation. My grays have different hues but [are purposely] on the dull side — bleak and cold."[24]

24. Ibid.

Études

Since the early 1990s, Pacquing's impressively wide range of work has been distinguished by its use of varying media, materials, references, moods, tempi, and tonalities, as much as by its allusiveness — its lack of obvious subject matter. His art refuses to conform to any single format or point of view, and the often-applied labels of "abstraction" or "conceptualism" fail to describe it. His approach is more like that of a composer-musician, in which the writing and the performance of the work take place simultaneously. Each suite of works has its specific intensity and logic, usually modulated by a counterpoint of wit. The impetus for his work is derived from his emotions at a particular time and from the changing conditions in which he finds himself; despite the seriousness with which he approaches art, he does not take himself too seriously.

His series of oil paintings *Self-Teaching Keyboard* (2004) is distinguished by its ironical tautology of mark-making, which creates a smoke screen behind which subjects subconsciously emerge.[25] No work is repetitious because each one uses a different starting point for its subsequent steps.

25. This series of oil paintings was prompted by a suggestion from Roberto Chabet.

In other works, such as the oil painting *People I Know (Fritz)* (2007), tragedy and wit combine. In this example, a hollow, jagged figure looms in the black and gray background wearing a pink bowtie and a bright blue belt. They carry a dark red flower—or it could be a pumping, bleeding heart? The quirkiness of the painting matches the character it depicts. The quizzically titled mixed-media *Abstraction Is Homeless* (2012) presents a bird's-eye view of an apartment or a city, sketched in flat, dark, violent shapes. The work is overlaid with splattered colors, collaged zones, a yellow "snake" coiled like a freeway around its body, and a flattened "cow" at its center; it looks like a vortex or spiral in which every painterly mark or gesture cannot avoid being representational.

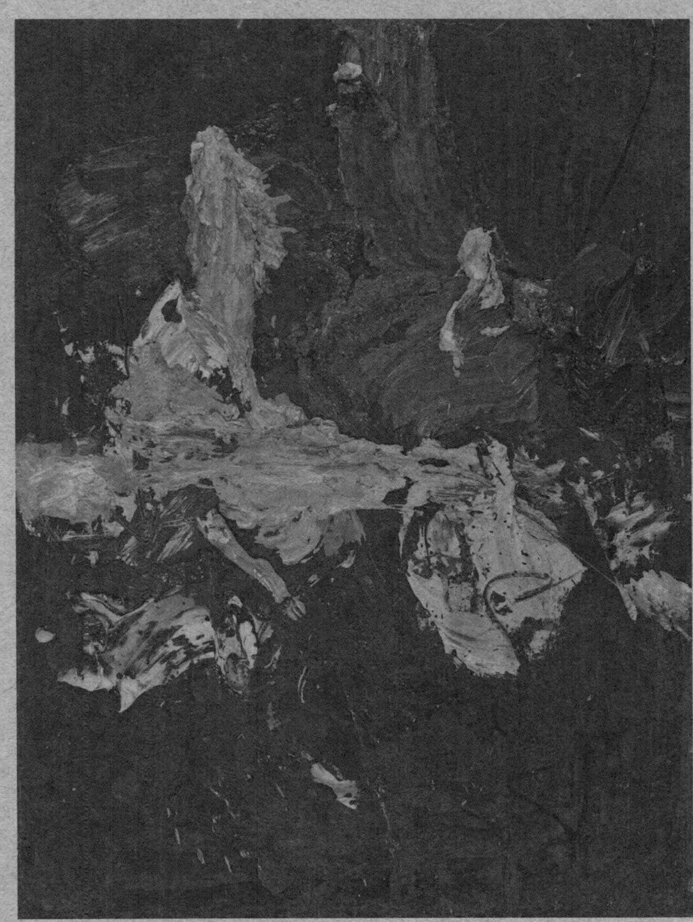

Fig. 1. *Carcass Series 04*, 2004–16, mixed media, 61 × 45.7 cm

Untitled, a series of small collages and montages Pacquing made around the same time, radiates a stronger sense of velocity and design, also spiced with incongruous humor. Self-consciously drawing on Surrealism and Dada, the images are tempered by classic modern graphics and then disrupted by intruding rogue elements of abstract painting.

The *Carcass Series*, an extended group of oil paintings of identical size made between 2004 and 2016, is less humorous and more sardonic. At first sight, the works seem to be "speed paintings"—expressionistic celebrations of color—an impression quickly contradicted when one recognizes depictions of slabs of imaginary meat cut from unidentified animals. Like a necromantic butcher, Pacquing moves and carves the "flesh" of the colors as he brings each cadaver back to life, giving it energy and identity (Fig. 1).

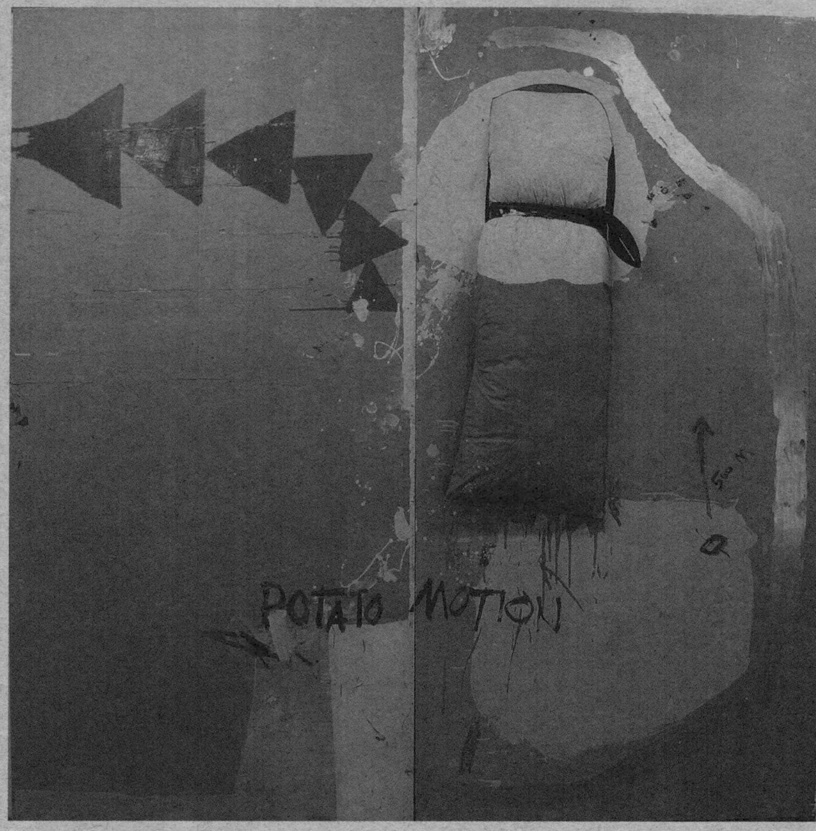

Fig. 2. *Days After Stream*, 2011, mixed media, 243.8 × 243.8 cm

Pacquing's slightly later paintings move away from a self-referential, internally rendered logic, where gesture, velocity, and color create palimpsests on densely layered surfaces. Instead, they offer a more imagistic approach with different elements overlaid and added to each other. At times, these works embrace absurdity, as in *Days After Stream* (2011), a brightly colored "nautical map" on which a painted pillow is strapped onto one of its "islands" with the words "POTATO MOTION" scrawled across its center, perhaps in reference to the American origin of this ubiquitous tuber (Fig. 2). Similar devices appear in the scumbled surfaces of plaster, paint, and color of the enigmatically entitled *F. Hole* (2012). Its verbal pun (and autobiographical reference) is partially explained by the body of the violin embedded at its center. Yet all we see is its back; the violin's resounding "f" holes are hidden (Fig. 3).

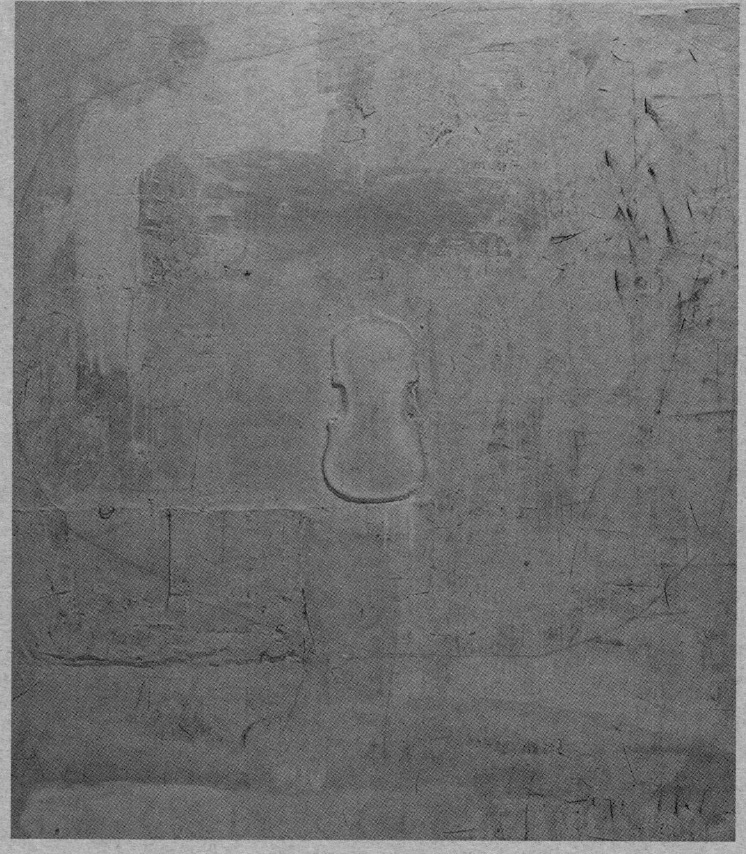
Fig. 3. *F. Hole*, 2012, mixed media, 121.9 × 139.7 cm

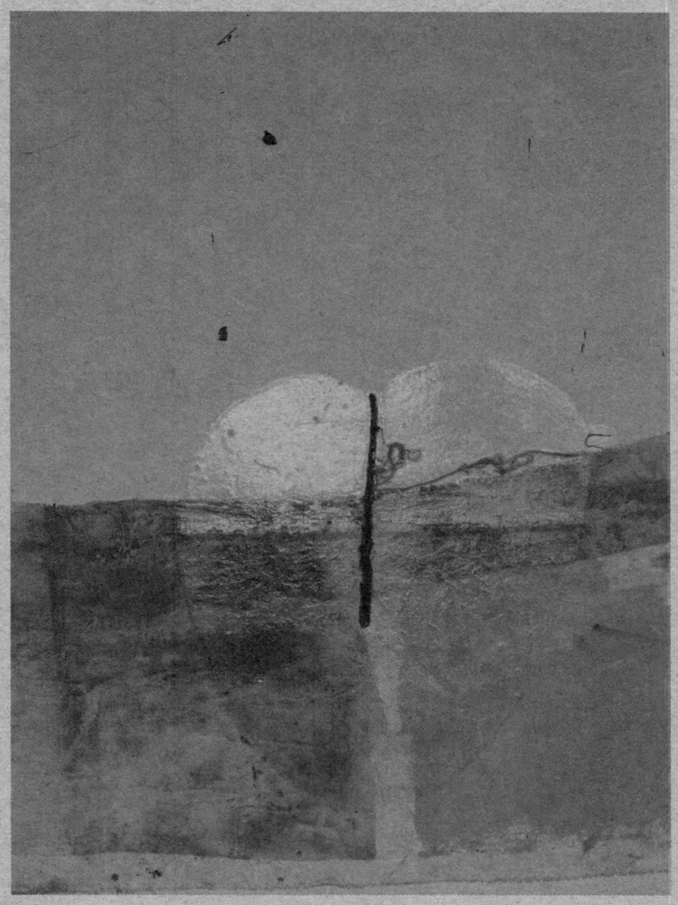

Fig. 4. *Hydroponics Series 7*, 2015, oil on canvas, 122 × 91.4 cm

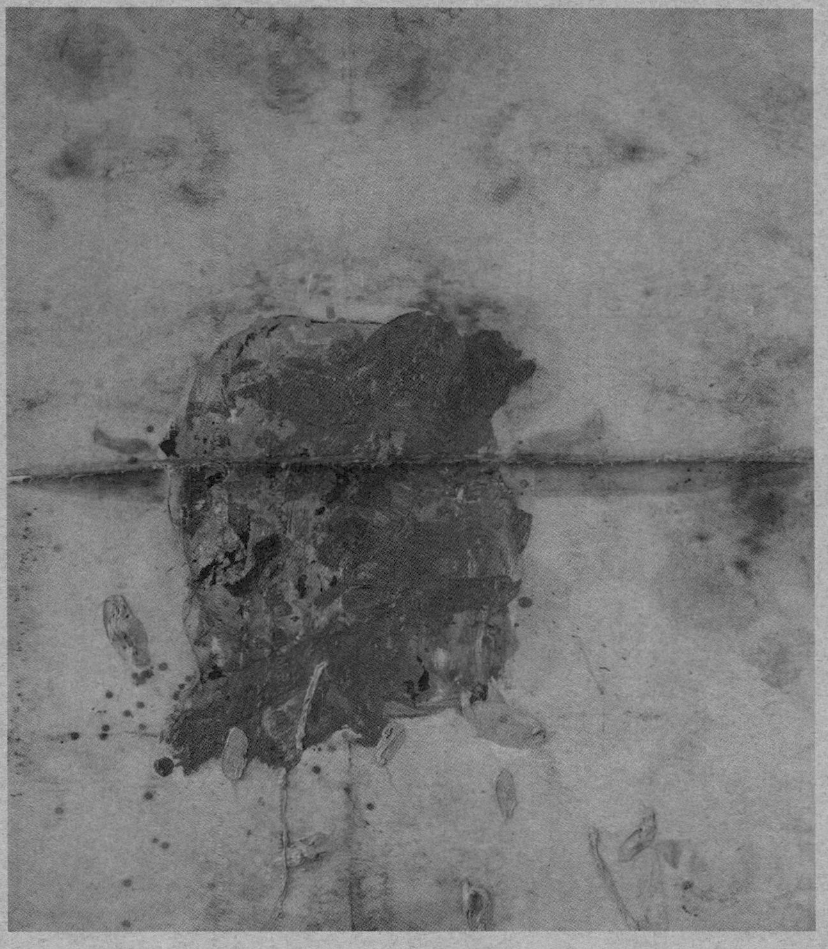

Fig. 5. *Tomato*, 2015, acrylic emulsion, rubber glue, oil on canvas, 152.4 × 133.4 cm

From 2014 to 2015, Pacquing developed a fascination with vermiculture and hydroponic cultivation techniques. These and quasi-taxonomic studies of the development of various plants informed a large series of works in oil and mixed media. In the *Hydroponics Series*, the scored-through and reimagined bodies of common fruits and vegetables, such as radishes, okras, bell peppers, bitter gourds, tomatoes, and non-specified organisms, appear to float, their bodies and roots visible, like strange, aquatic denizens of another world (Fig. 4). In their environmental concern, these works prefaced his series *Half Full*, an ironical statement about the current state of Pacquing's existential "glass," which continued his exploration of multicellular growth in different forms and media. Focusing on these themes, his paintings became less gestural as they increasingly embraced three dimensions, covered by cracks, fissures, and excrescences (Fig. 5).

Around the time of his 50th birthday, in 2017, Pacquing decided to stop using oil paint and return to the various commercial house paints and building materials—plaster, fillers, and tile adhesives—with which he had started. Sculpture became increasingly important as well and, as with his montages and assemblages, he used recycled or reclaimed materials that he could manipulate and transform. His large floor sculpture *Quorum Sensing*, a clear statement about the failure of politics, is composed of slats of reclaimed wood; on one end, like a head, a large "basket" has been "woven" out of slats, while others splurge away from it, spilling across the floor (Fig. 6).

Slit and Thrust, a series of multimedia works (also the title of a 2017 exhibition), pushes further in this direction and reflects an external, more natural influence. A keen walker and mountaineer, Pacquing knew the wild landscape of Nueva Vizcaya quite well.[26] After a severe typhoon, he volunteered to help the indigenous Kalanguya people reestablish a sustainable agricultural community and participated in a shamanistic fertility rite there. During this, he was particularly impressed by a sacrifice in which a wild boar was slit open, its heart punctured with a sharp stick and its blood allowed to run freely in an act of propitiation. The simple movements of "slit" and "thrust" stuck in his mind, prompting a series of magisterial, diptych-like assemblages of the same name, in which two heavily modulated, white, almost adjacent surfaces are partitioned by vertical strips of unruly "other" materials that project or recede like traumatic wounds. These "white" paintings are all depicted on black grounds.

26. A mountainous region in Luzon, north of the province where Pacquing was born.

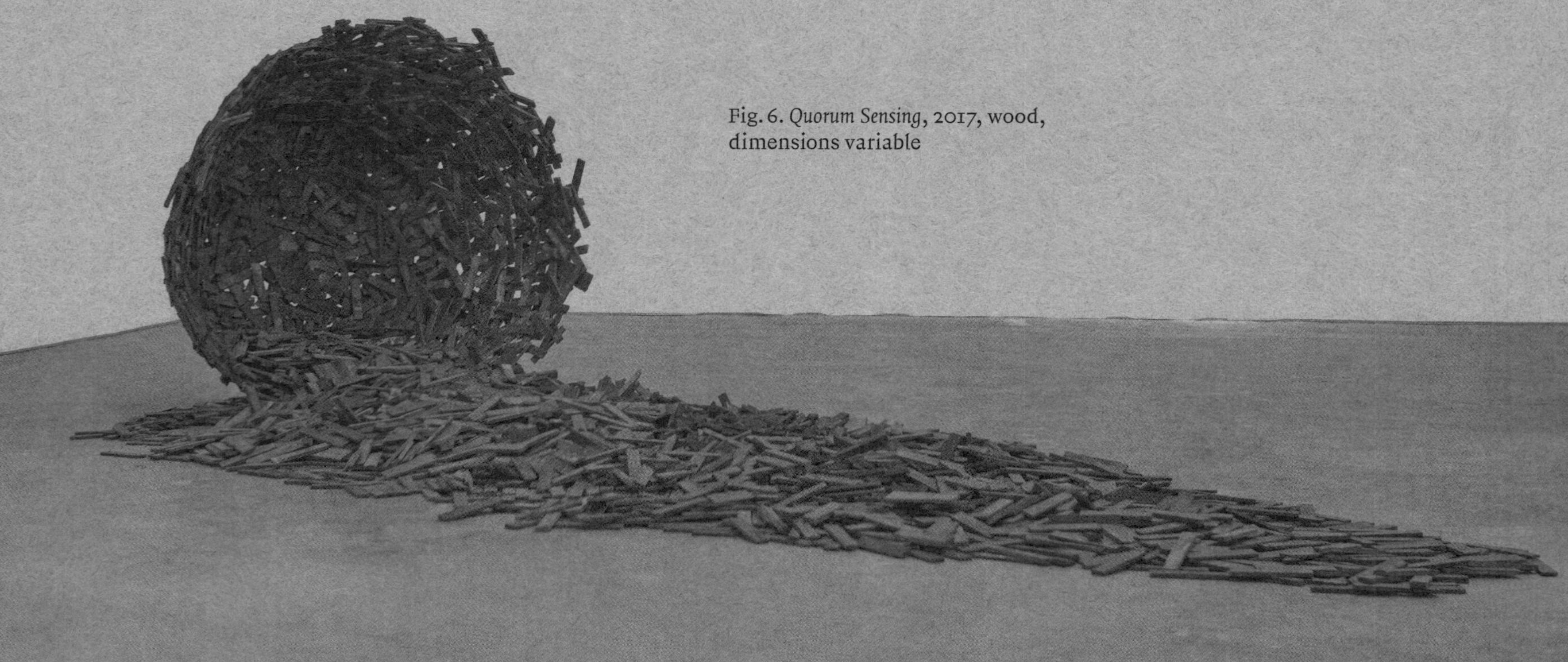

Fig. 6. *Quorum Sensing*, 2017, wood, dimensions variable

Pacquing's sculptures and constructions address numerous topics on scales ranging from the extremely small to the environmentally immersive. For the 2010 exhibition "Earth Mounds" at Finale Art File, Manila, he brought together paintings, collages, sculptures, and installations, all of which fell under the taxonomy of domes. Termites' nests were his initial inspiration: "[They] are far more intricate in structure, and far more impressive...when compared to the existing scale of human construction." But he was also "thrilled by the architectural detail and structural engineering" of human-made versions, from Filippo Brunelleschi's dome for the Florence cathedral and the Al-Aqsa mosque in Jerusalem to basilicas, cupolas, stupas, and igloos across the world.[27]

27. Bernardo Pacquing: *Artist Portfolio* (Manila: Silverlens, 2020), np.

With the 2018 commission of *Earth Mounds* for a seaside resort in Davao, Mindanao, came the challenging opportunity to build an ideal outdoor dome. Pacquing chose local driftwood as the primary material and decided that two main considerations should govern how the work developed. Given that driftwood is irregular in shape, he wanted the sculpture to have "visual balance from all viewing angles and distances." At the same time, its mass—10 feet in height by 20 feet in diameter—also had to have structural as well as visual integrity: "The challenge was to compose, fit/refit, and connect each joint using only brass rods held in place by adhesive.... This was crucial since my intention was to...accommodate the weight of a full-grown man should he decide to climb to the top of the sculpture."[28]

28. Ibid.

The following year, Pacquing further developed this idea in *Domes Village*, a network of four wooden domes, one geodesic, linked by three consecutive hanging bridges, to be explored, climbed over, and appreciated as art, in River Park, located in the newly built New Clark City in Tarlac. Situated in the first green, smart, disaster-resilient metropolis planned in the Philippines, the work expresses through its materials the city's qualities of strength, resilience, interconnectedness, and survival. The domes were constructed using recycled local hardwoods from remnants of houses buried by lava a century before; this type of bricolage also evoked still-present memories of the disastrous 1991 Mt. Pinatubo volcanic eruption that had occurred in the nearby Zambales Mountains.[29]

29. See "Domes Village," Silverlens, November 30, 2019, www.silverlensgalleries.com/exhibitions/2019-11-30/domes-village.

Between February 2020 and January 2022, Pacquing's work focused on the COVID-19 virus and the strict lockdown conditions it entailed. During a visit to his wife, he was trapped in Singapore, spending an entire term cut off from his studio. Faced by what he felt was the city's enforced cleanliness and overregulation, compared to that of the Philippines, he experienced claustrophobia and depression. Oil paint was in short supply, and he used what he could get, commandeering grocery cardboard boxes as "canvas." His first work there, *Code Orange 1–8* (2020), echoes the Singaporean lockdown code in a series of chunky abstract collages made of brown, unpainted, die-stamped cardboard. These were followed by *1-Beta Chain*, 15 small oil paintings executed on thick cardboard montages with red impasto paint—a color he had rarely used—smeared, dripped, and poured over their blocky supports.

Pacquing marshaled his resources in 2021 to embark on *Red Objects* (2021), four large (6 × 10 ft) diptychs of oil on canvas, which obliterated the floor of his tiny Singapore apartment. Made up of different shades of red, with flowing traces of black dancing across them, the roughly scumbled surfaces were somehow talismanic: "While gesturing with massive strokes, splattering thick daubs of oil paint, it dawned upon me that I was like a shaman reading the bloody innards and guts of an animal while making a sacrifice. As I worked, I was sifting my feelings through the paint as it passed over the wide floor of the canvas—as if I was looking for symbols or signs."[30] Under the title *Disquietude*, these dark works fight impotence by enacting empathetic concern and energy in the face of pandemic fear and oblivion; he exhibited them together after his return to Manila in 2022.[31]

30. See note 6.

31. Bernardo Pacquing, *Disquietude* (exh. cat.) (Manila: Silverlens, 2022).

Speaking of this time—and of the past, present, and future as well—Pacquing responds with a typically honest comment:

> *A connection binds my every work from the beginning to now as I look for perfection without knowing what it is. Driven by chaos and uncertainty, I keep trying to make sense—to find resolution. COVID was terrible, but cathartic. I just hung on, continued, and tried to wade through.*[32]

32. See note 6.

"Untitled #3" After J.S. Bach's Partita No. 2 "Chaconne", 2019, assemblage, 100.3 × 152.4 × 81.3 cm

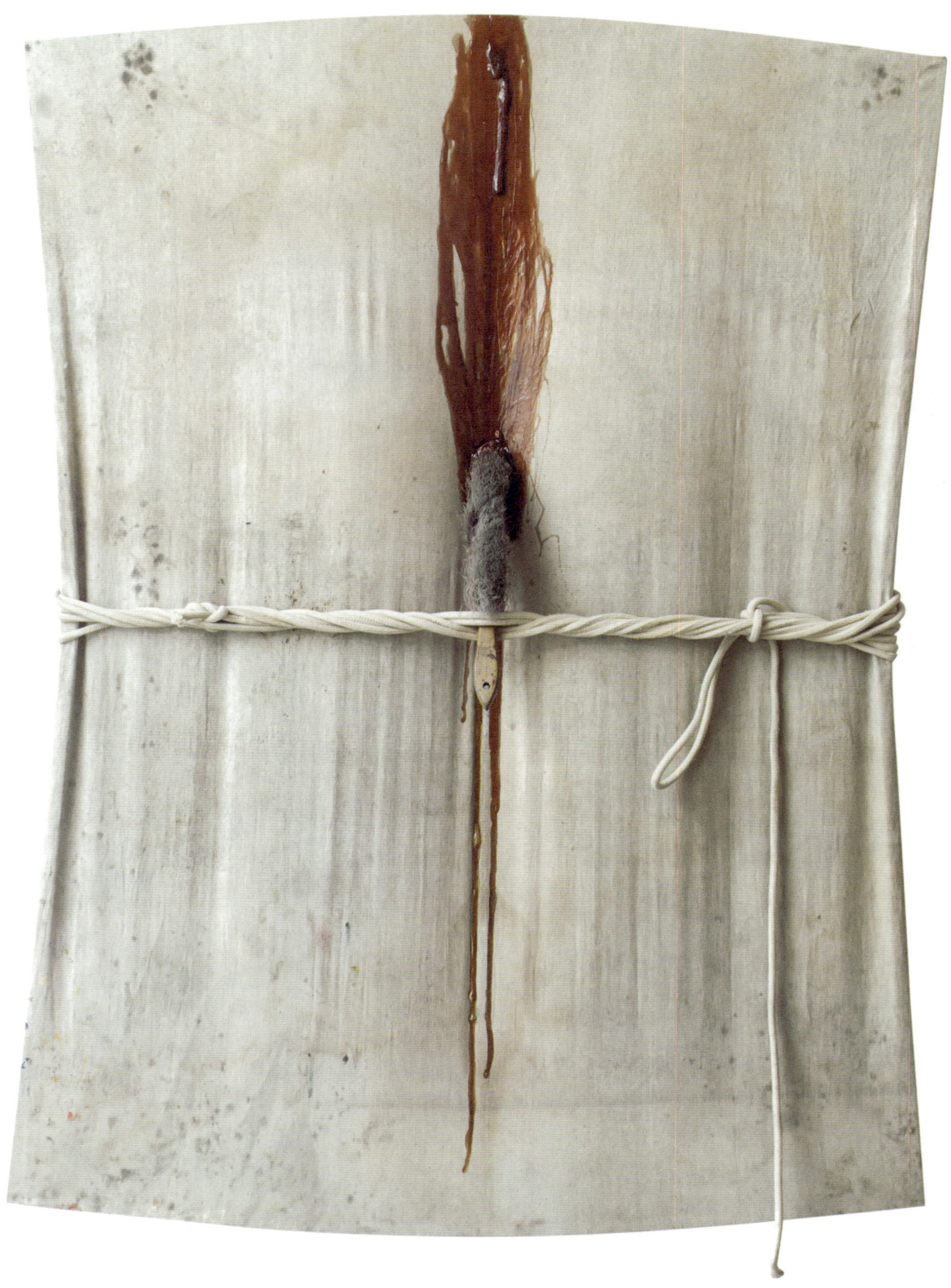

Untitled #4, After J.S. Bach's Partita No. 2 "Chaconne", 2019, assemblage, 160 × 121.9 × 10.2 cm

Vagueness of Dynamics 05, 2022, oil, house paint, assemblage on canvas, 152.4 × 121.9 cm

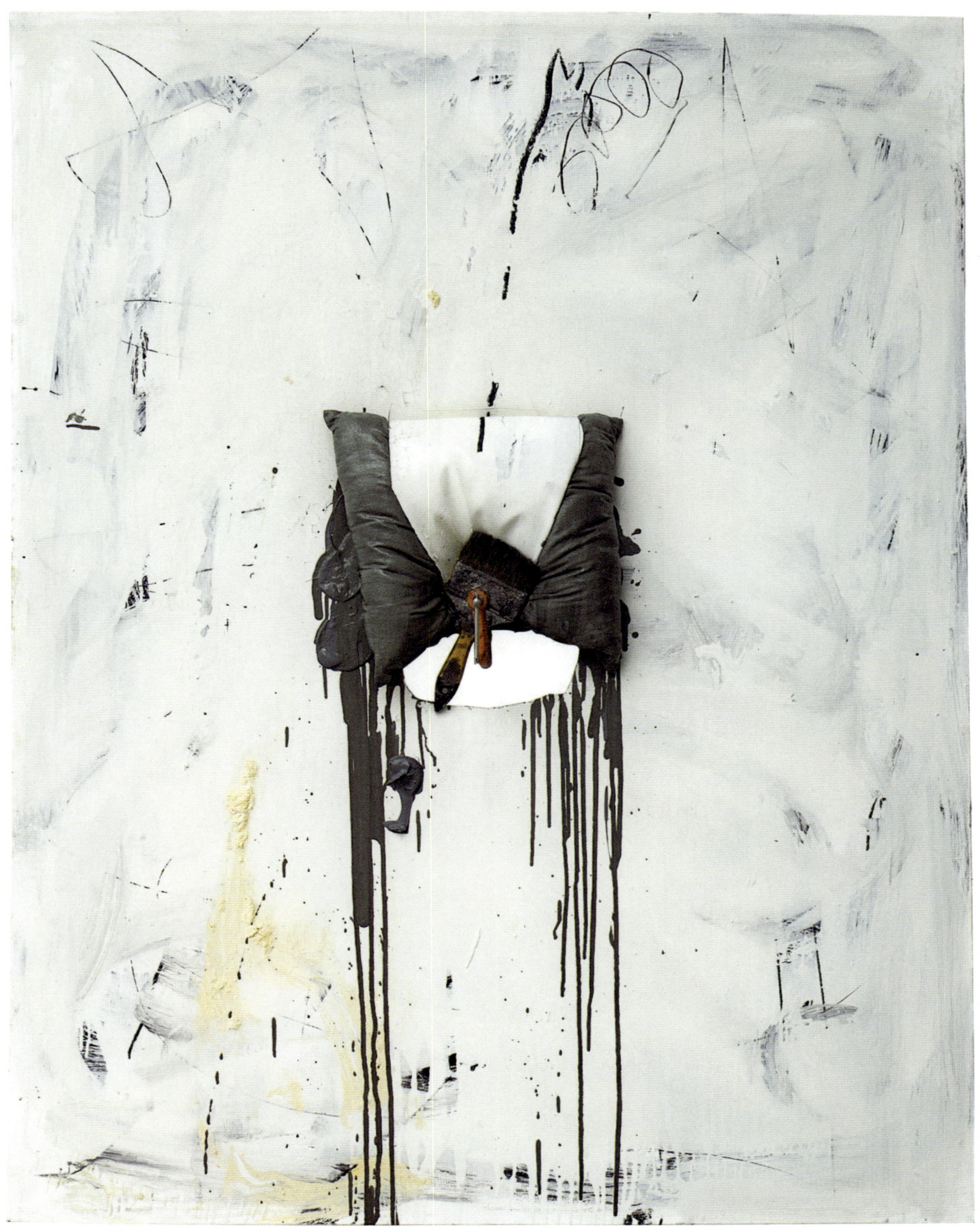

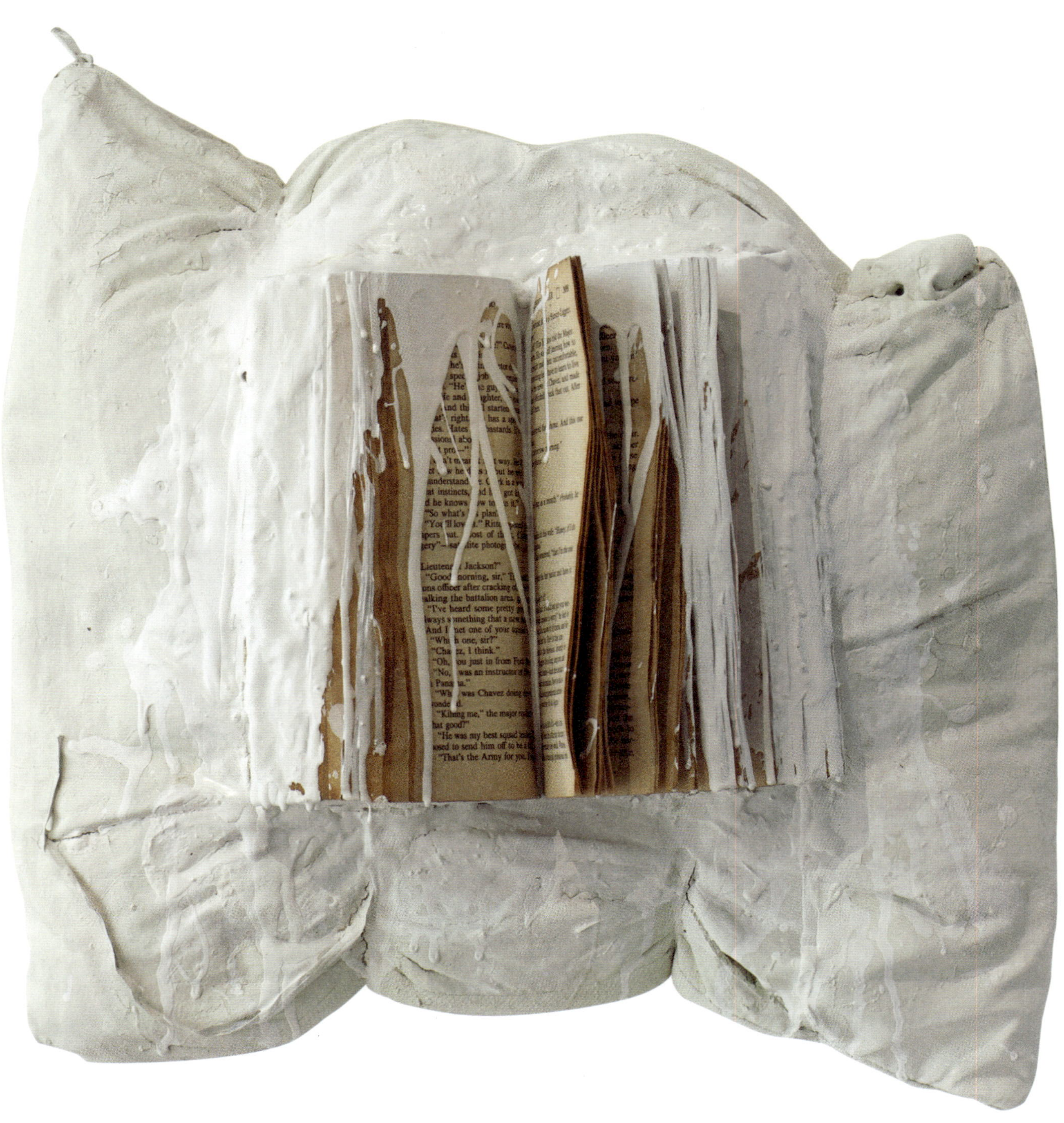

Anticipatory Anxiety #2, 2017, mixed media, 36.8 × 35.6 × 14.6 cm

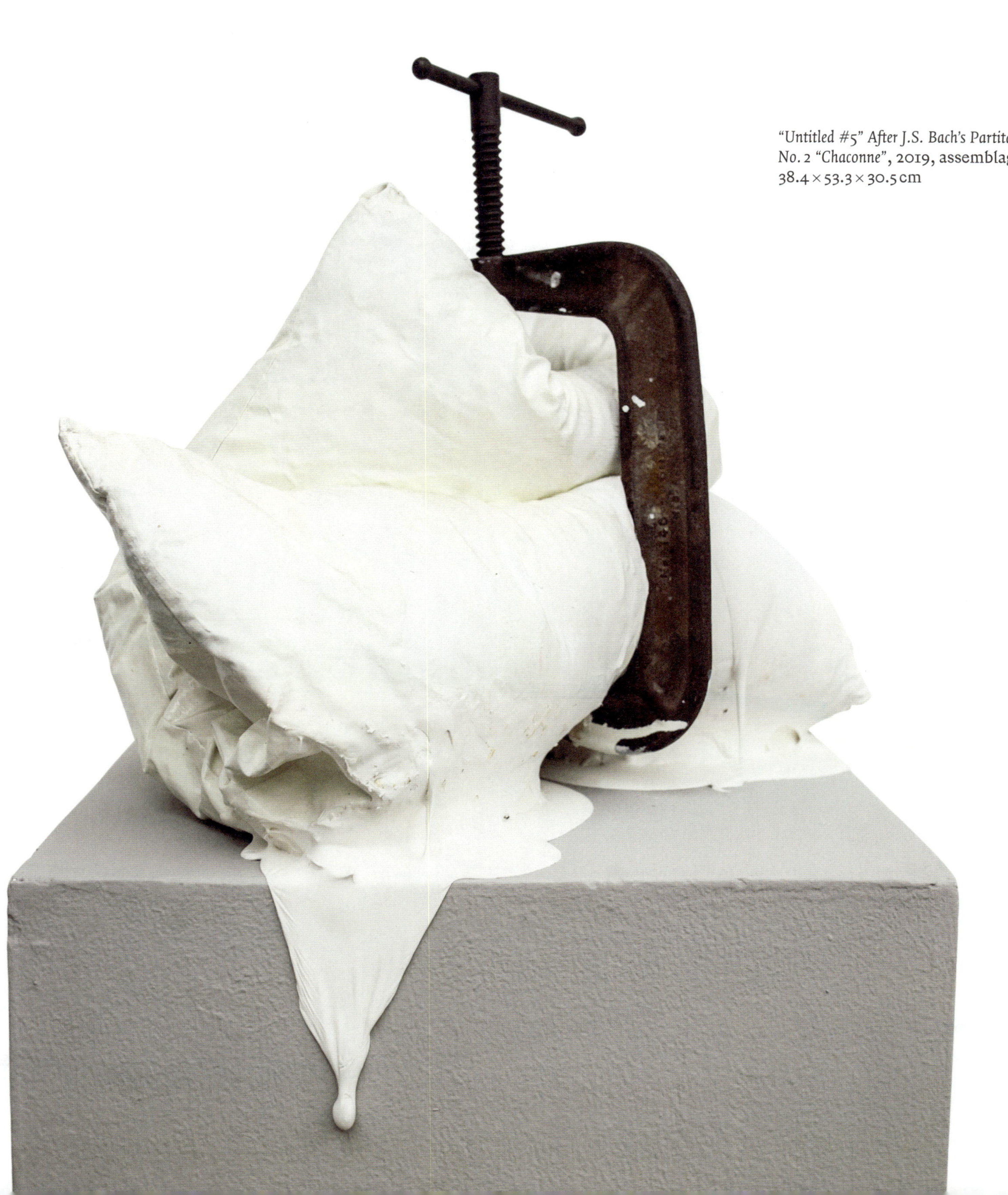

"Untitled #5" After J.S. Bach's Partita No. 2 "Chaconne", 2019, assemblage, 38.4 × 53.3 × 30.5 cm

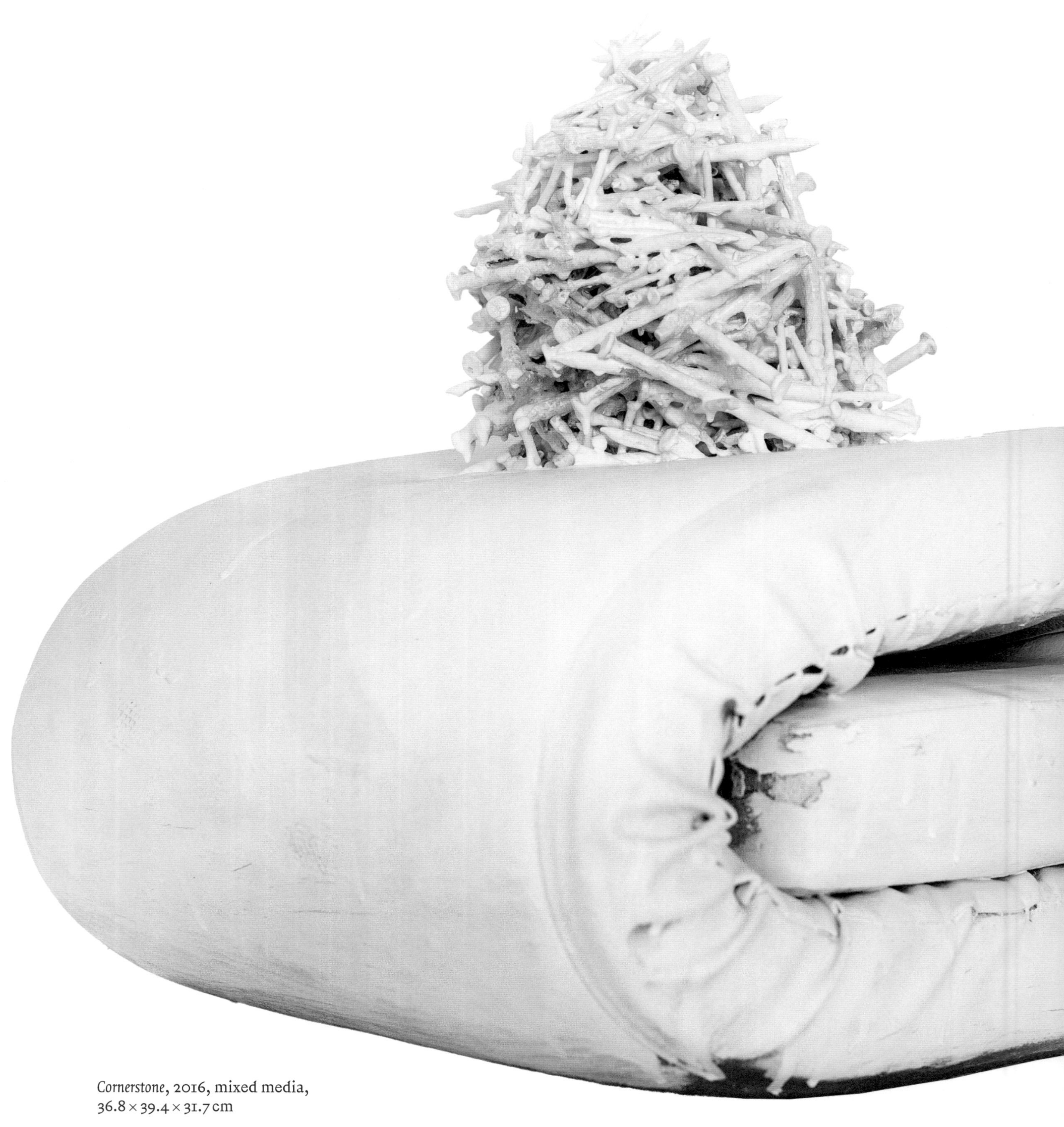

Cornerstone, 2016, mixed media,
36.8 × 39.4 × 31.7 cm

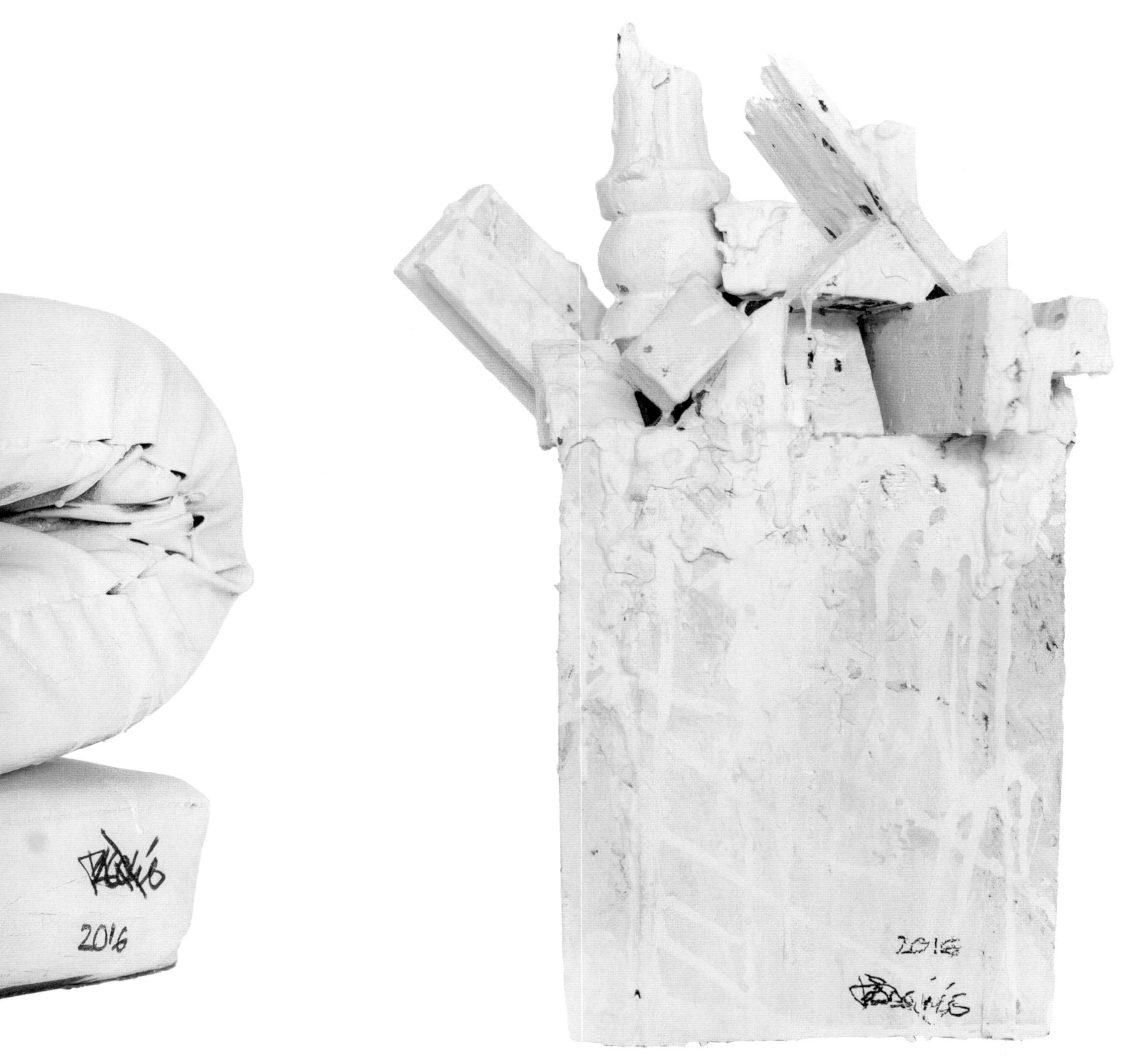

Controlled Demolition, 2016, mixed media,
33 × 12.7 × 12.7 cm

Totem Pole, 2016, mixed media, 50.8 × 22.9 × 22.9 cm

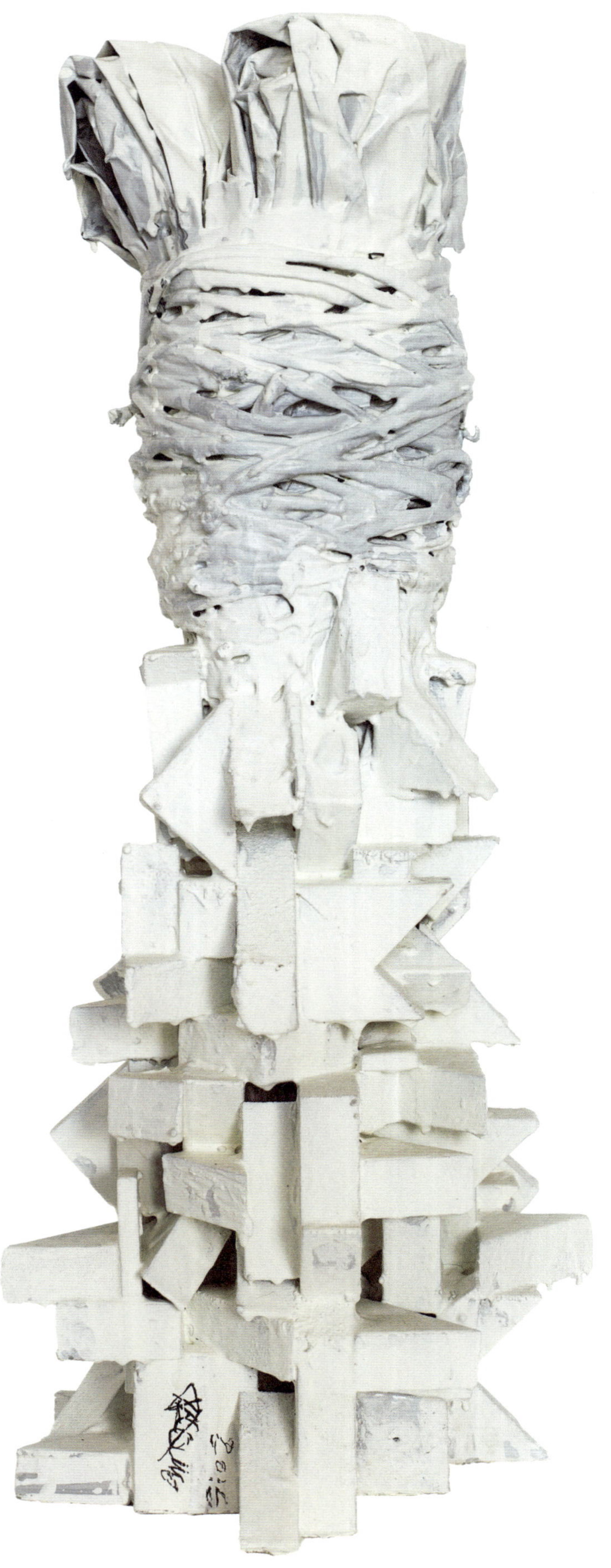

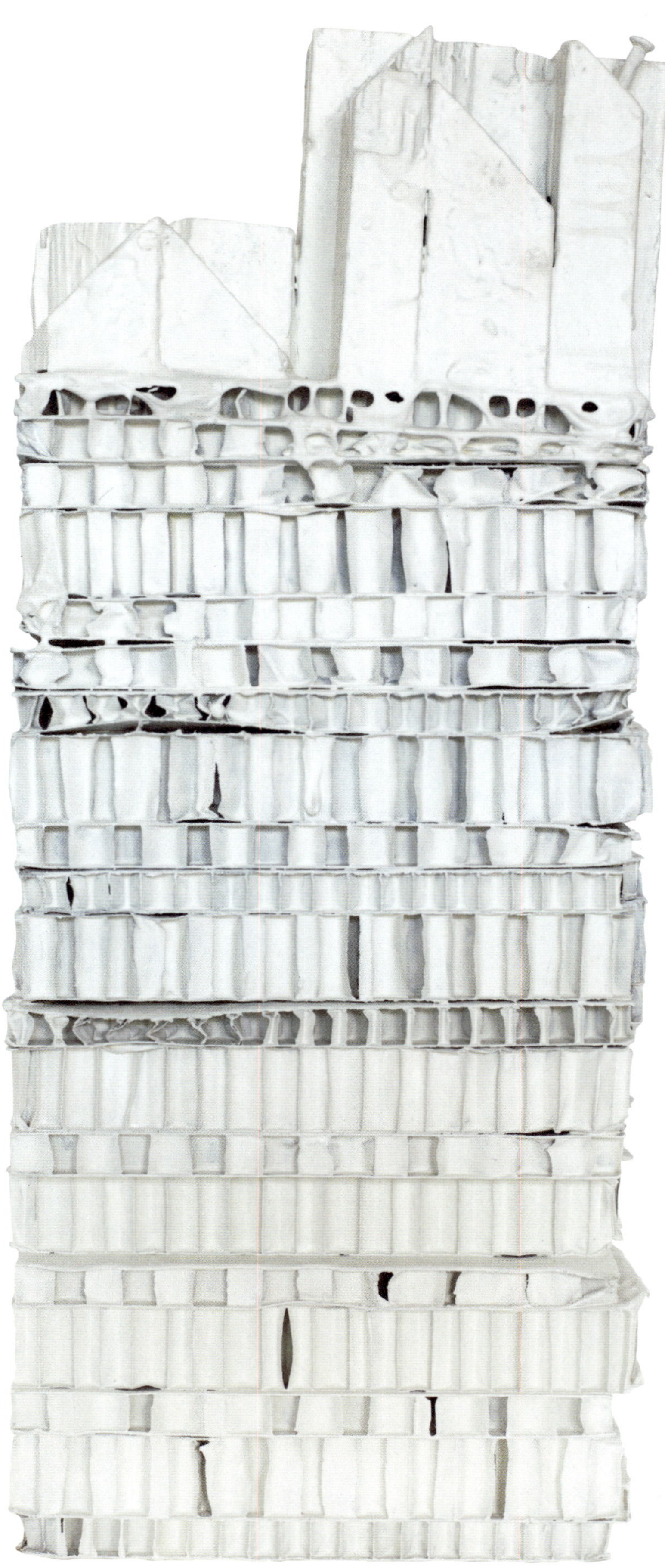

Tower, 2016, mixed media, 50.8 × 21.6 × 15.2 cm

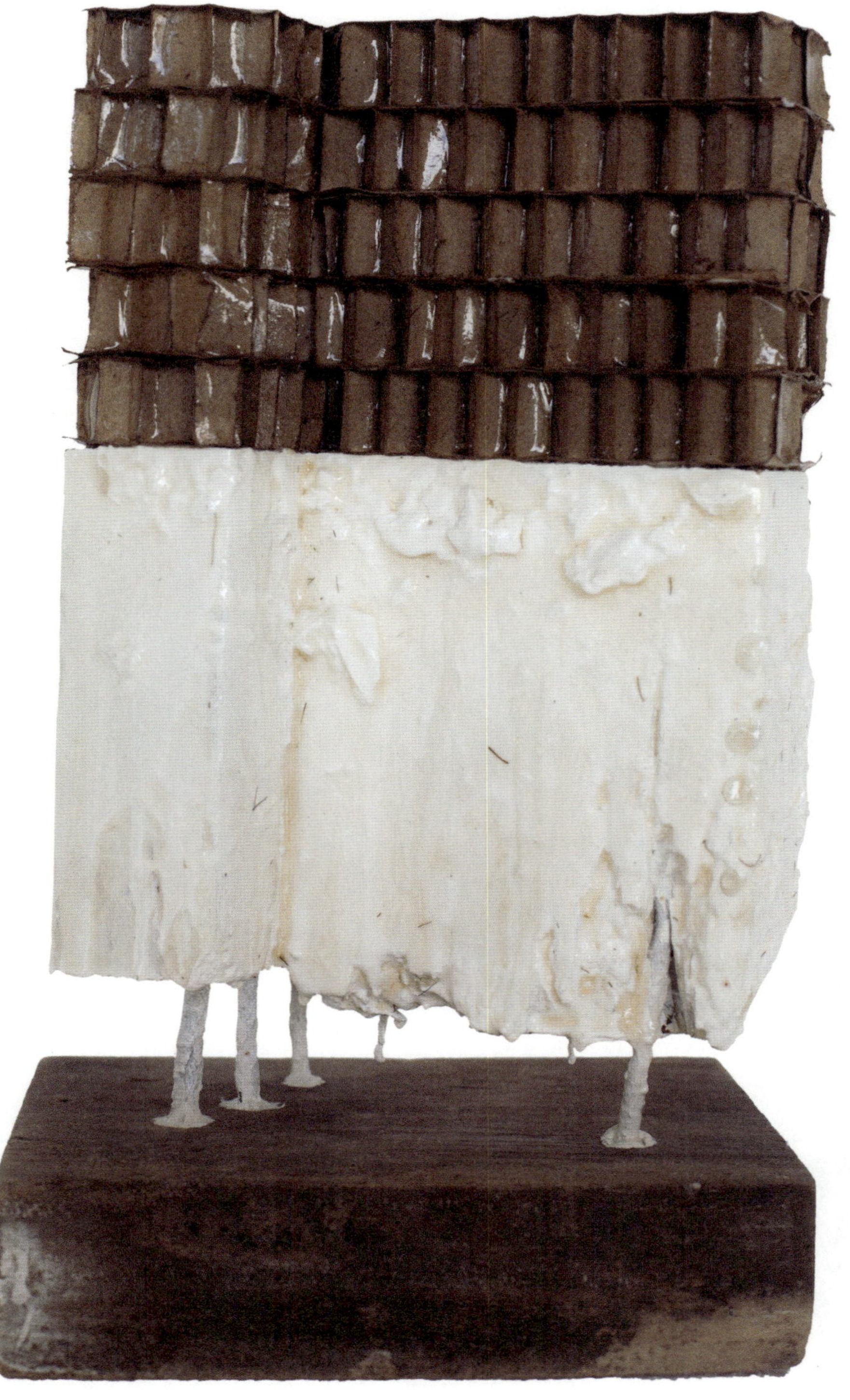

Tenement, 2016, mixed media,
30.5 × 16.5 × 14 cm

Quorum Sensing, 2017, wood, dimensions variable

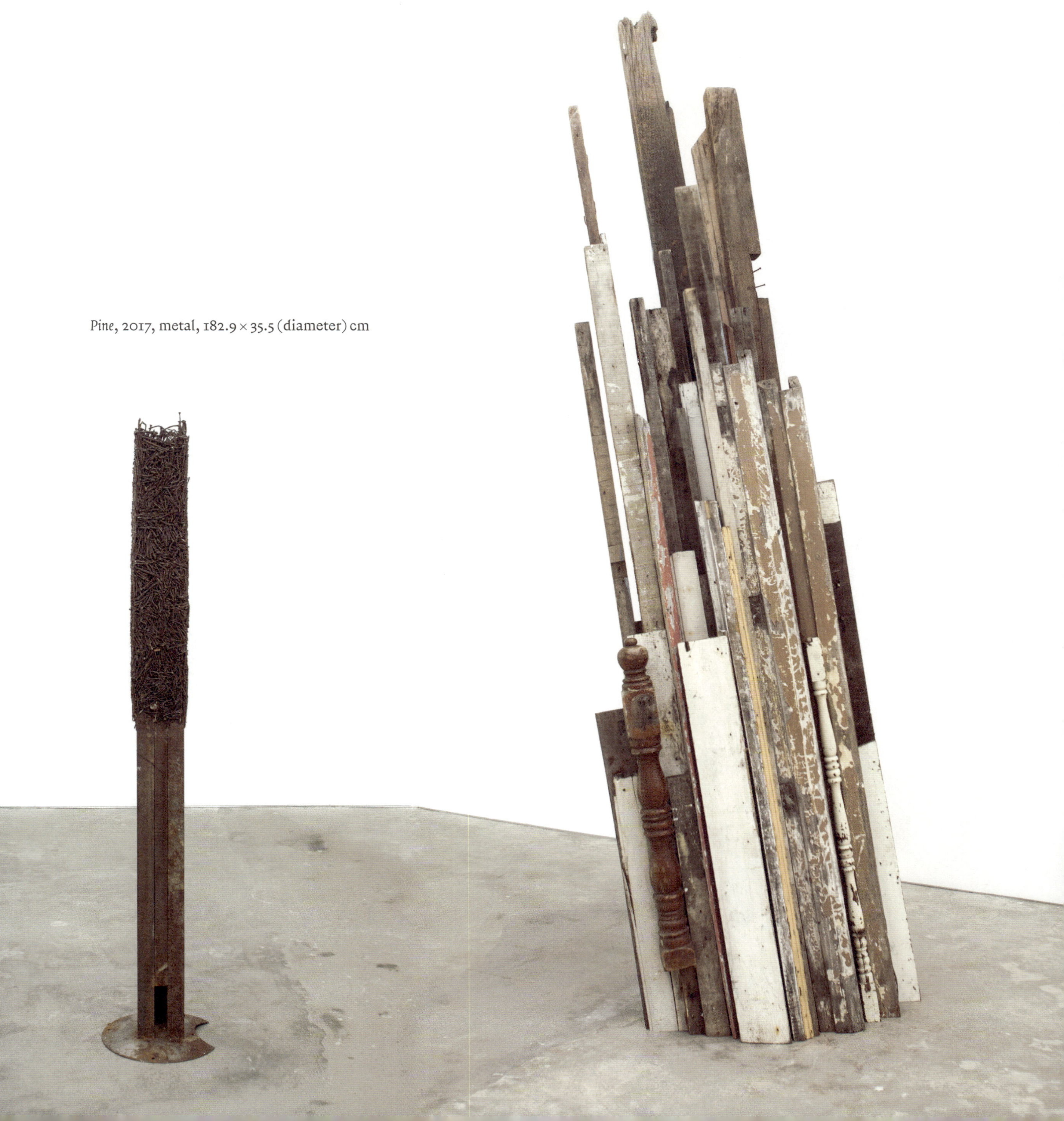

East Wind, 2017, wood, 330 × 96 (diameter) cm

Pine, 2017, metal, 182.9 × 35.5 (diameter) cm

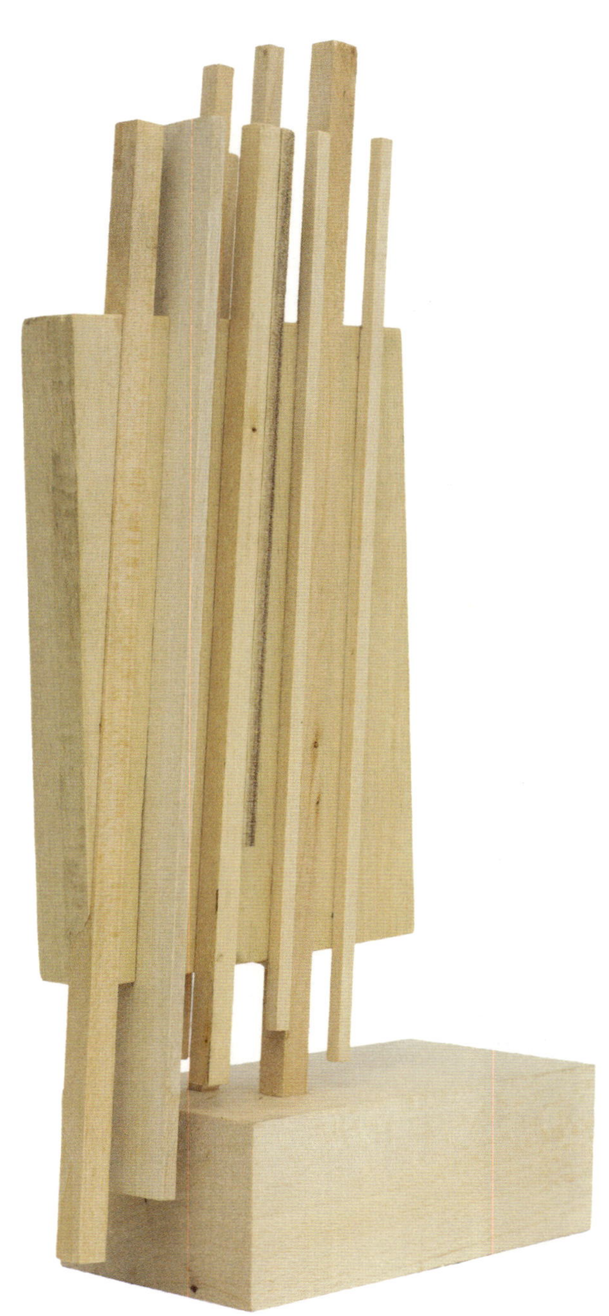

Untitled 03 – After Lissitzky, 2019, wood,
35.6 × 19.7 × 7.6 cm

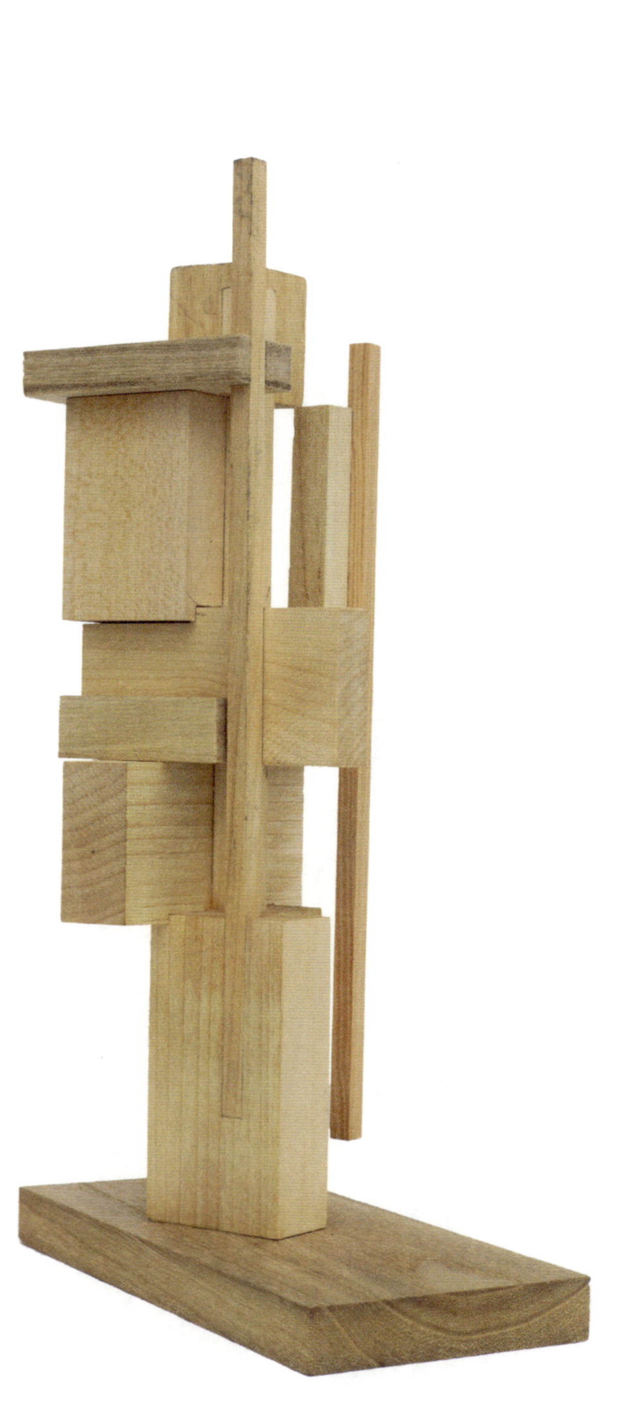

Untitled 11 – After Lissitzky, 2019, wood,
36.2 × 21 × 10.8 cm

Untitled 01 – After Lissitzky, 2019, wood,
17.2 × 20.3 × 14.6 cm

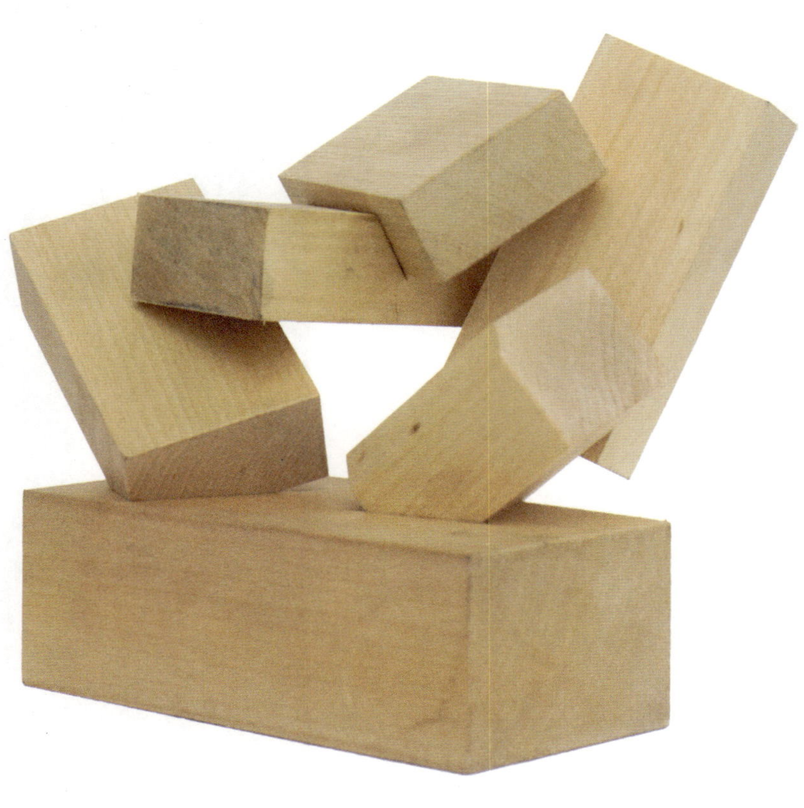

Untitled 02 – After Lissitzky, 2019, wood,
40.6 × 15.2 × 8.3 cm

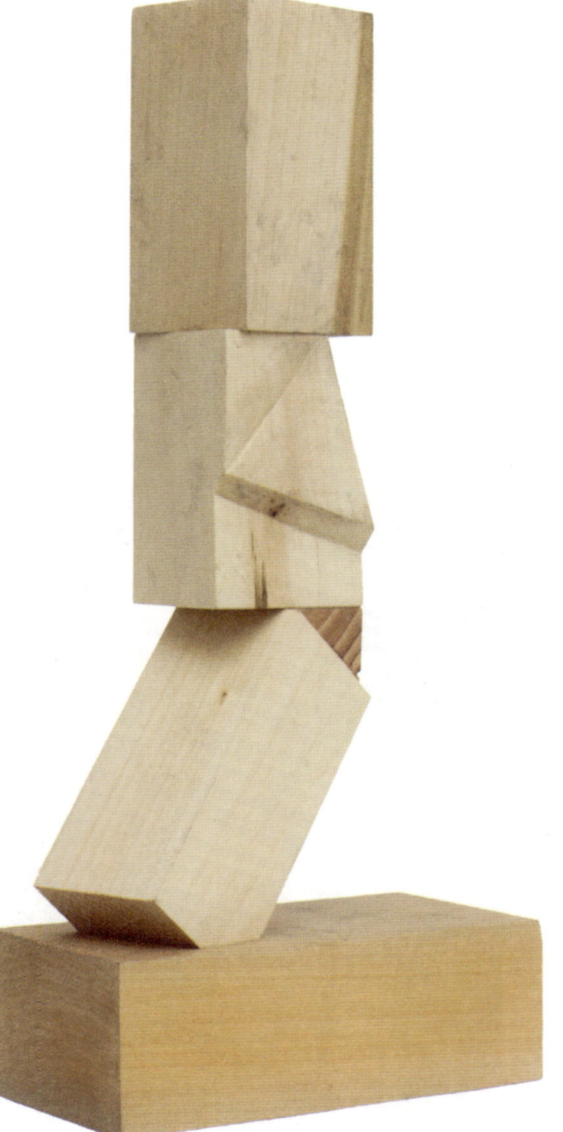

Untitled 08 – After Lissitzky, 2019, wood,
15.9 × 21.6 × 24.1 cm

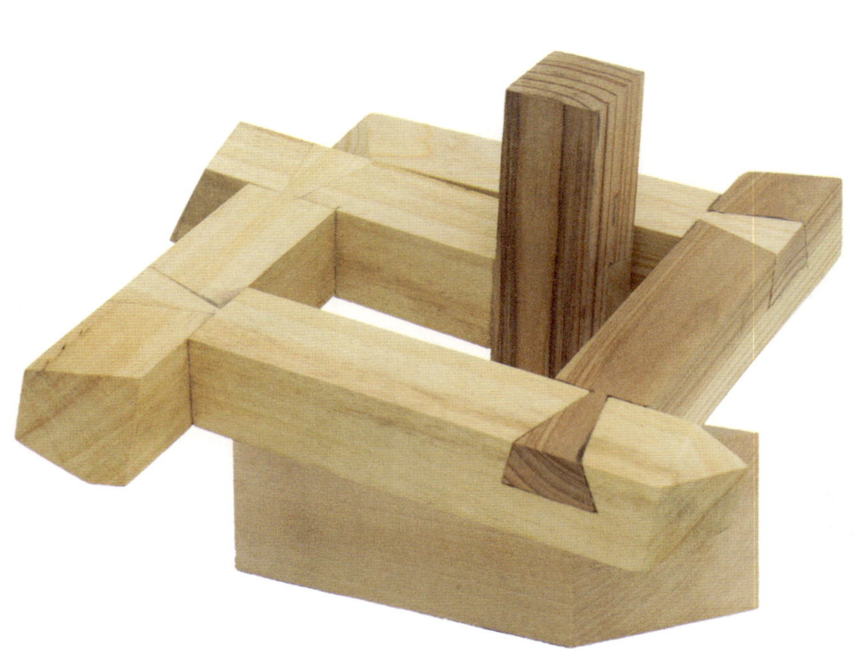

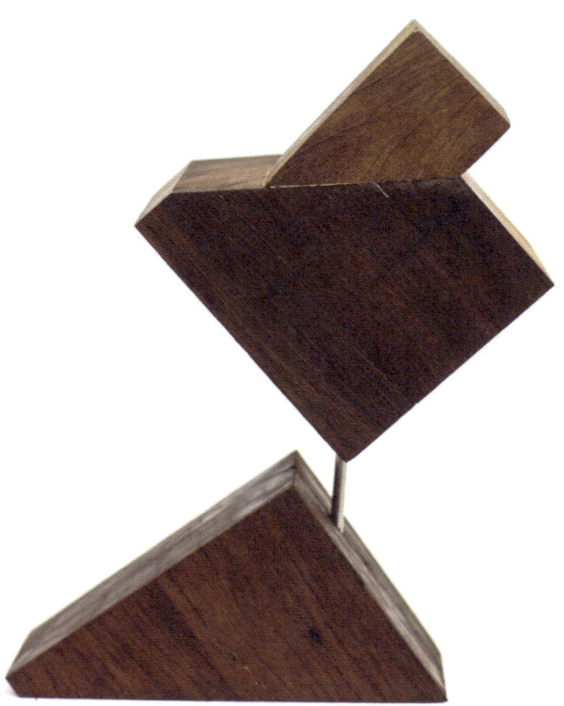

Wood work 01, 2019, assemblage on wood,
28 × 26 × 4.9 cm

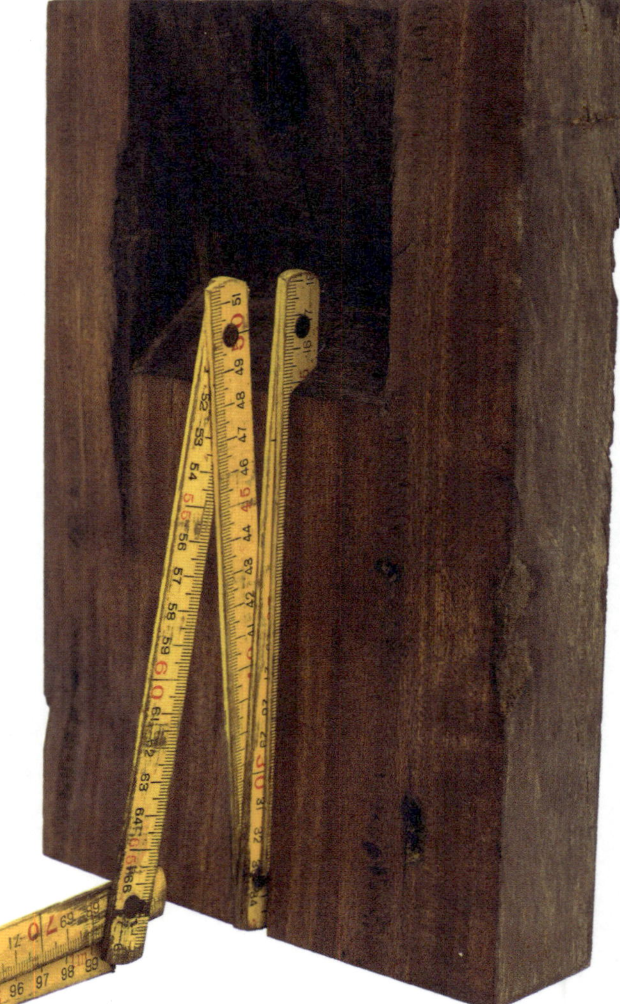

Wood work 04, 2019, assemblage on wood,
23 × 17.5 × 9.5 cm

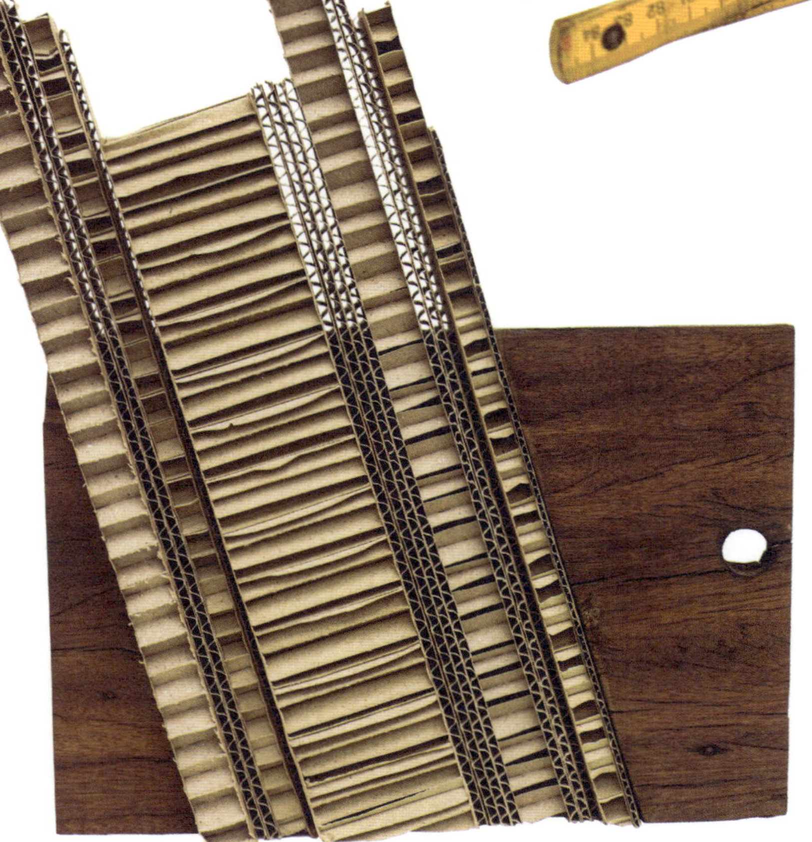

Wood work 05, 2019, assemblage on wood,
28 × 26 × 4.9 cm

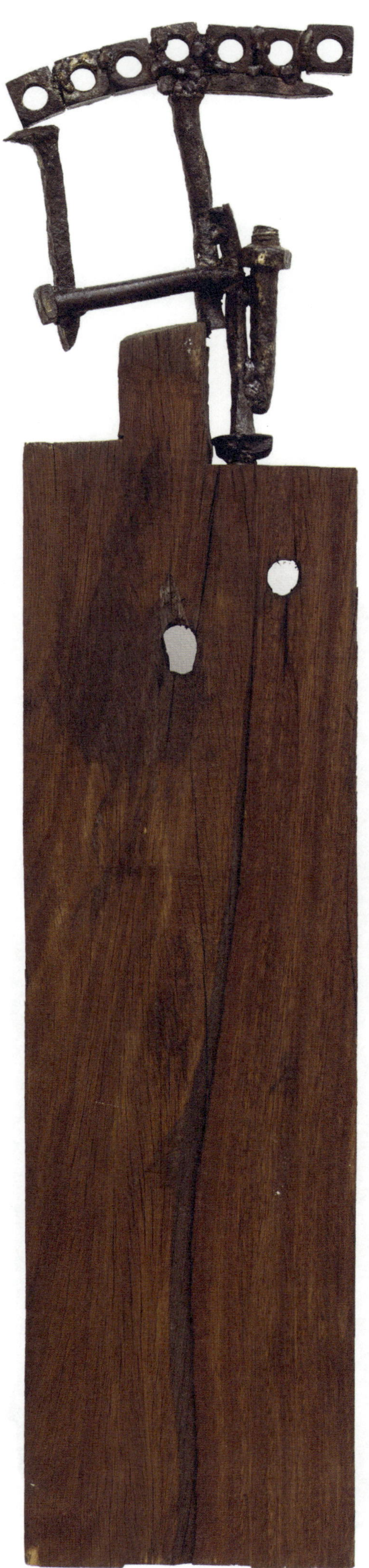

Wood work 14, 2019, assemblage on wood, 82 × 18 × 9.4 cm

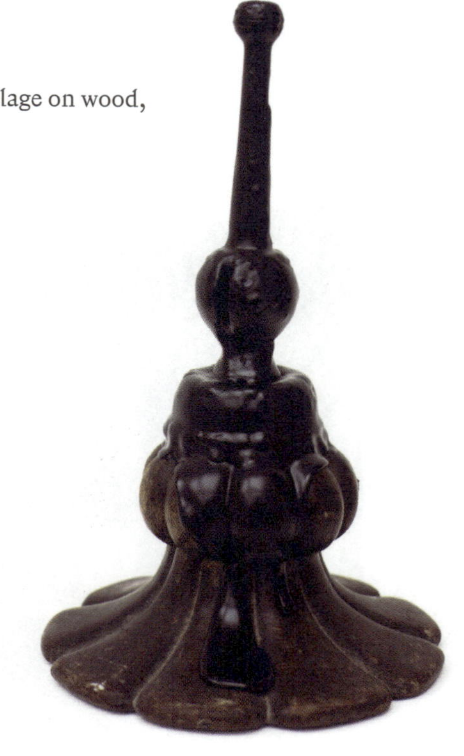

Wood work 15, 2019, assemblage on wood, 26.7 × 7 (diameter) cm

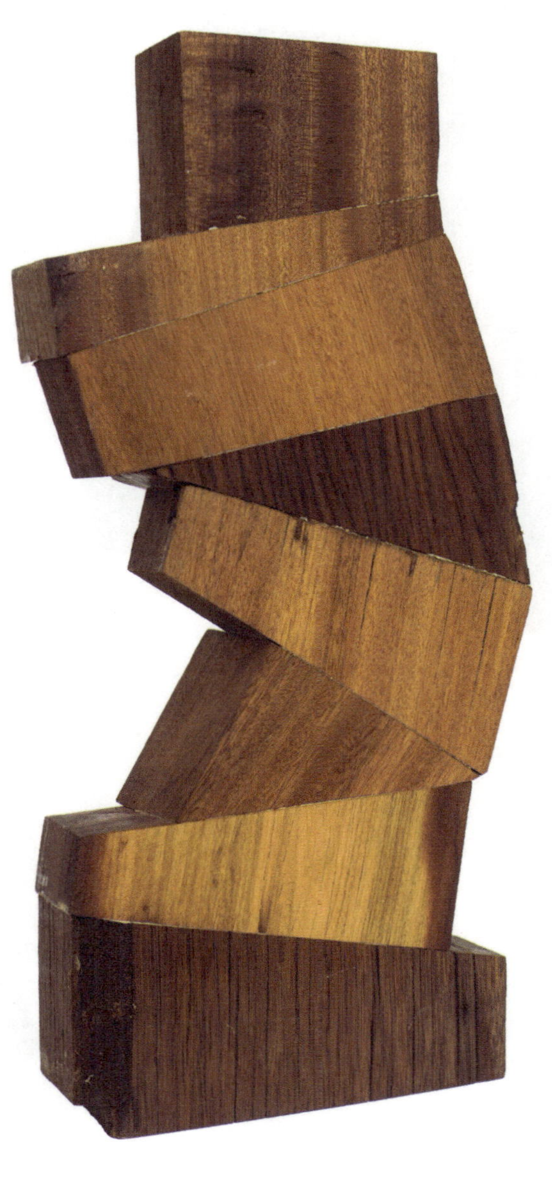

Wood work 12, 2019, assemblage on wood, 43.6 × 20 × 5 cm

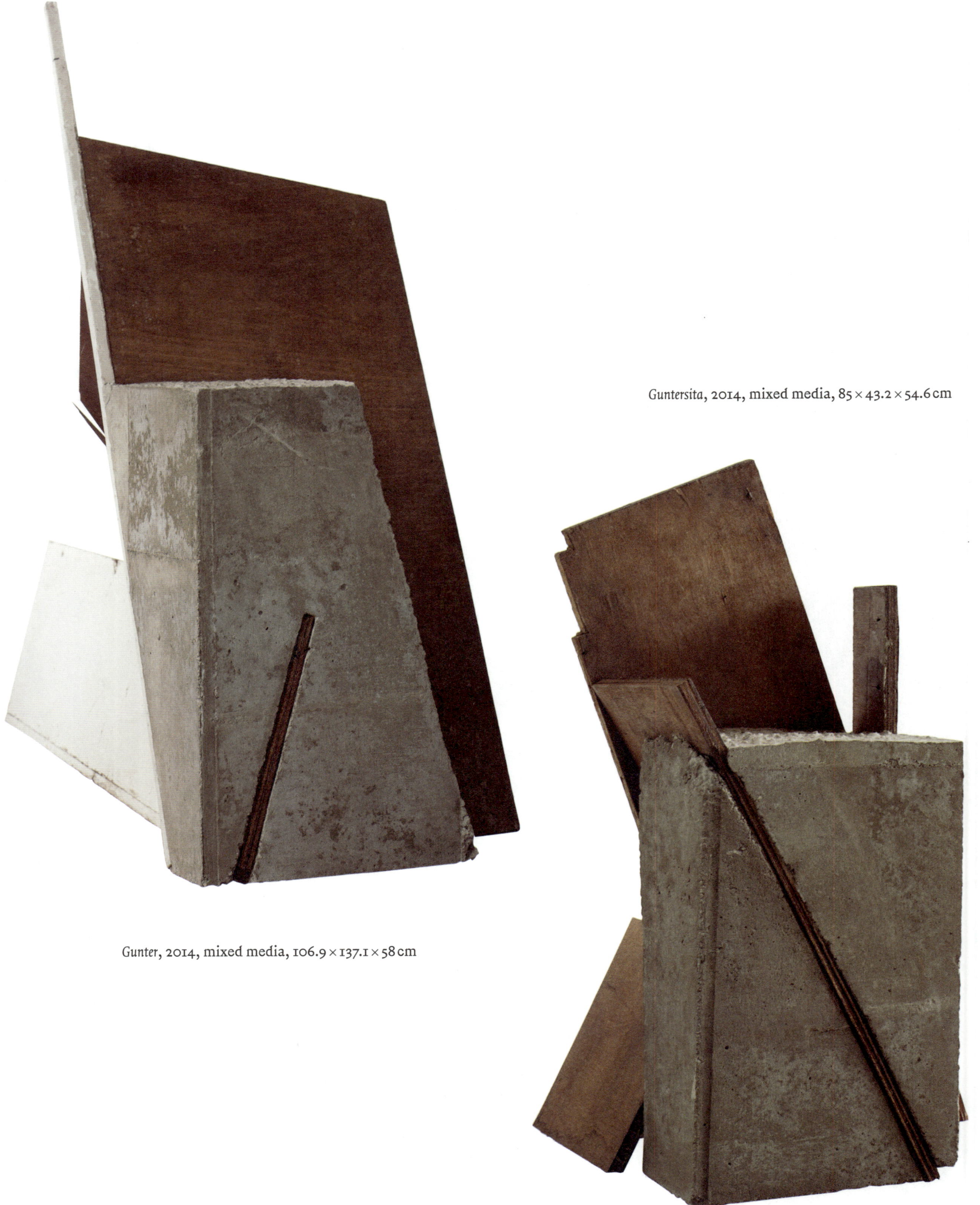

Guntersita, 2014, mixed media, 85 × 43.2 × 54.6 cm

Gunter, 2014, mixed media, 106.9 × 137.1 × 58 cm

Doing Dirty Abstraction: Bernardo Pacquing in conversation with Russell Storer

Bernardo Pacquing's studio, Manila
Monday, July 31, 2023

Russell Storer: *To start, can we talk about how you came to work the way you do?*

Bernardo Pacquing: I really wanted to study fine arts. At that time, UP [University of the Philippines] was the number one school. My dad was a bit upset because he wanted me to be in a Catholic university, so obviously not UP. He mentioned at the time that he thought I would become a Communist there! Thankfully, I was accepted by UP, and just to please my dad, I majored in visual communications, which was more practical than fine arts. But my heart really was in painting. I did well in the visual communications program. After university, I immediately joined the Cultural Center of the Philippines [CCP] as a graphic designer and worked there for two years.

RS: *What year did you start there?*

BP: I started at the CCP in 1990. At the time, we were designing graphics to represent the seven arts of the Philippines for the first edition of the *CCP Encyclopedia of Philippine Art*.[1] I asked my art director if I could design the graphics for the Visual Arts [section]. There I met masters and contemporary artists, like Lao Lianben, Gus Albor, the Zobels, and the Joyas. It was great fun doing those compositions. However, I became exhausted doing graphic arts, and in 1992, I decided to quit the CCP to become a full-time painter. It was a big decision.

1. The seven arts of the Philippines, which formed the framework for the CCP's programming, are architecture, theater, dance, visual arts, music, literature, and cinema. The first edition of the *CCP Encyclopedia of Philippine Art* was published in 1994.

During those years, I was living in Sampaloc, where our old house was, which needed to be restored and which I then did. I really love carpentry and woodworking and restoring things. There, I was surrounded by materials, which was extremely stimulating for me. Those were, in fact, my first materials and art experiences: painting the plywood, which first needed to be dismantled from the house, with house paint that I have been using ever since, roof paint, some waterproofing paint, and even some tar. Through that restoration, I was introduced to a nontraditional way of painting. And slowly, little by little, I learned how to paint with oil. That was the beginning (Fig. 1).

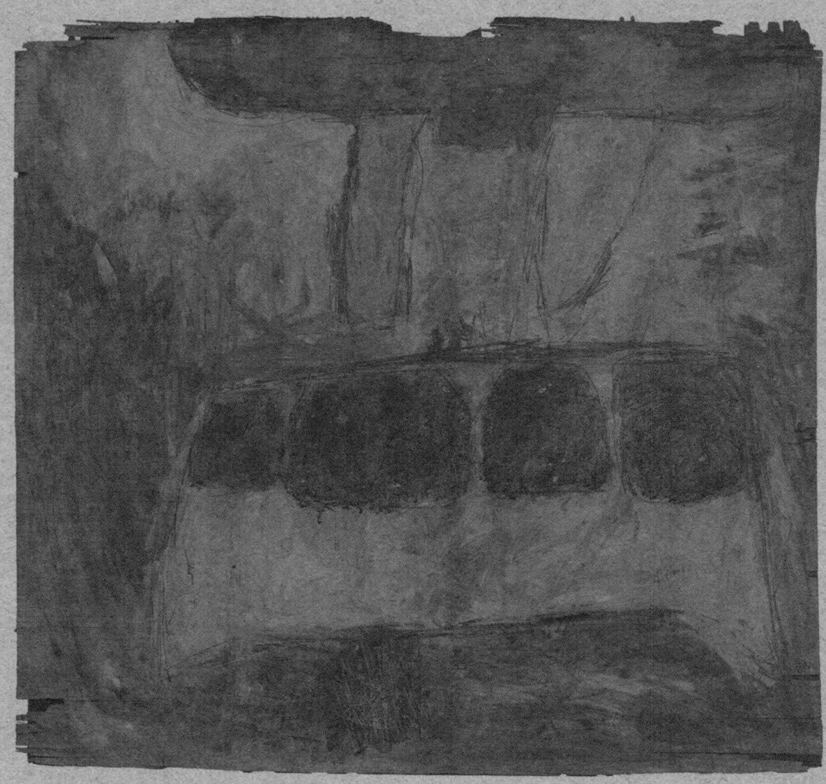

Fig. 1. *Untitled*, *c.* 1990, mixed media on plywood, 91.4 × 91.4 cm

RS: *Why did you choose to work in abstraction, rather than figuration?*

BP: I guess my earlier background as a graphic designer trained me to be very precise in design, composition, and even font size. We would literally paint the letters perfectly. For me, it was quite boring and very restrictive. Because of that, I became very tired of graphic arts. My intuitive side wanted to grab paper and charcoal, or a lead pencil, and to draw crude doodles in a manner completely opposite to that used in graphic arts — I wanted a total release from the restrictions imposed by graphic arts. I guess that is why I chose abstraction over figuration. For me, abstraction truly expresses how you feel deep inside you. It can be very emotional, expressing your feelings of anger, frustration, happiness, contentment, and so on. Realizing that about yourself is a big step (Fig. 2).

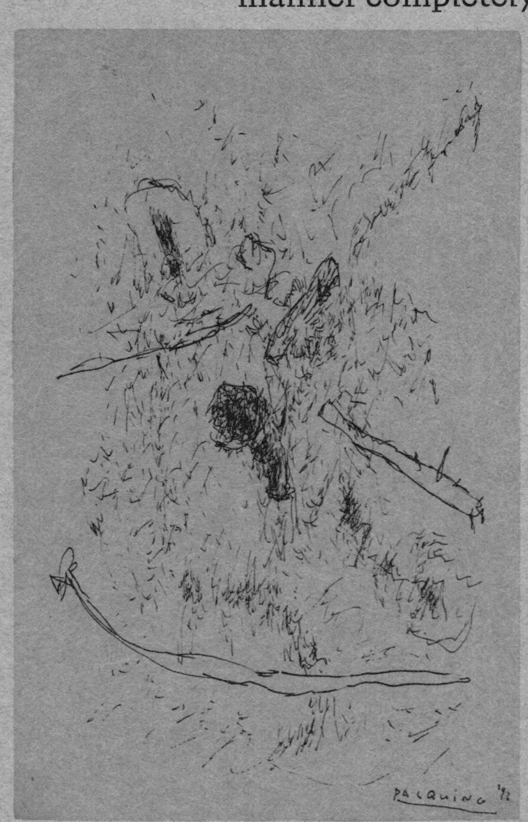

Fig. 2. Artist's doodle

RS: *You had a community of like-minded artists around you. How did that help you to develop your work?*

BP: Yes, and naturally I had more friends in studio arts than in graphic arts [at UP]. They were sculptors, painters, printmakers. Chatting with them, you felt their sensibility and learned so much from them. It was exciting to hear them mention artists I had never heard of; one of them, for instance, idolized [Georg] Baselitz, which then inspired me to see his work. That is also how I discovered [Chaïm] Soutine and Eva Hesse, the latter a favorite of another friend, and a really good sculptor called Richard Serra. The works of other artists help you understand where you want to go, how you wish to define yourself, which sector of abstraction you want to focus on.

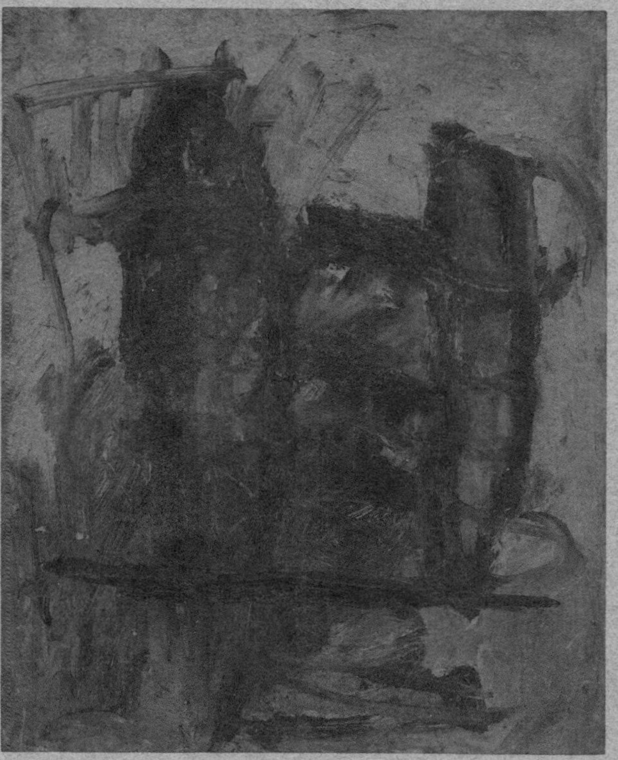

Fig. 3. *Untitled*, c. 1994, mixed media, 30.5 × 25.4 cm

There were also a lot of what we called "pretty abstractions." In contrast, jokingly, we called what we preferred, what we were doing, messy, dirty abstraction. And it was more fun! (Fig. 3).

RS: *And does this so-called "dirty abstraction"—the use of everyday materials and of working with that materiality—reflect your environment, the landscape of Manila?*

BP: Yes, it does. Manila is a dirty and very polluted, noisy place. I am surrounded by all that, which is naturally expressed in my work.

The materials of the city all around me are rusty, moldy, damp, and I am exposed to those kinds of materials. In my art, I take up the challenge of finding beauty in these overlooked and messy – but also lovely – expressions of what Manila is.

I am also very fond of walls. On my street, or anywhere in Manila, one sees government workers trying to paint a tunnel or an underpass of EDSA[2]; at the same time, there is always a puddle of muddy water [nearby], so every time a car passes, it splashes a wall. And a worker is there trying to clean it with white paint. Then, when it is teatime, they just go off to tea and never come back.

2. Epifanio de los Santos Avenue, also commonly referred to as "EDSA," is a major highway that runs through Metro Manila.

That sensibility is classic and I love it, just as I love the walls. The workers have short sticks with brushes because there is no budget for longer ones, and they just paint like this [*gesturing as if painting a low wall*]. And what about the upper part? It cannot be nicely painted. That is Manila, and such incidents are my inspirations.

Also, when you ride a train, you see the walls under the tunnels, where the poured concrete looks quite barbaric. You can see that the plywood was not evenly placed when they poured it; the moldings are still there, rotting, as are the markings of the engineers. And it is quite messy. Of course, people do not really care because it is inside the dark tunnel. But for me, it reflects how things are done in Manila, and how we live here (Fig. 4).

Fig. 4. *Damp Mortar*, 2003, oil and house paint on canvas, 182.9 × 457.2 cm

RS: *Given that, do you feel that there is a social dimension to your practice?*

BP: At first, I thought my work did not really touch upon social issues, which I was not particularly curious about. But then, looking back now, I can see that it does. My art reflects the people living in this place. It seems that here, we build to destroy and destroy to build.

Even government projects are literally built and then abandoned, becoming ruins because of the corruption and graft involved in the original sale.

It is strange, but it is real; we do not look back to reimagine old structures and try to preserve them. It is sad. A specific building preserves so much history. And, of course, during World War II, Manila lost its history; and after the bombs flattened all the concrete, buildings become a carpet of gray stuff.

We have remained that way ever since. We have wars in Mindanao. Every Filipino is always living in and with ruins. They have become a part of us.

RS: *Would you say that the materials you use lead or determine your work?*

BP: Yes. I treat every available material in a very different way. When you select a material, there is an immediate question: Will I present it "as is"? Sometimes, I choose not to, and repurpose it instead. And sometimes, I am inspired by it and come up with creative ideas based on the original object or material.

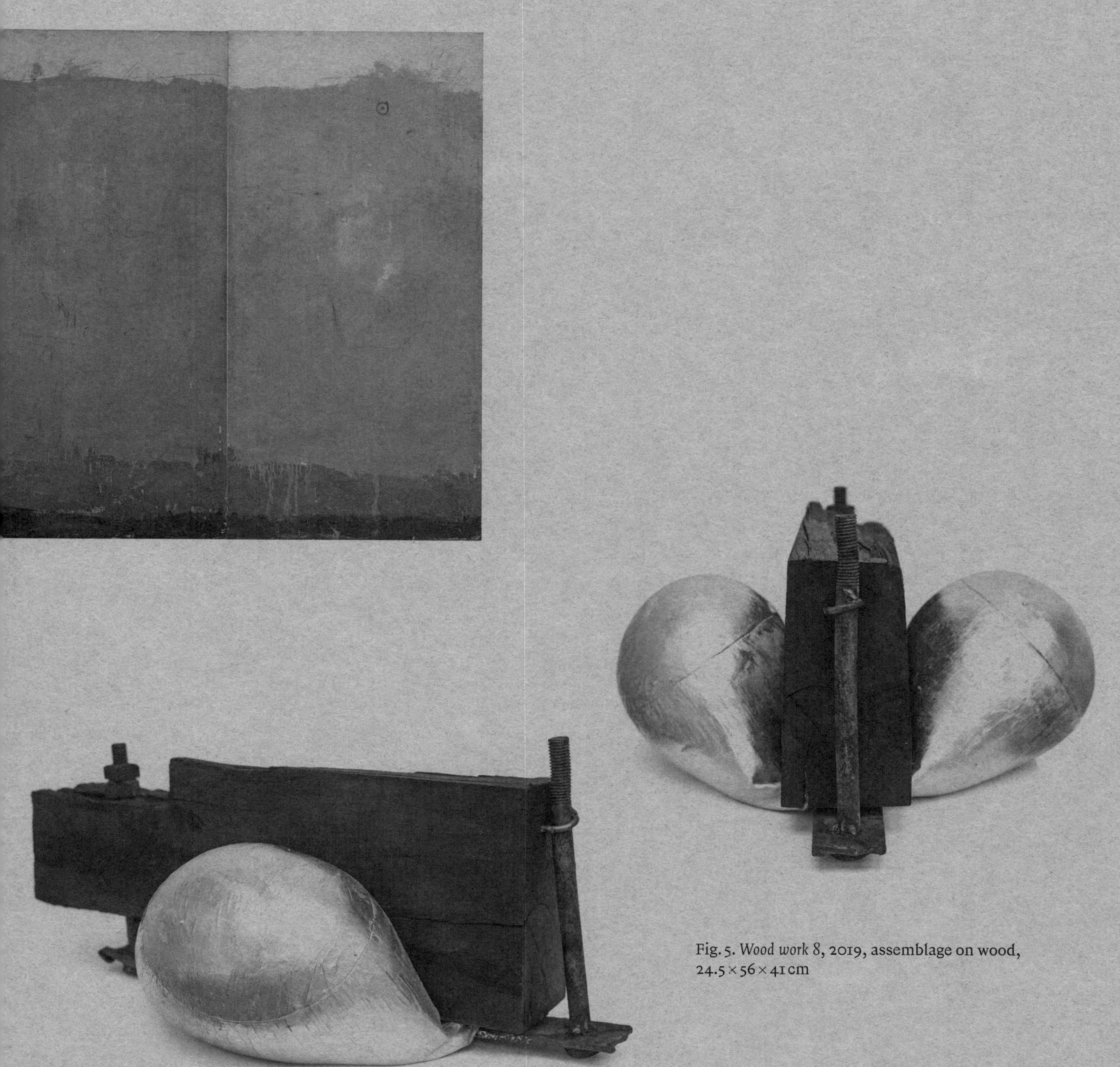

Fig. 5. *Wood work* 8, 2019, assemblage on wood, 24.5 × 56 × 41 cm

Other times, I feel the challenge to mix a material with its opposite; for instance, to dip an old, soft pillow into concrete or water so that it becomes a bit harder. And then, the big question is: Should I present it as a pillow? Obviously, it looks like a pillow. However, I can also combine it with other objects, transforming it into a sculptural element. Every available material inspires a different treatment; so, for example, you can mix a rubber tire with wood or combine it with concrete (Fig. 5).

Fig. 6. *Untitled*, *c.* 2012, mixed media on plywood, 58.4 × 116.8 cm

RS: *Has your process changed over time? In the beginning, you had mainly these materials on hand, so you drew on them. Now, you can choose whichever material you wish to work with.*

BP: My process evolves. Nowadays, there are hundreds of different industrial paints and very exciting new materials. In addition, however, I have also kept specific materials over the last ten years knowing that one day I would use them. I just do not yet know how.

For example, my studio is an old, 1970s house. It is very dark, done with typical plywood of the period called Danara. It has a plywood finish, with a hardwood-colored wood stain. I took down all the dividers in the rooms to open up the space. And I then, literally, used all the plywood in my collages and exhibited works. My biggest assemblage was 16 by 32 feet, made completely from parts of this house. For instance, that work [*pointing to a work hanging on the wall*] is a cupboard, a cabinetry part (Fig. 6). This work [*pointing to another work*] is where the teaspoon would lie on a spoon rack and you can still see the joinery of the sidings.

RS: *Do you look for materials or objects that create a tension by being a bit irregular or awkward while also containing a kind of a harmony?*

BP: That is correct. And that also affects how I treat materials such as rusty nails, old tires, and pillows. I have even collected dried paint rings left by old cans of house paint to use them in collages. When the piece is done, one cannot really see that a feature came from a can of paint. People ask: "Where did you get that? What is that? Oh, okay!" And it is nice to have that kind of response.

RS: *You also create a physical tension in your works where you bind things and hold them together. Could you talk more about that?*

BP: I actually created work for "Zero Infinite" at Silverlens Manila in 2019 about tension and how it affected me. It consisted entirely of canvas works, where the tension of the canvas was ratcheted up on the stretcher almost to its breaking point (Fig. 7).

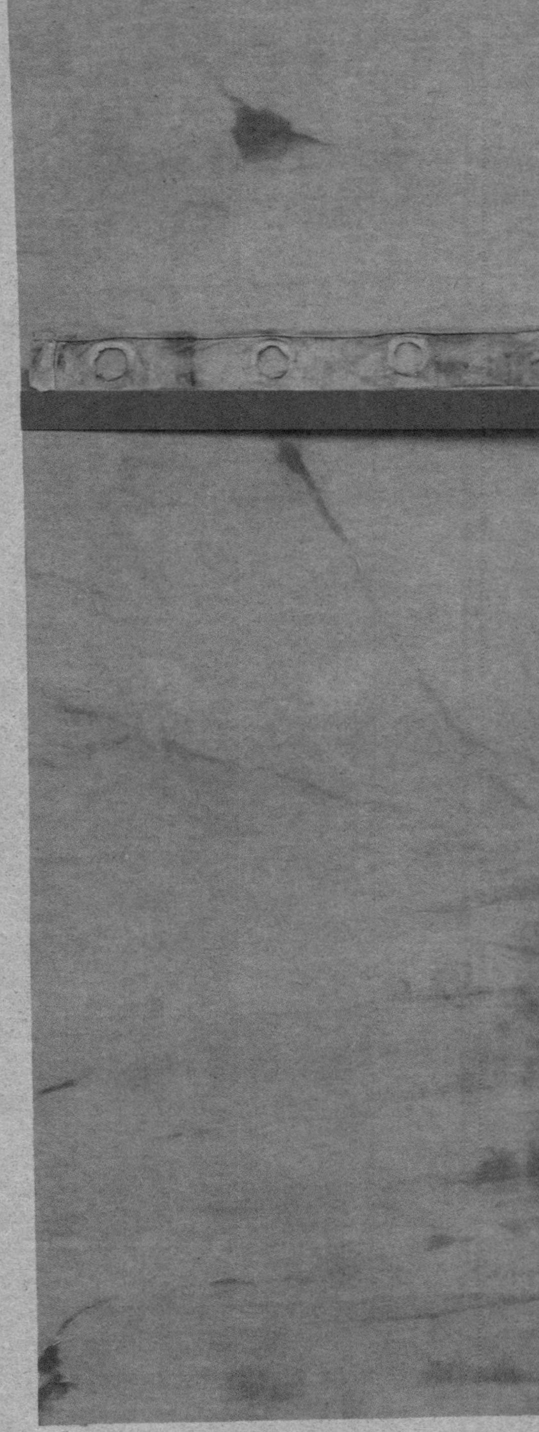

I would add on a lot of industrial paint to make the canvas stronger, hoping that it would hold up along the whole stretcher. The entire show was based on Bach's solo violin piece, which for me, is the most difficult solo violin piece ever written.[3]

3. J.S. Bach, *Partita No. 2* "Chaconne", composed between 1718 and 1720.

The composition, for me, evokes the limits of human skill, because you feel how difficult it is for a player to master and play the piece. And there is the continuous tension between the movements of the violinist's fingers and the play of the jumping bow. My exhibition intuitively expressed my feelings about that composition.

For instance, I clamped a pillow to the point of tearing it, and then I covered it in concrete so that the pillow became harder and harder, even while it was being squeezed extremely hard. And the process of pouring concrete over a pillow was very exciting, more exciting for me than the final outcome. I love the feeling of pushing something to its limits, as I did with the paintings when I ratcheted them to their limit while controlling the tension so that they would not break. Just for fun, I actually wished to find the limit; so, I added an additional paint layer to break the canvas intentionally. I loved it!

RS: *I think that time is a central component in your work. You seem to be capturing the history of these materials as well as their potential future transformations.*

BP: Of course, eventually, pillows will rot, even when covered in concrete. Wood will rot. House paint on a canvas will flake, eventually, and I do not really care—it is okay.

RS: *Which takes us back to your description of the city around you. You live between Singapore and Manila. And obviously, they are very different cities. The materials are different. The environment is different. How did that shift affect the way you work?*

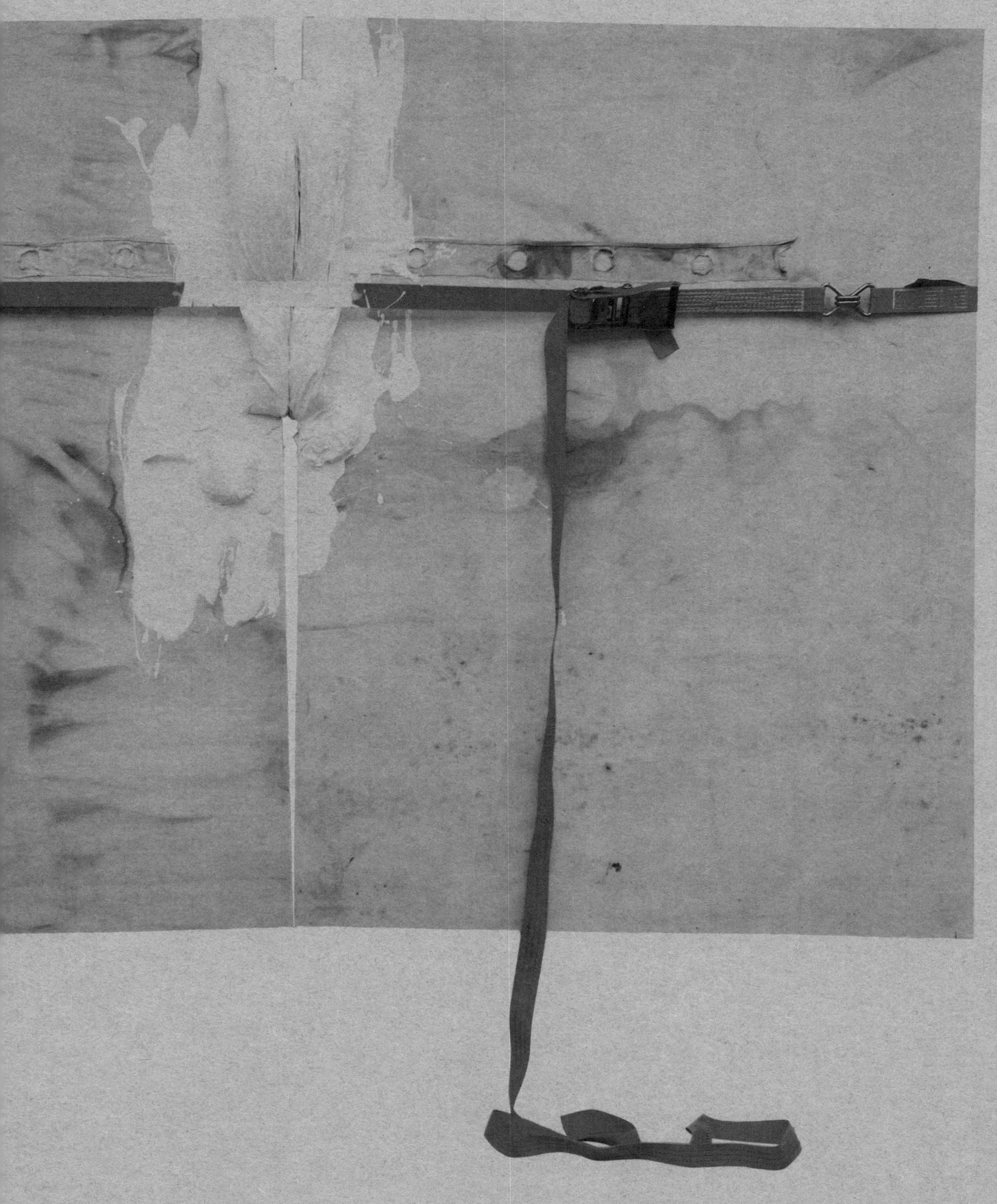

Fig. 7. "Untitled #1" *After J.S. Bach's Partitia No. 2 "Chaconne"*, 2019, assemblage, 182.9 × 280 × 17.8 cm

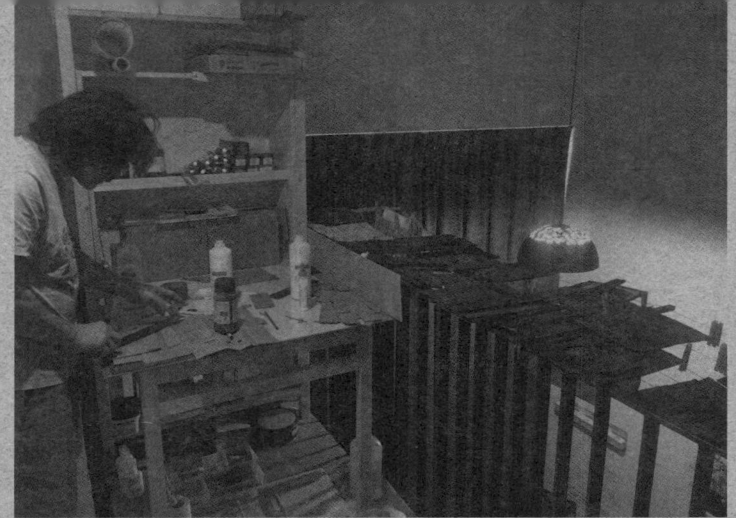

Fig. 8. Bernardo's Singapore studio, 2021

BP: I was stuck in Singapore for two and a half years during the pandemic, and it was quite depressing. My friend warned me beforehand, saying, "Bernie, your work will change. Singapore is a very, very clean city, very structured, a very depressing place for you. I think your work will change, [it will] become cleaner and more structured."

During COVID, I had no materials. I was living in a tiny apartment with my wife. My first-ever collages during the pandemic were made from the boxes of oil paints that I ordered online. And then, after that, I applied oil paints to those cardboard boxes and did some collages as well. Then, I began using grocery boxes gathered from our online orders to create collages. I would say, jokingly, to my wife, "This is First World cardboard," which is very different, of course, from the grocery boxes in Manila (Fig. 8).

I ended up doing collages out of very clean, die-cut boxes (Figs. 9a, 9b). I also applied paint to the cardboard for the collages. At first, these were bright, warm colors, like oranges, yellows, and reds. And then, as time went by, months and months later, I slowly realized that the pandemic was very serious. My work became darker and darker, and the colors were like a bloody red. My depression was peaking at that time. After 80 or so collages, I became exhausted with cardboard, and I began to search [how] to do larger works, and I was able to use some canvas. Because our space was so small, as I already mentioned, my first canvases were four by five. After that, I tried a six-by-ten canvas that was really big for our apartment. I had to alternate between pinning it to the floor and then to the wall—and back to the floor again. All the walls and floors were covered in plastic. My wife would joke that it was as if I had killed someone, covering the walls and floors with plastic to make it easier to clean all the red away. When I had my canvas on the floor, I literally felt as if I were scouring the innards of an animal. Or I felt like a shaman inspecting an animal's entrails for signs (Fig. 10).

So, that is what was really happening to me during the pandemic.
And I survived.

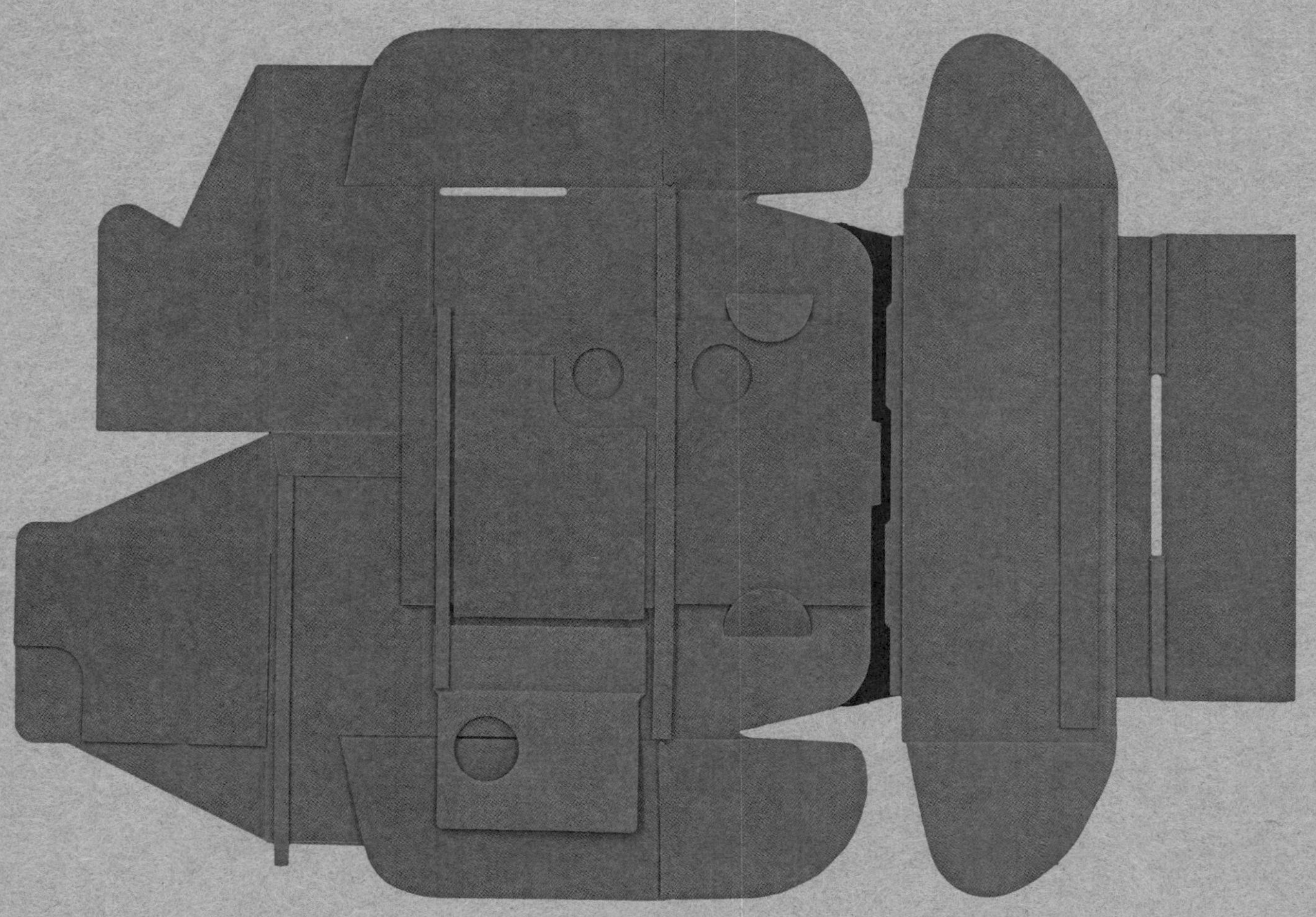

Fig. 9a. *Brown Study #19*, 2023, cardboard, 78.1 × 62.9 cm

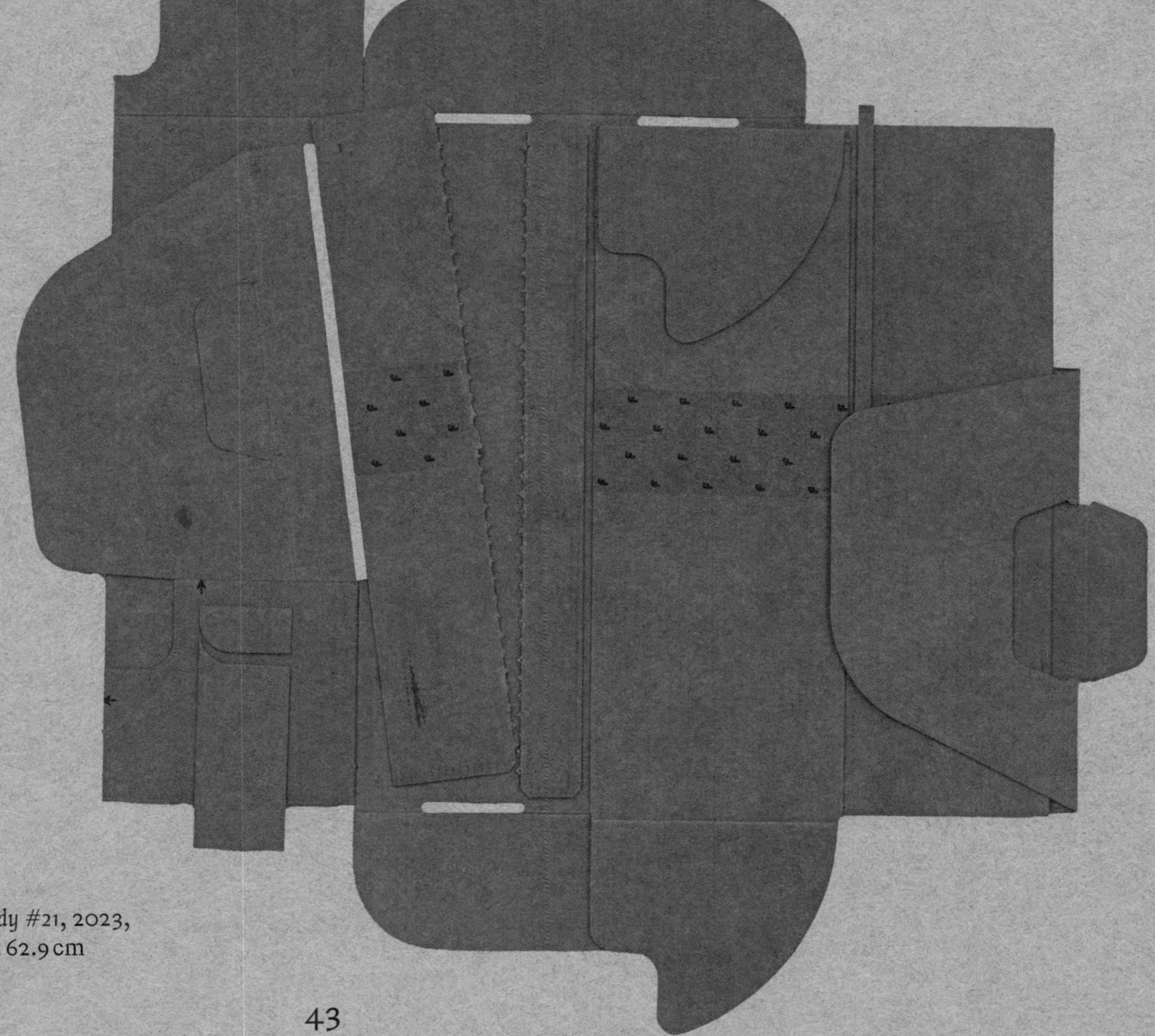

Fig. 9b. *Brown Study #21*, 2023, cardboard, 78.1 × 62.9 cm

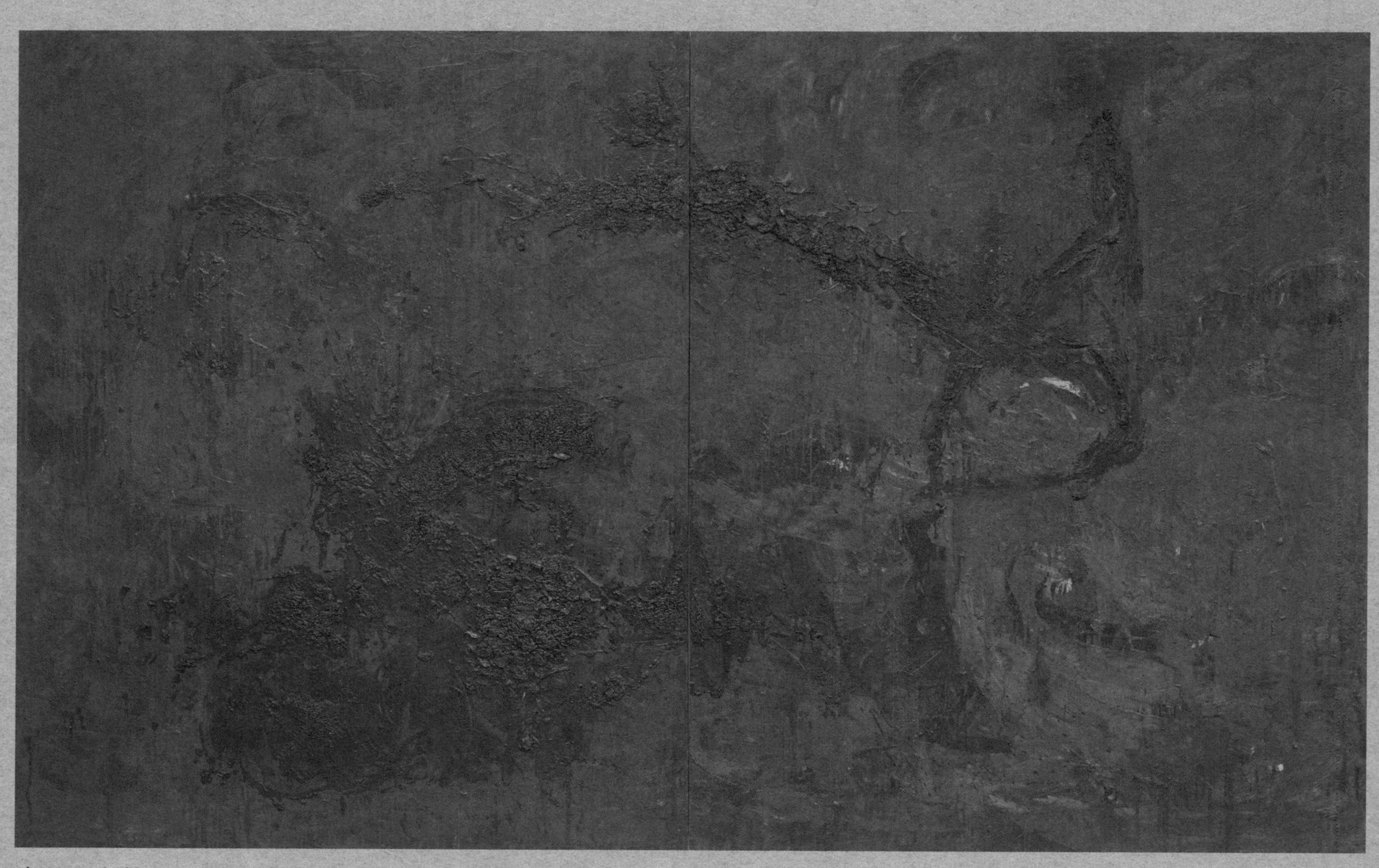

Fig. 10. *Red Object #04*, 2021, oil on canvas, 182.9 × 304.8 cm

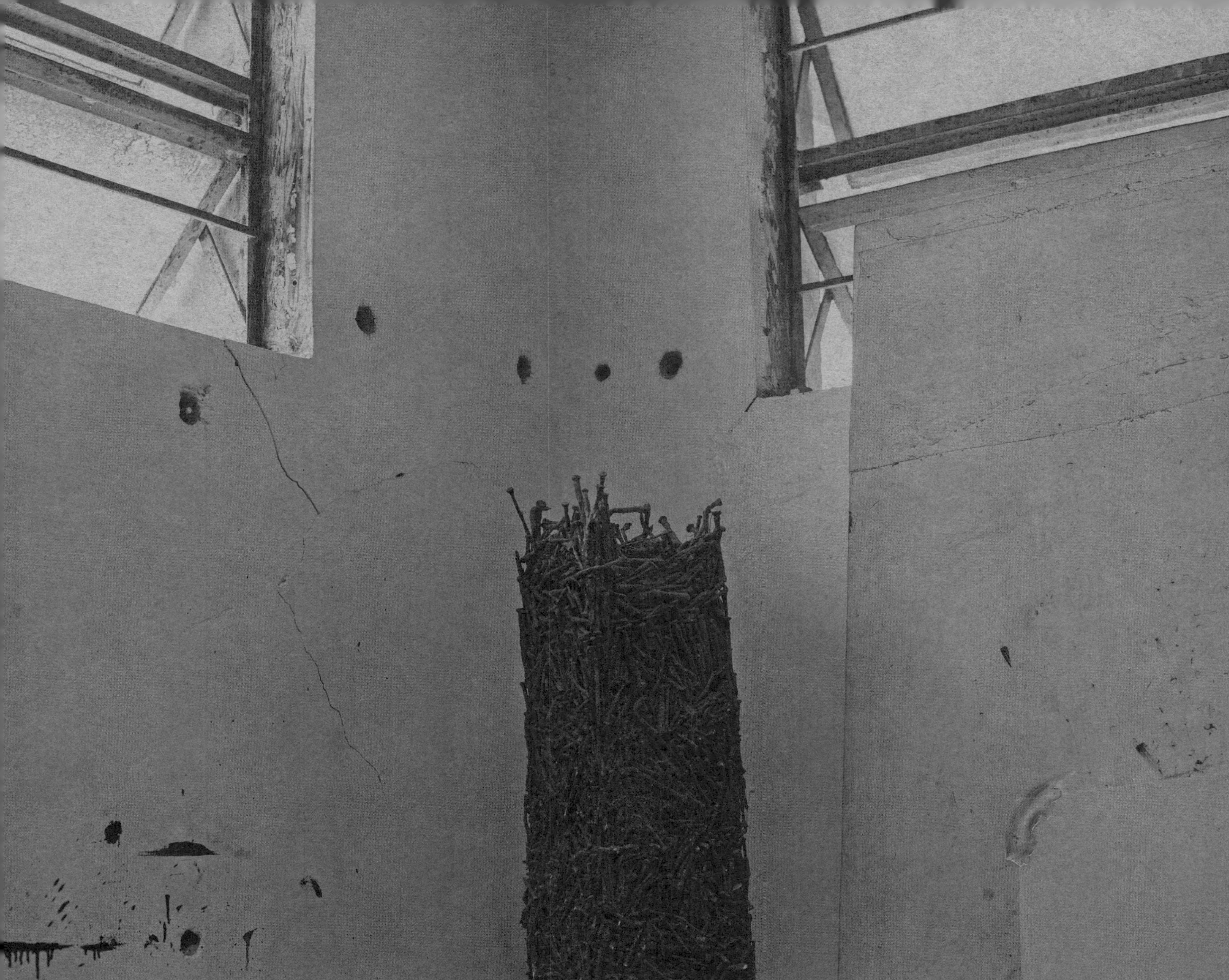

Fig. 11. Bernardo's Manila studio, 2022

RS: *Moving back to Manila, did your work change again?*

BP: In Manila, I slowly returned to doing assemblage on canvas, which I had always enjoyed. I made use of some old materials [I had] previously collected. I had truly missed my studio, and it felt like I was home again. And I slowly went back to my real environment — that is, to rediscovering rubble with mold, which I loved. In Singapore, I have some woodworking space, but I cannot even use my chisels and mallets because of noise regulations there. So, when I am back here in Manila, I can create again, be reunited with the real me and with all my old wood and collected materials. I am now preparing for my next one-man show, after the one-on-one red paintings. Its theme this time is ruins and rubble. And so far, so good; I'm enjoying it (Fig. 11).

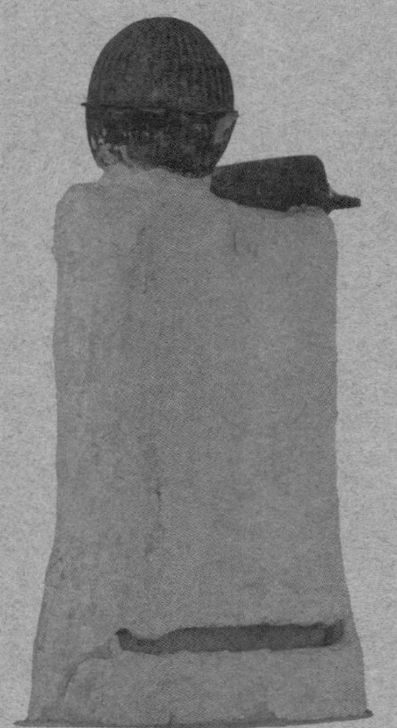

Fig. 12. *Arc de Triomphe*, 1998, mixed media, 47 × 30.5 × 12.7 cm

RS: *I am interested in your artistic trajectory from your earlier identity as a painter to your work with assemblage. Did you move from there into sculpture, or was sculpture always a parallel practice?*

BP: I would say that it has been a parallel practice. At first, I started with assemblage or wall works using canvas and plywood. But somehow, after making them, there was always a sense that I had mastered this and now I wished to do more. Then I would think: What if I did it this way—same material, same approach, same treatment—but in three-dimensions? That way, you can mix the malleability and fragility of various materials together. And that is how I evolved into doing sculptural work, which was a really exciting development for me (Fig. 12).

RS: *Looking back over 30 years of practice, do you see distinct phases in your work? For instance, there is the "Builder Bernie" and then there are other, different Bernies.*

BP: I really do not know, because at the age of 56, I am still actively learning—and evolving. I am hungry to learn and to define myself using my environment and to see how I will treat and use materials around me. As you know, there are no preparatory studies for my works. It is all just intuition.

RS: *You are an artist who is seen as responding to an urban environment, so I am also interested in your recent shift to the outdoors and your relationship to nature.*

BP: Yes, I can become fascinated with everything and anything. At one point, I became fixated with hydroponics and with harvesting my own tomatoes—it was really fun. I was also fixated on worms, vermiculture, for a while. I guess that was because of our farm.[4] I think one's interests are a reaction to the environment one is in.

4. Located in Santa Rosa Malico, Nueva Vizcaya, the farm grows a local arabica coffee at 1,600 meters above sea level.

My fixation with domes started with termites. Restoring the old [family] house in Sampaloc, I rediscovered plants, soil, and termites. I wanted to understand how termites made a dome, which I think is a perfect structural form; from igloos to large cathedrals, we always seem to build domes. I then moved on from domes and became fascinated with engineering structures and the materials used, and I realized that I would like to experience building my own dome. What would it feel like, I wondered, to make one? So, I constructed domes out of parquet flooring in my studio. Then, at one point, Isa [Lorenzo] messaged me, saying "Bernie, there is just so much trash here. What can you do?" They have a resort in Davao, surrounded by mounting piles of driftwood. So, I made a dome out of their driftwood, which was extremely exciting. Of course, termites almost brought it down. A natural cycle, no? (Fig. 13).

Fig. 13. *Earth Mounds*, 2018, driftwood, 300 × 600 (diameter) cm

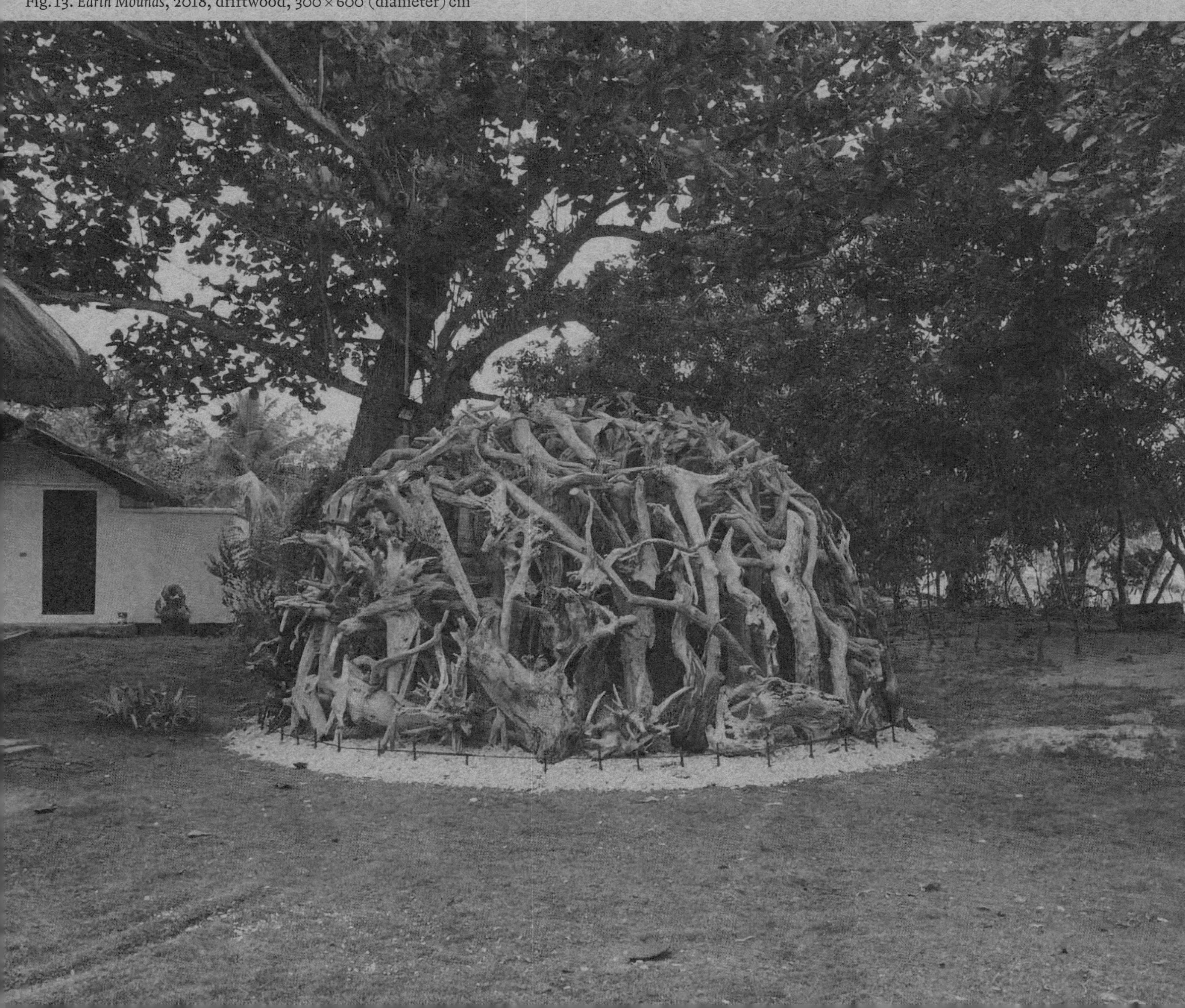

RS: *That is a bit like the urban cycle here, is it not? You build it, and it breaks down.*

BP: That is right. It breaks down. The Clark project, for me, was the largest project, and it was an honor to work with 200- and 300-year-old wood. That would be a dream come true for any carpenter. And when I got those materials, I began building right away. Rachel [Rillo] then mentioned that there were Dutch artists, partners, and engineers who could help me with the armature, the structure. Their manner of treating the old wood is very complicated. They first take a piece in order to date the age of the wood, and then send it to a laboratory in Laguna to test the wood for possible twists or warping and for its breaking point. I do not understand them or the need for this – and they cannot understand me – I just want to work. I just wanted to start right away and viscerally create the dome. They had a different sensibility. They are so structured when it comes to process and materials. Typical Dutch! And then, they were invited by Isa to go to the resort and see my driftwood structure, and they were completely stunned. "Oh, my goodness! How were you able to do this?" they asked. I am the emotional one, and they are the scientific ones.

For me, it is just like painting: just throw it down and keep doing it. And for them, it is all science and numbers. But then, working with wood is truly fantastic. It is an experience. Of course, the wood will rot, full of termites again. It goes back into nature. Everywhere you go there is a cycle; and I guess, that is it. It is what it is. You just have to enjoy it.

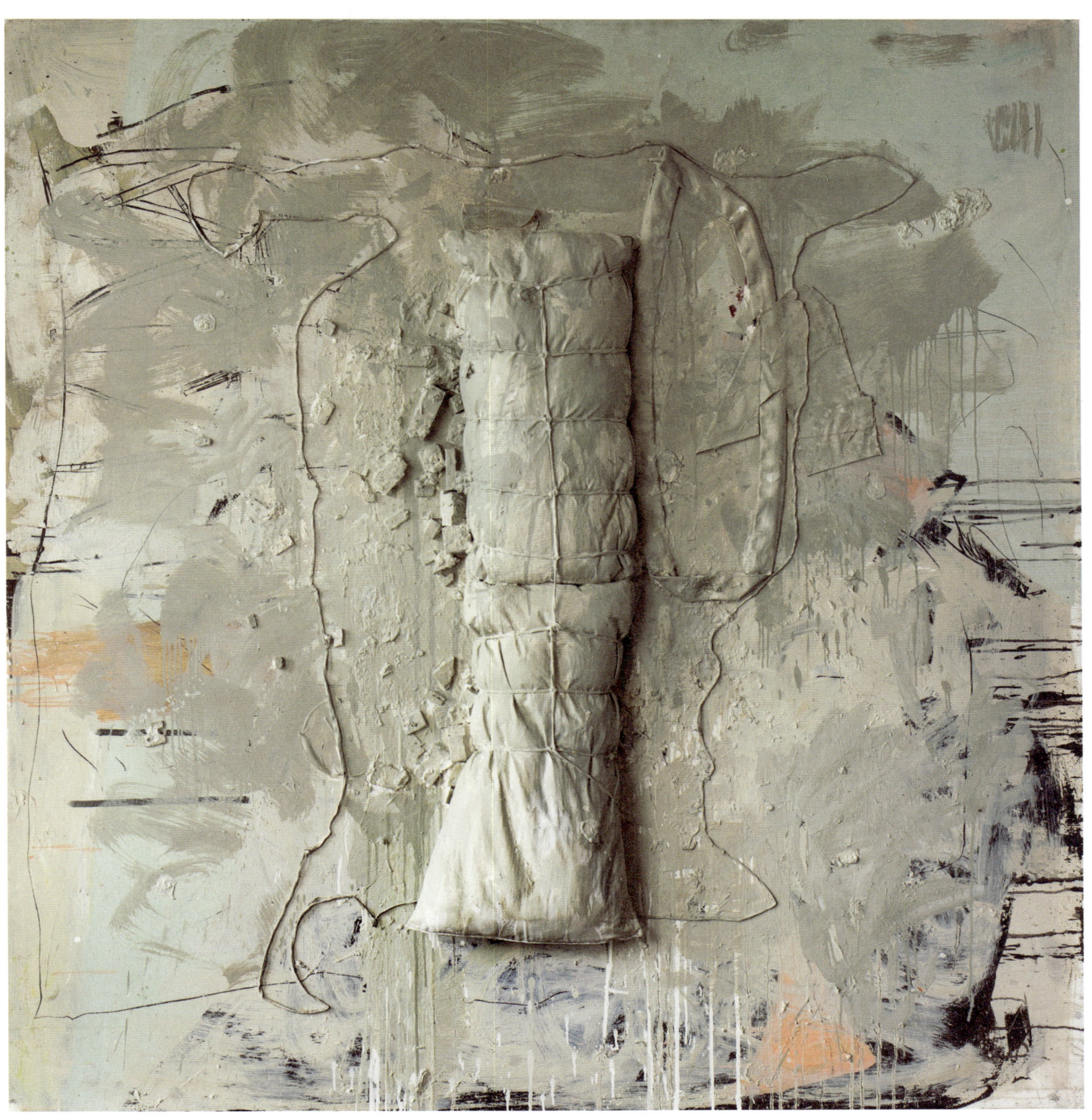

Effigy, 2016, paint and assemblage on canvas, 203.2 × 203.2 cm

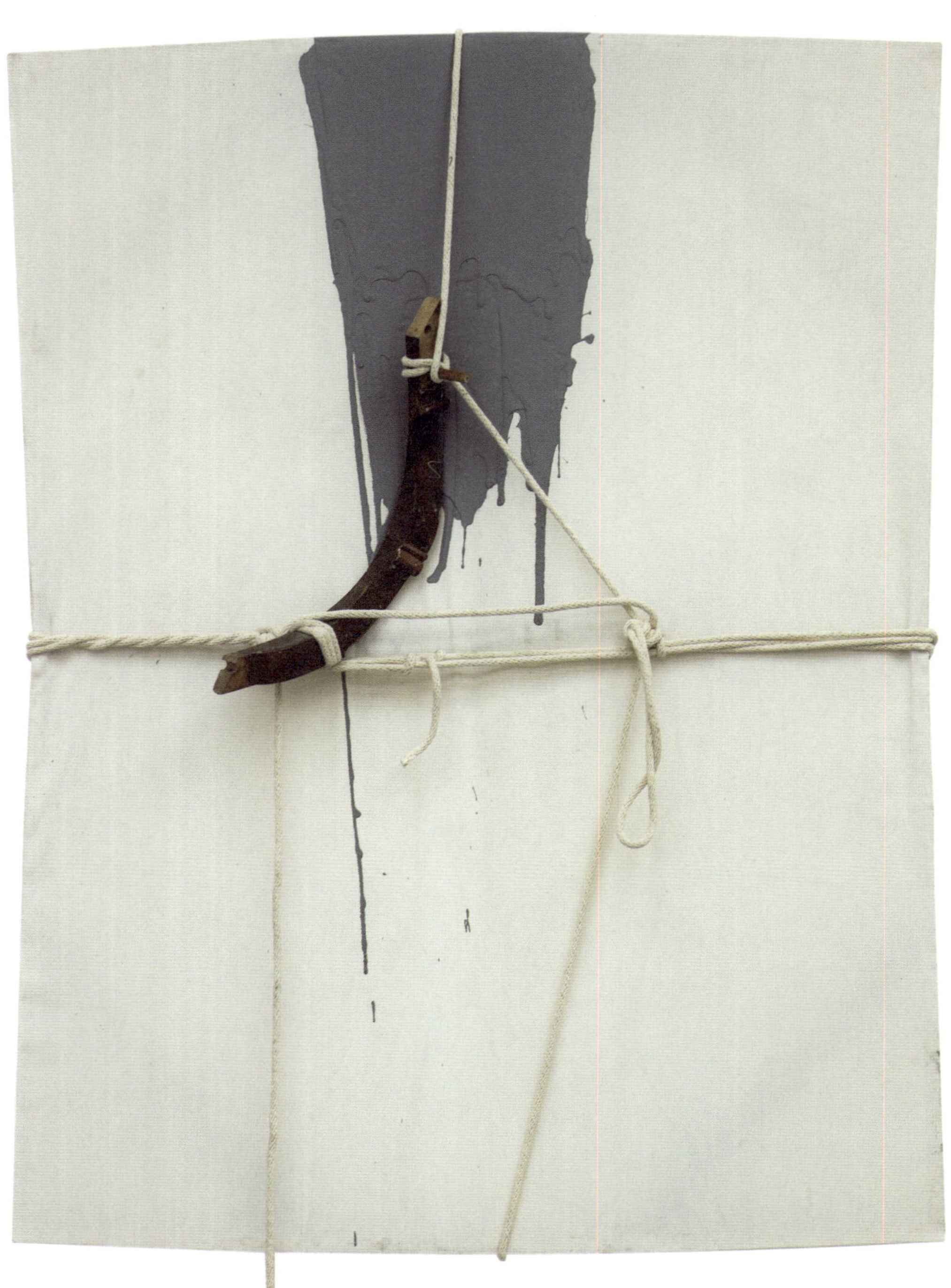

Vagueness of Dynamics 02, 2022, oil, house paint, assemblage on canvas, 152.4 × 121.9 cm

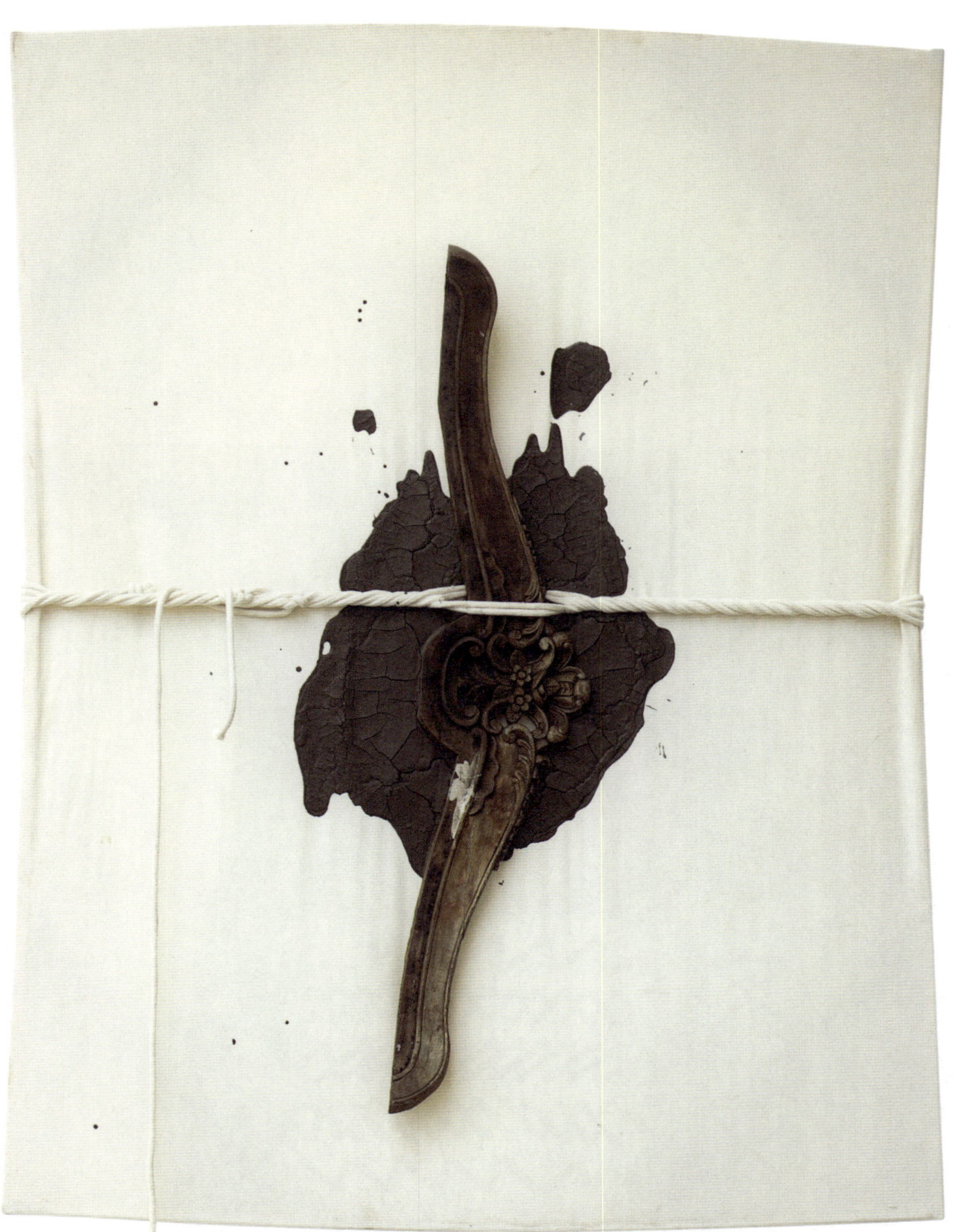

Vagueness of Dynamics 04, 2022, oil, house paint, assemblage on canvas, 152.4 × 121.9 cm

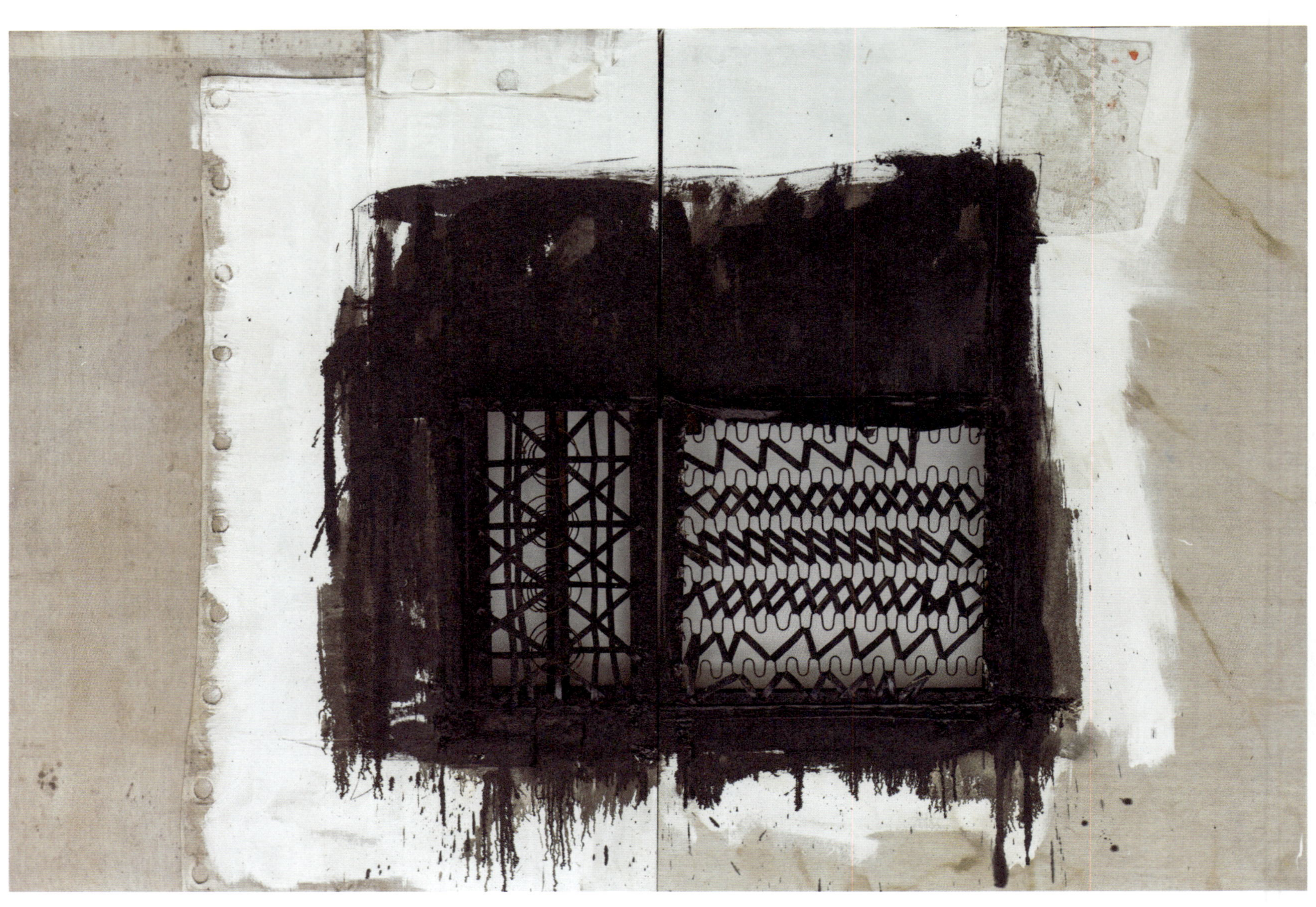

"Untitled" After Malevich's Black Square, 2019, assemblage on canvas, house paint, 213.4 × 274.3 cm (diptych)

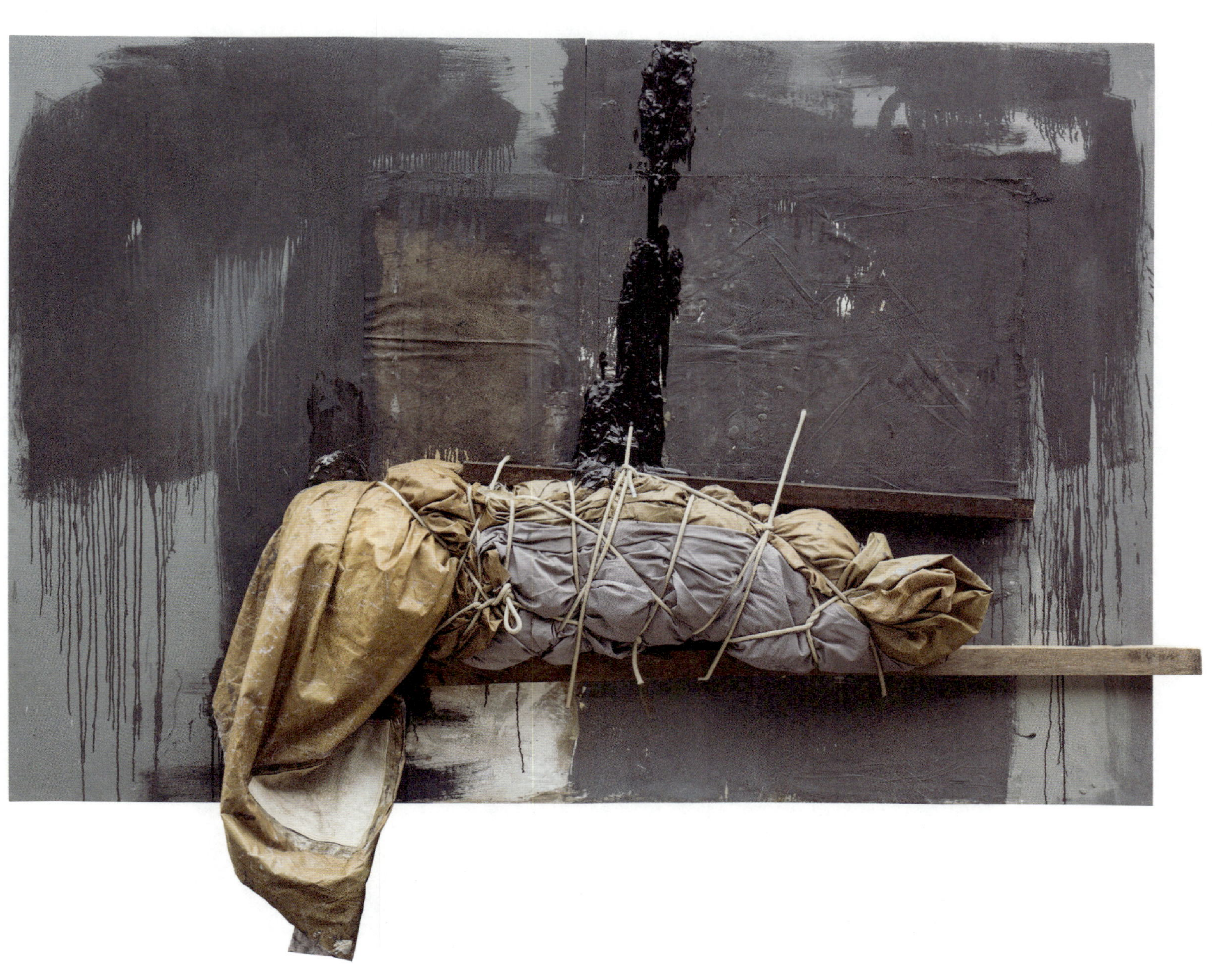

Crimped Tent, 2019, assemblage on canvas, 182.9 × 274.3 cm

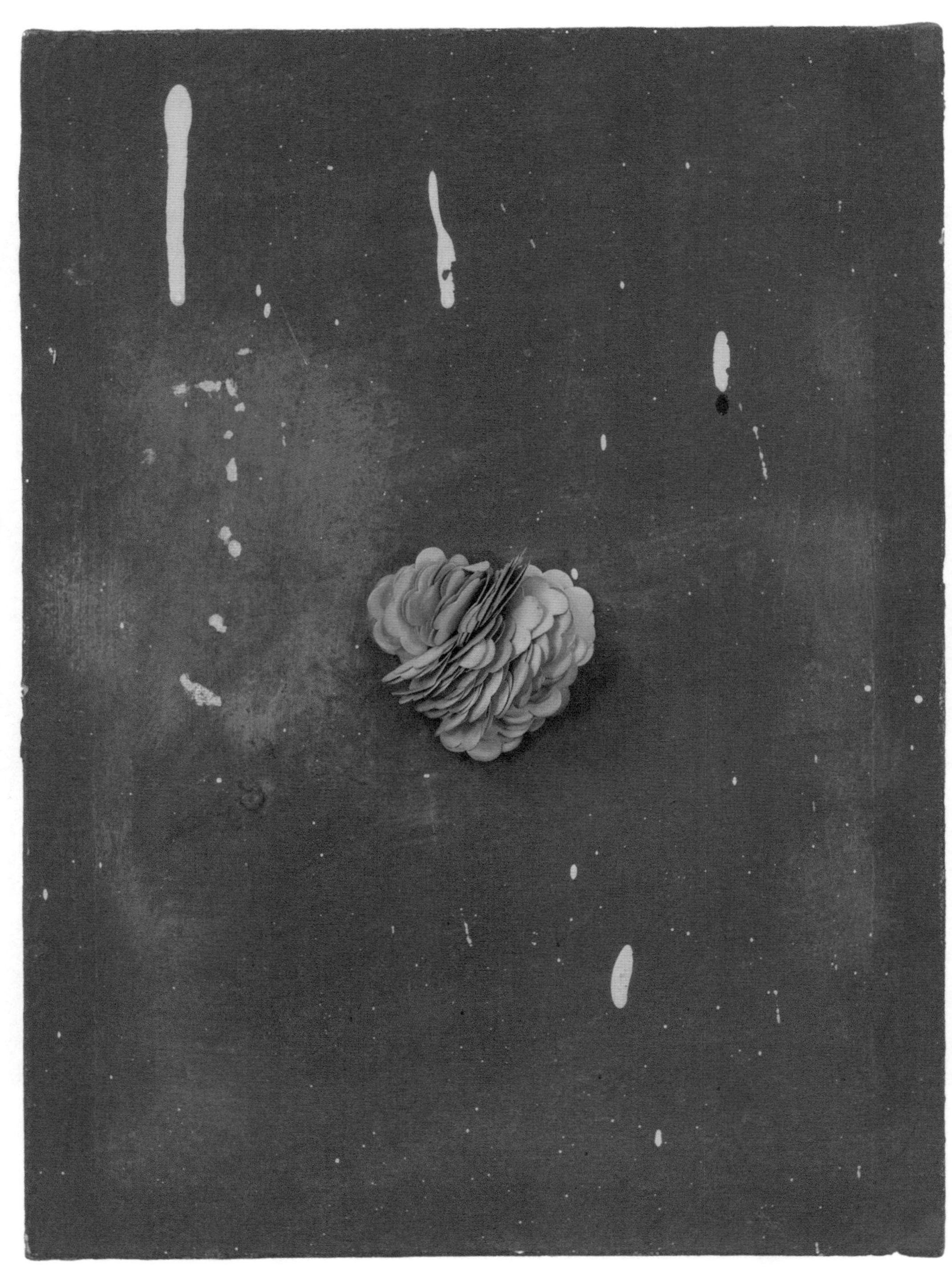

Mahjong Series 01, 2005, mixed media, 30.5 × 22.9 cm

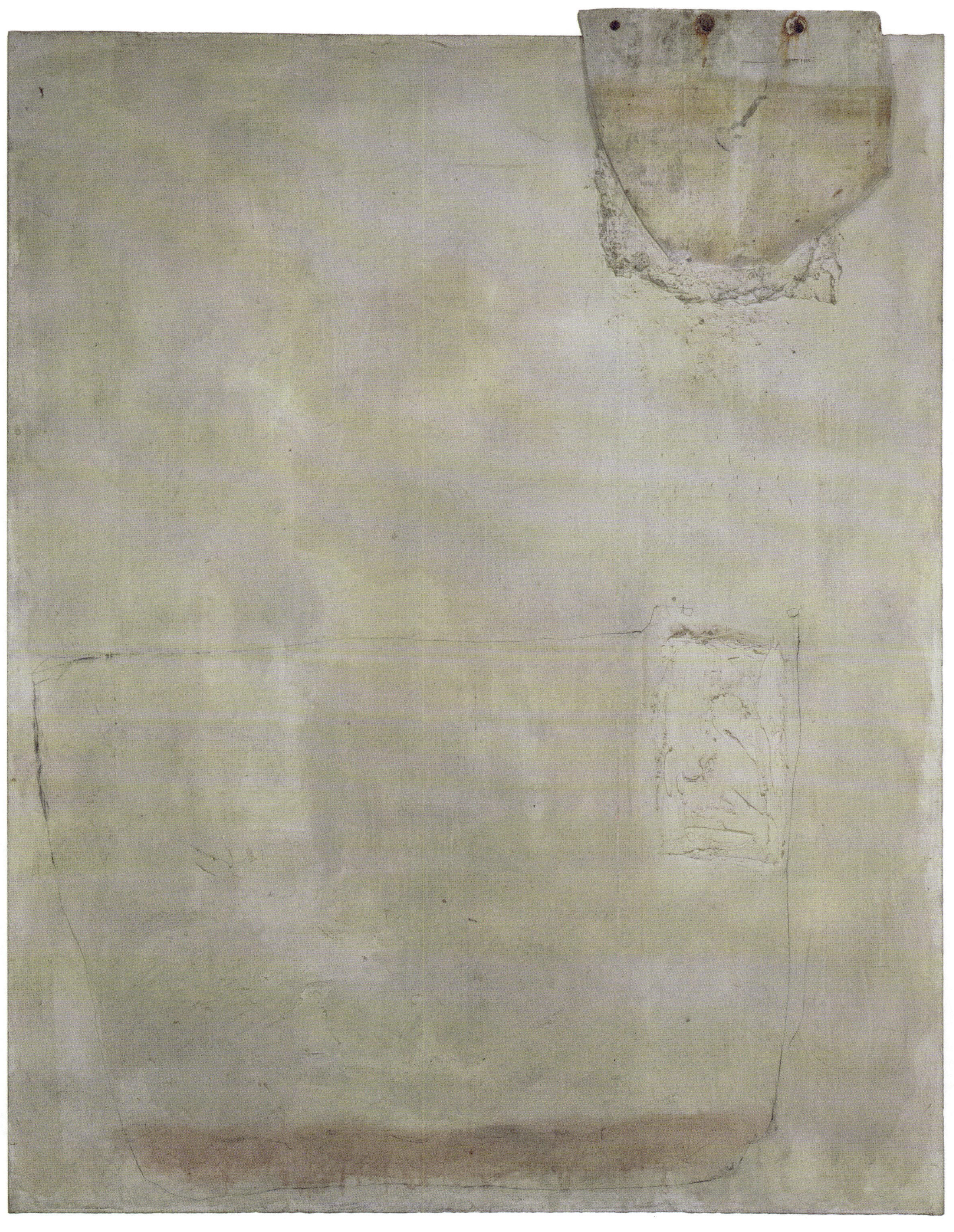

Waterline, 1999, broken ceramic, house paint, graphite pencil on canvas, 152.4 × 121.9 cm

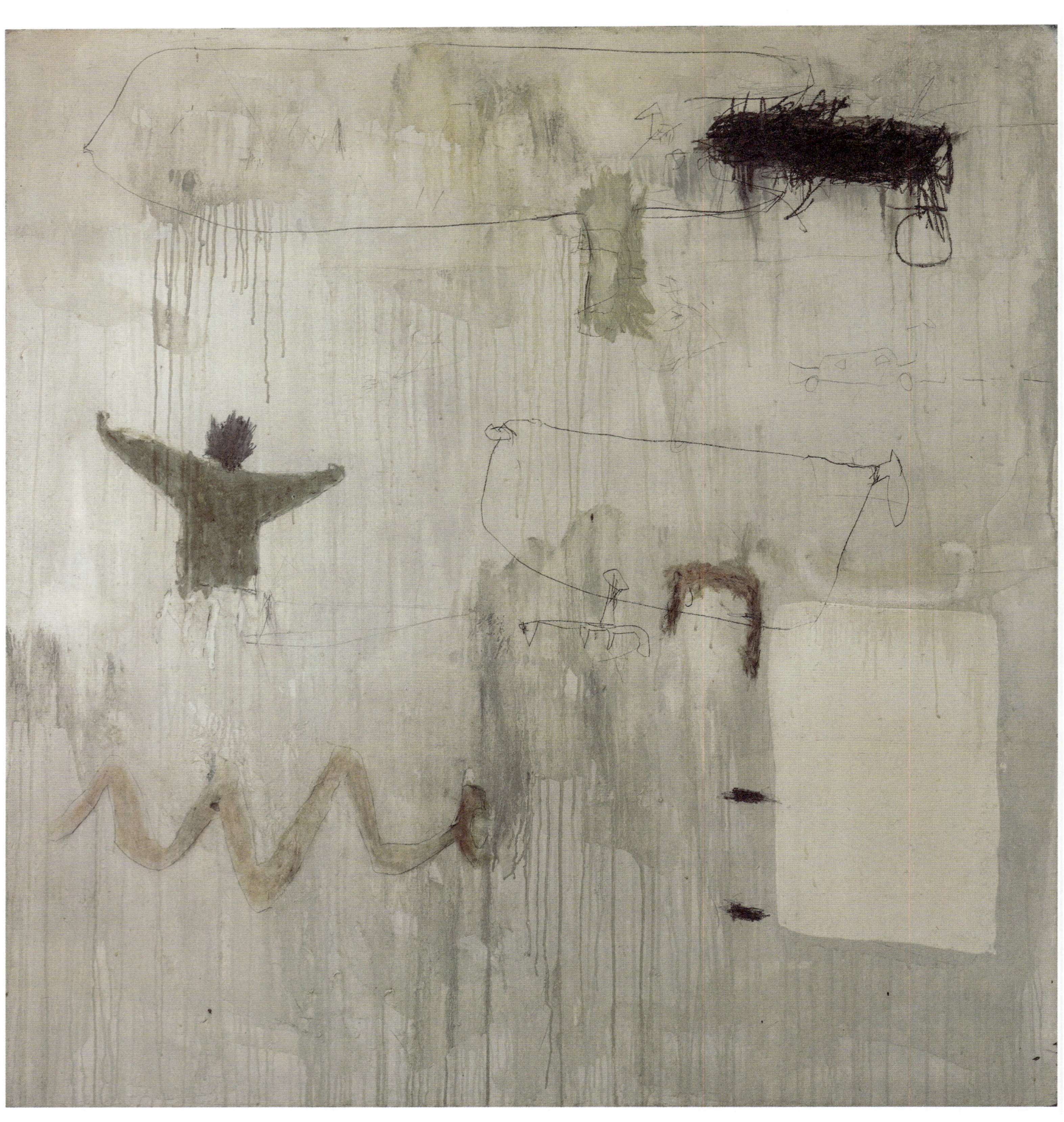

Poems and Letters, 2000, graphite pencil, house paint, oil on plywood, 121.9 × 121.9 cm

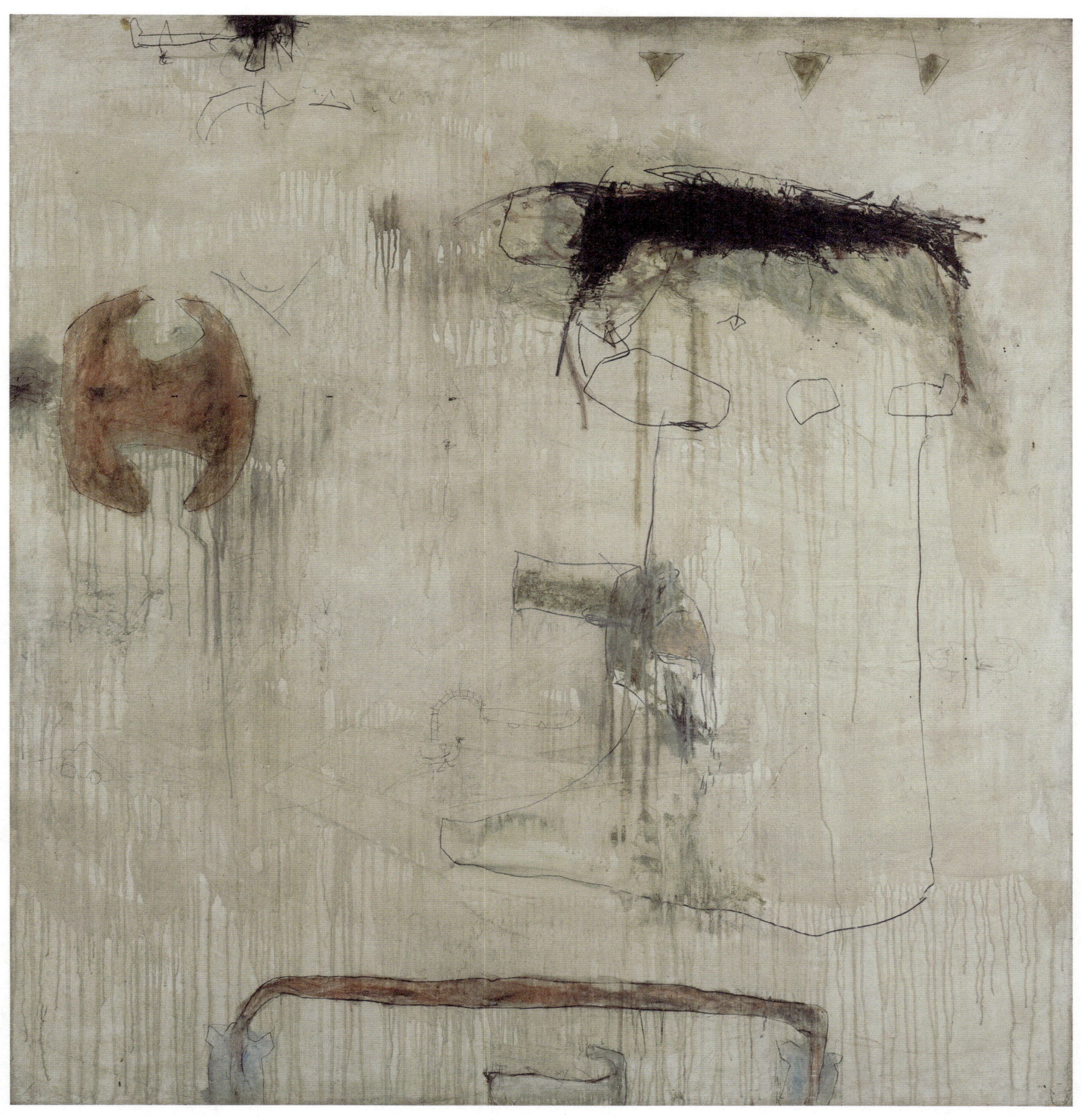

Poems and Letters, 2000, graphite pencil, house paint, oil on plywood, 121.9 × 121.9 cm

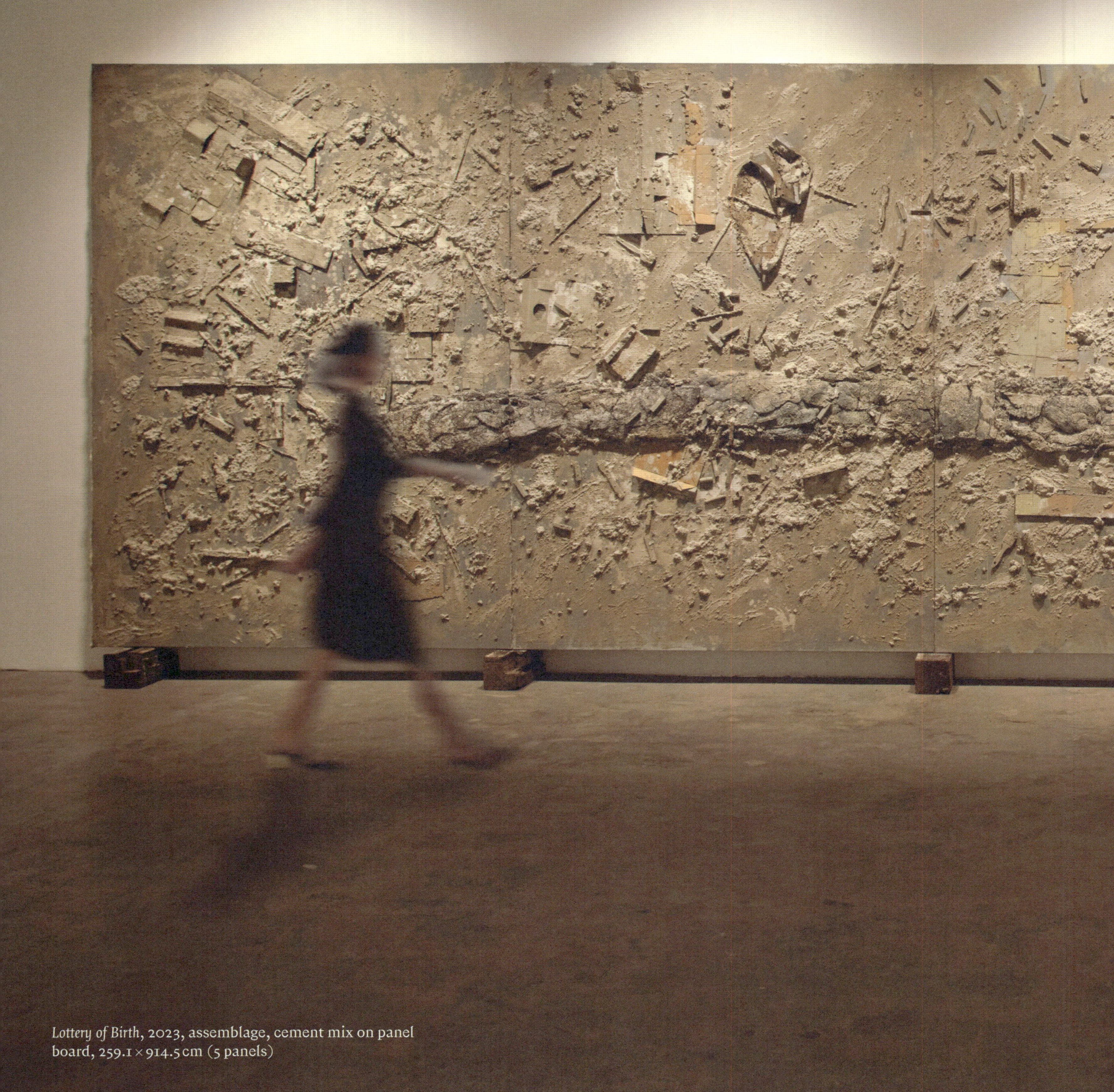

Lottery of Birth, 2023, assemblage, cement mix on panel board, 259.1 × 914.5 cm (5 panels)

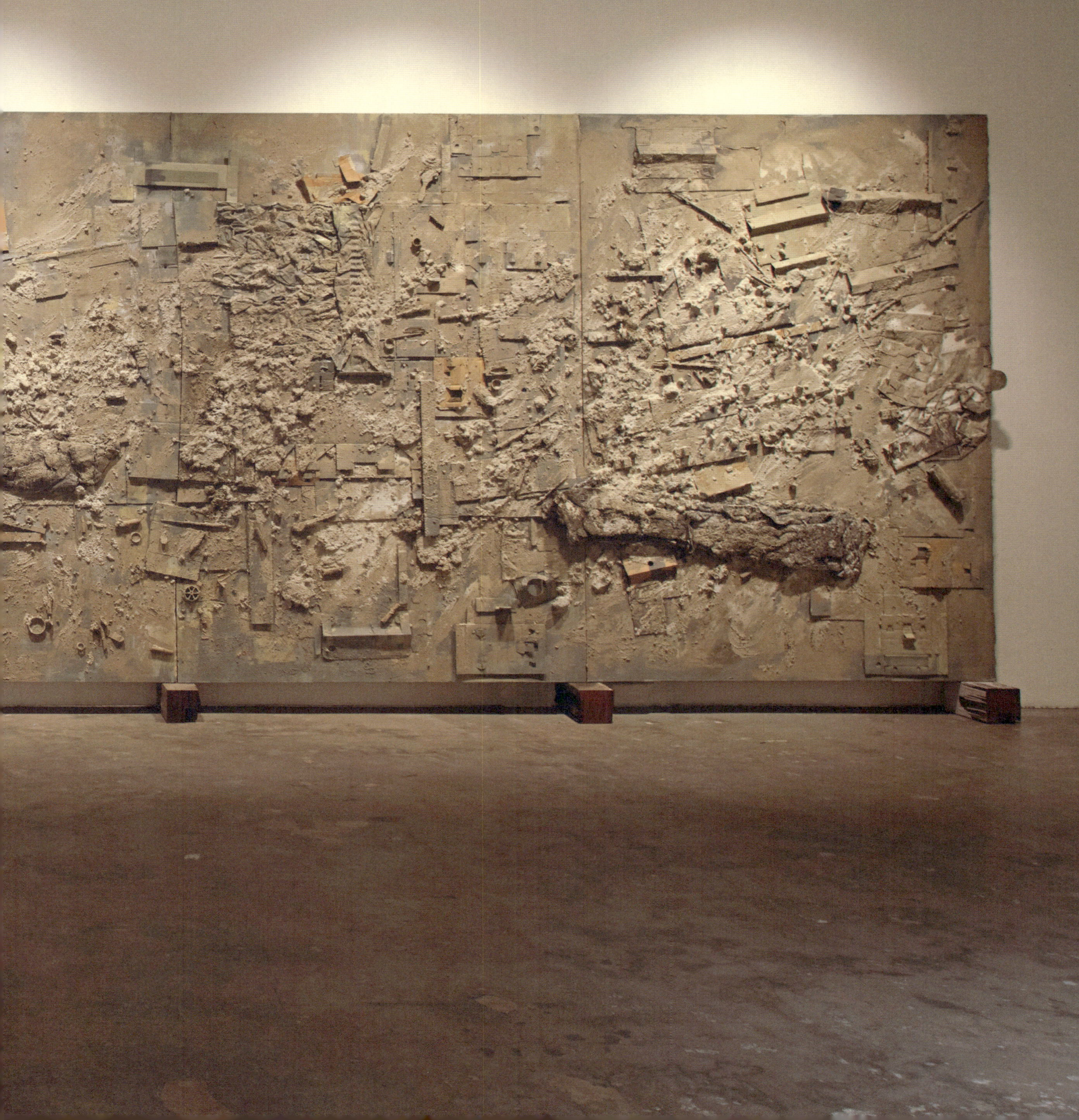

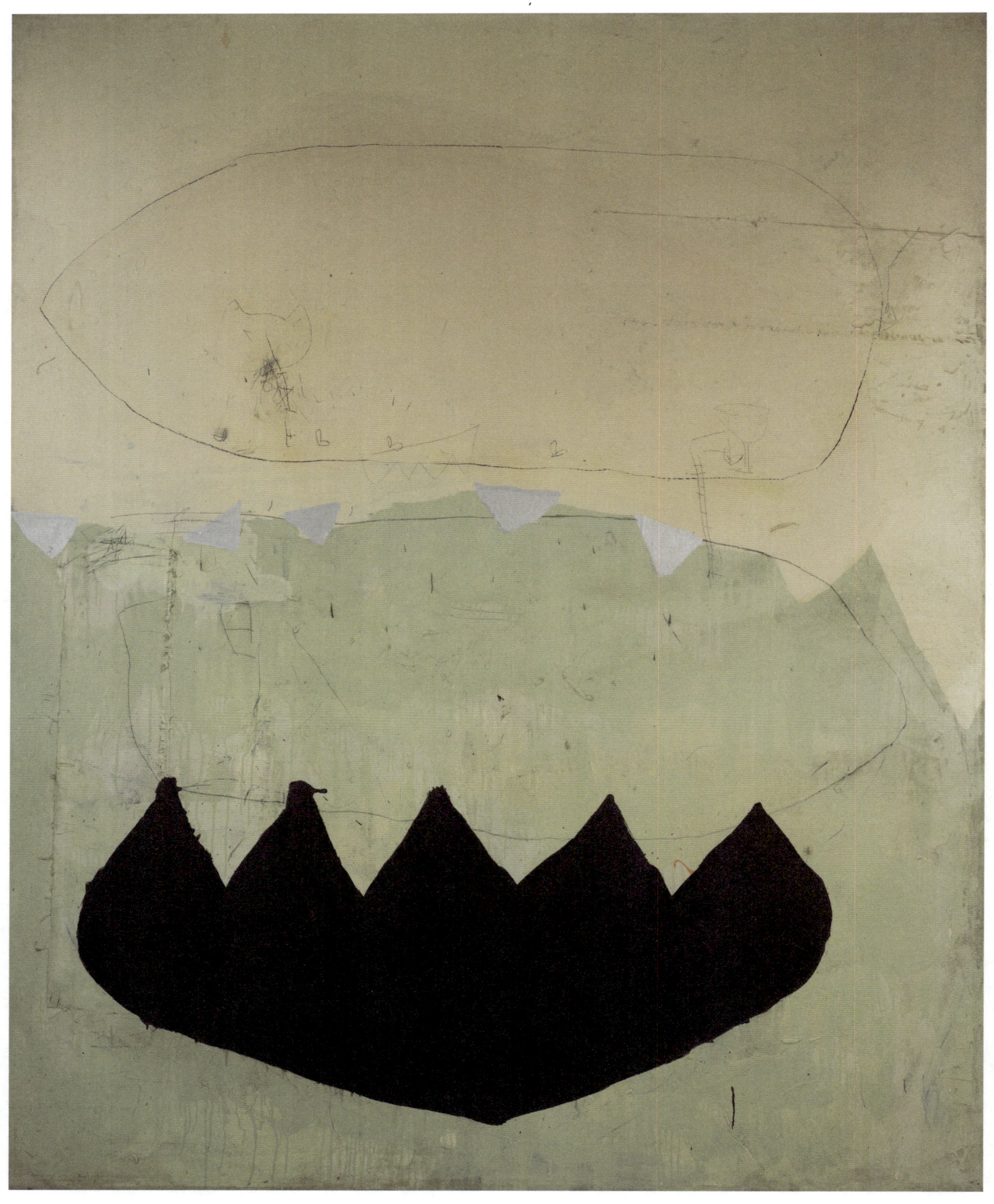

Untitled, 2001, house paint on plywood, 182.9 × 152.4 cm

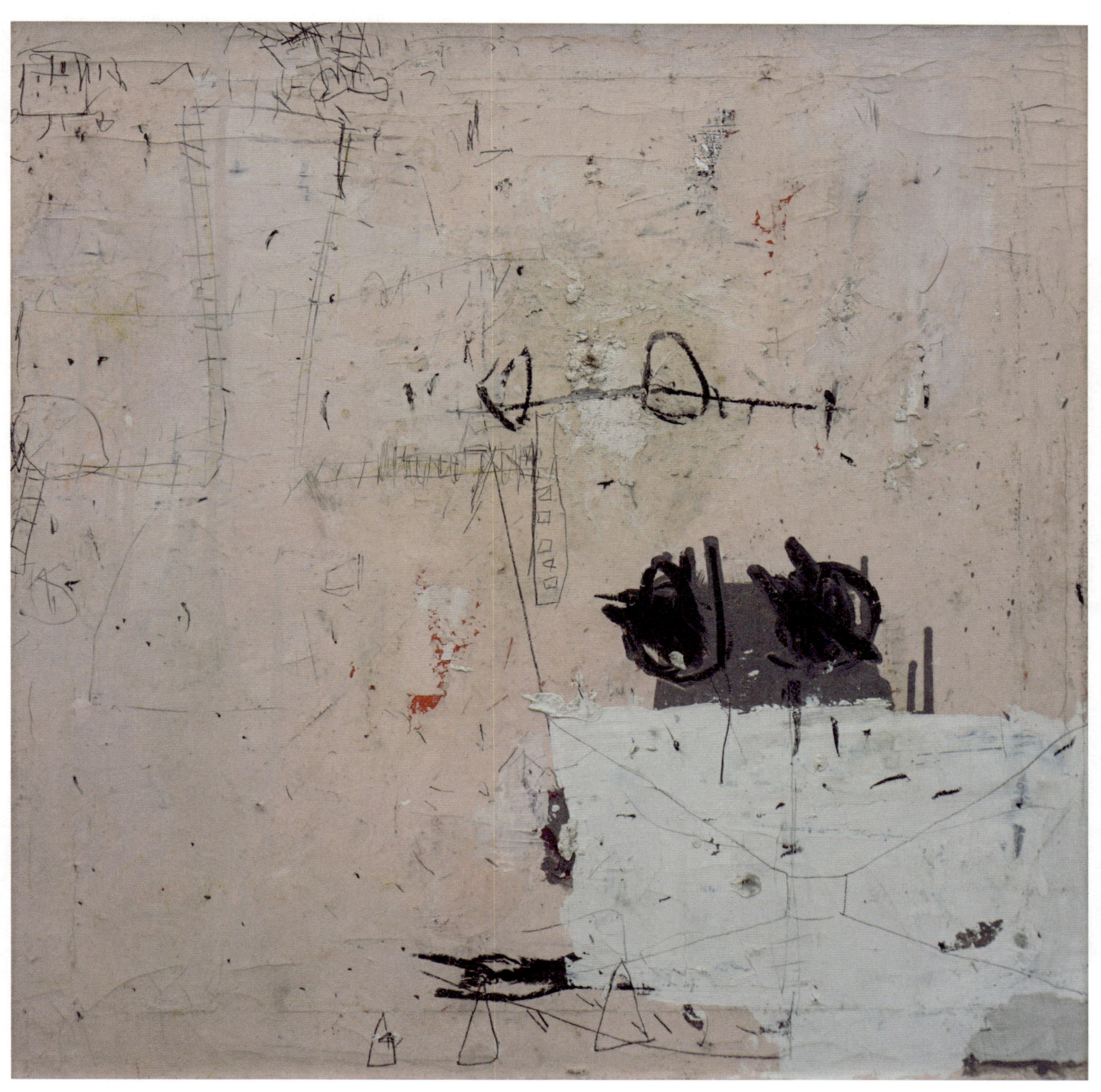

Pink Painting III, 2005, oil on canvas, 61 × 61 cm

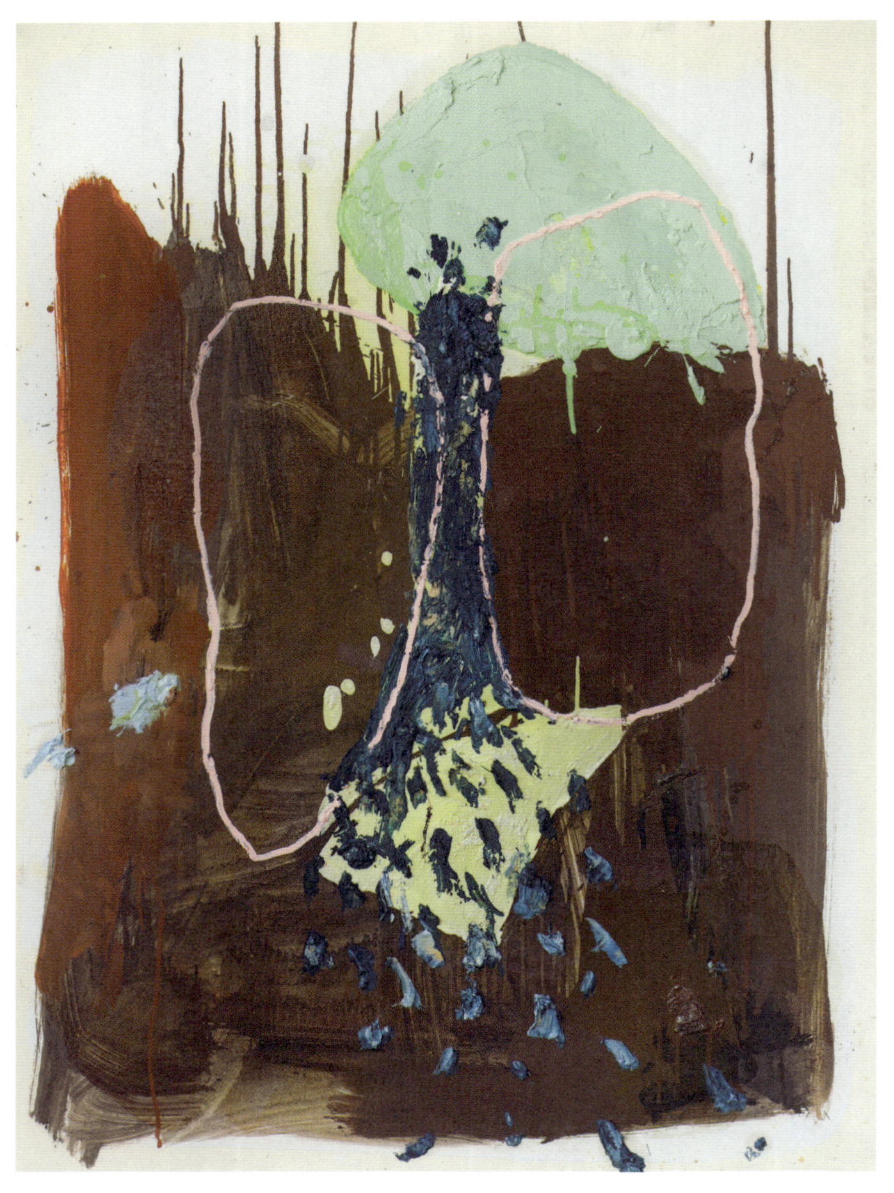

Hydroponics Series 4, oil on canvas, 2014, 122 × 91.4 cm

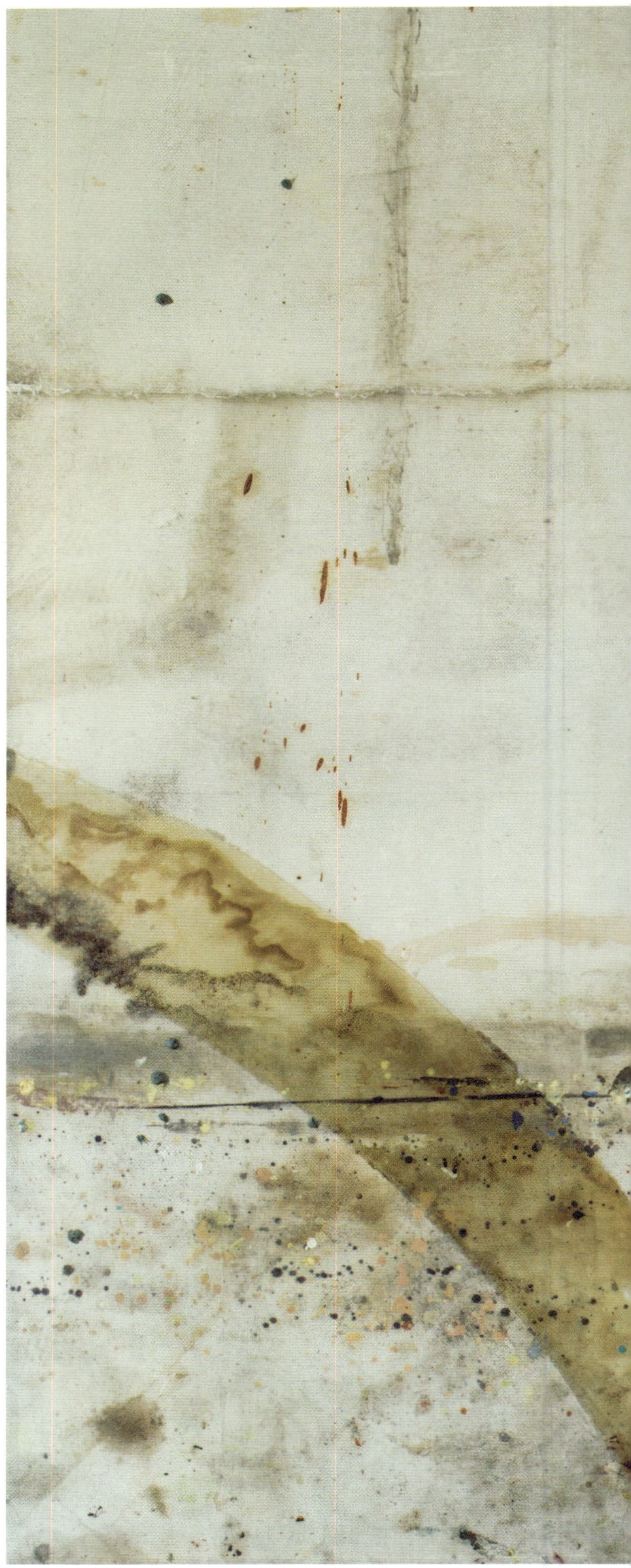

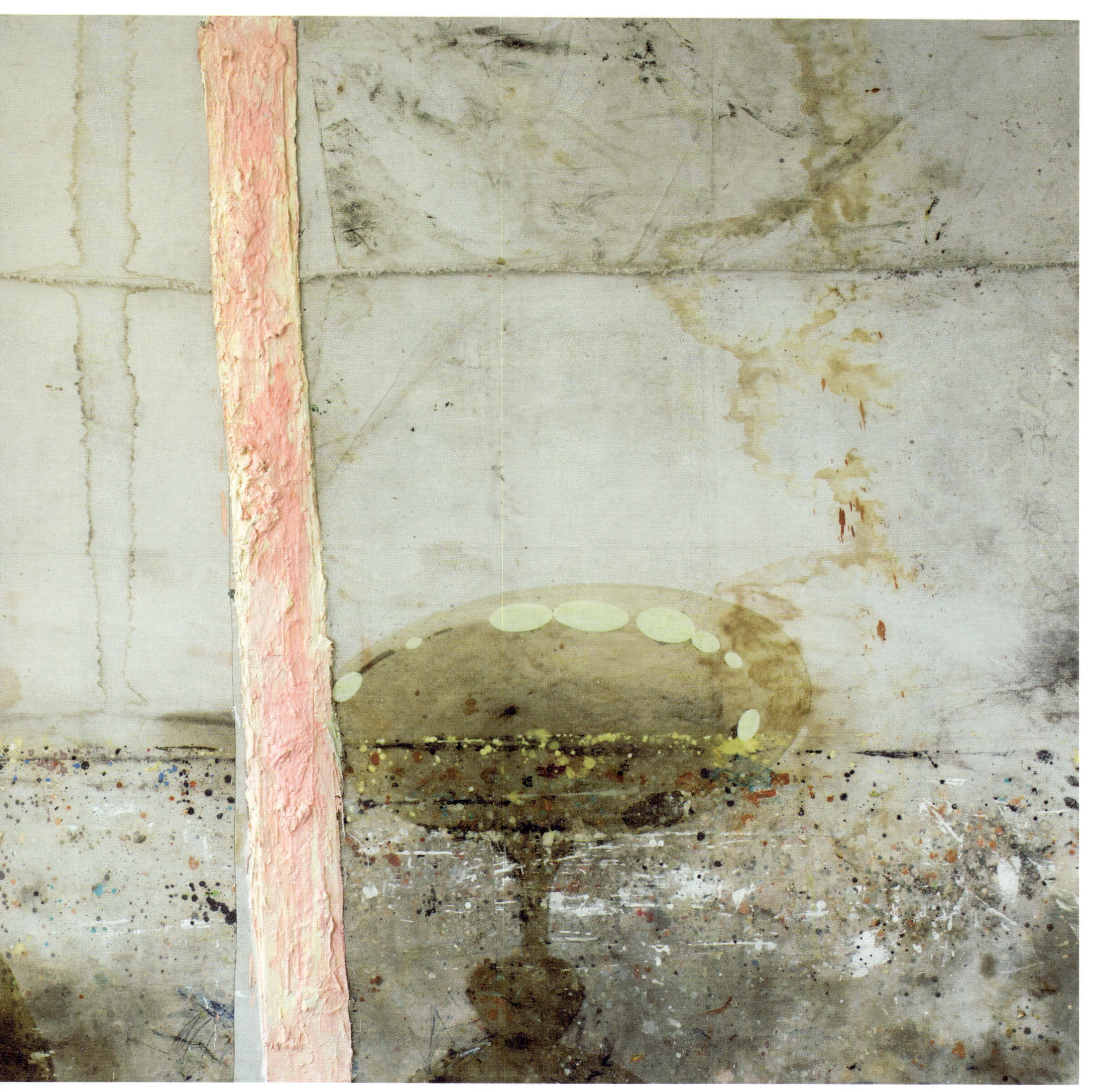

Kangkong (Ipomoea aquatic), 2015, mixed media, 182.9 × 274.3 cm

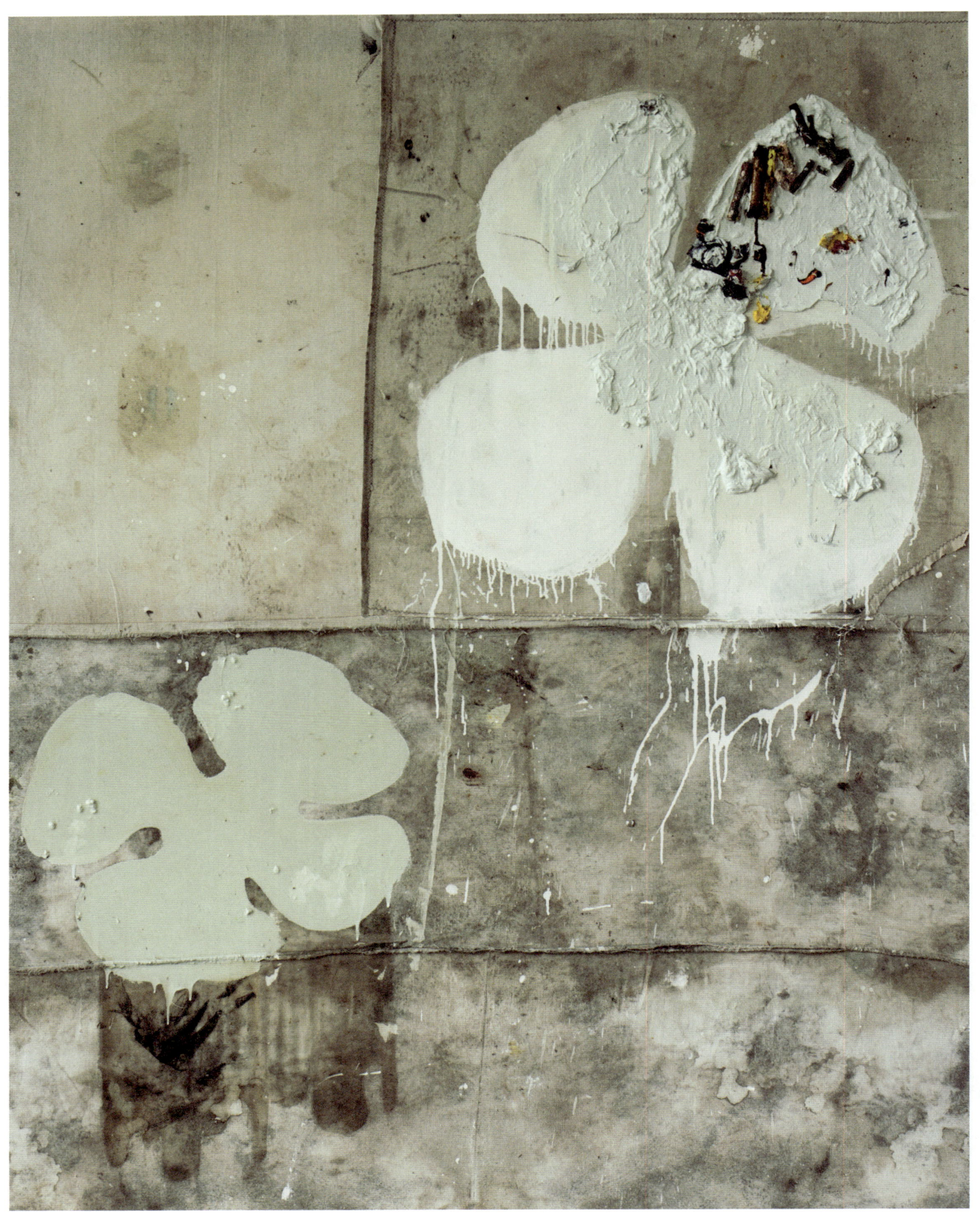

Blossom, 2016, oil on canvas, 167.6 × 137.2 cm

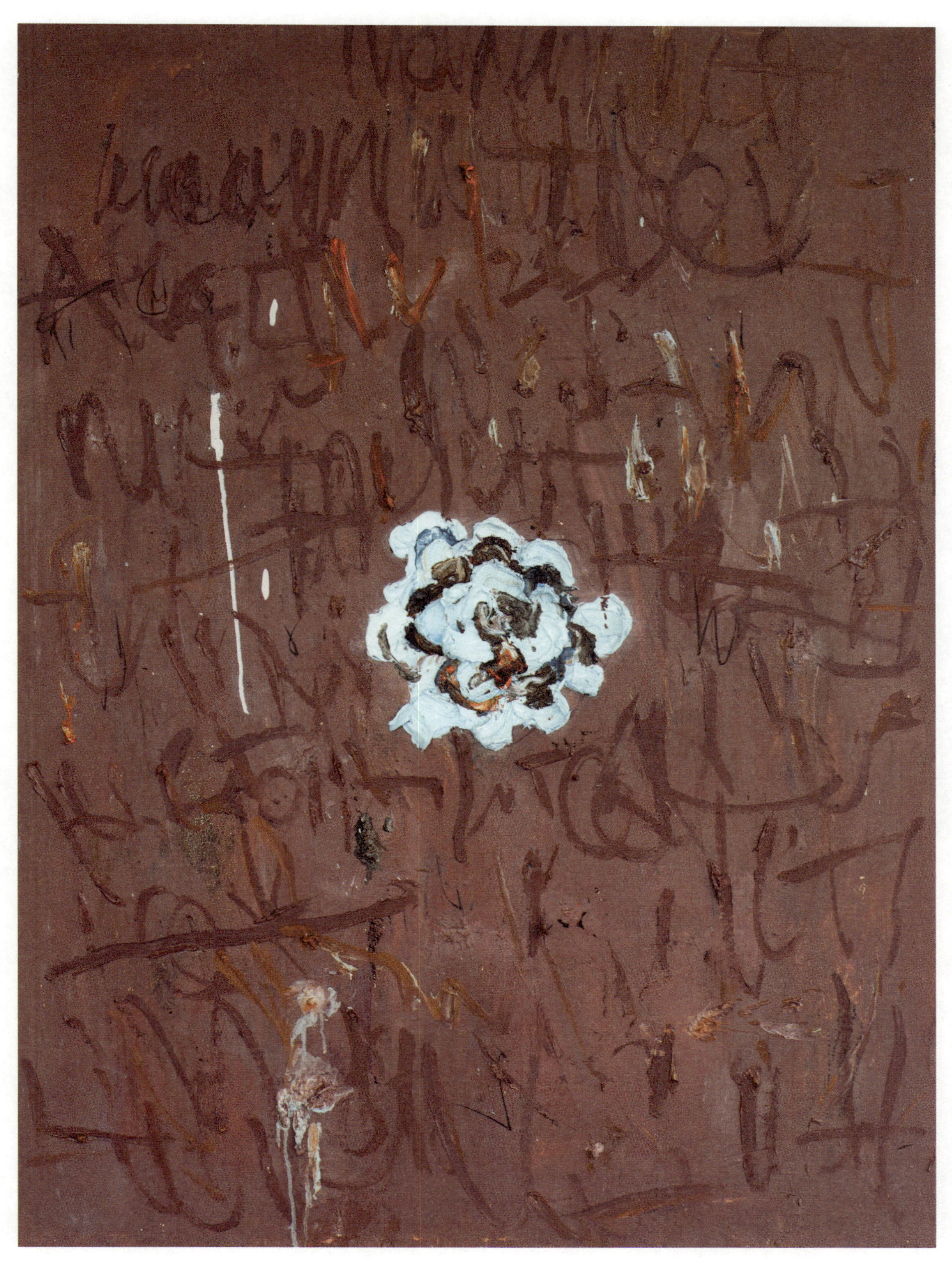

Hydroponics Series 1, 2014, oil on canvas, 122 × 91.4 cm

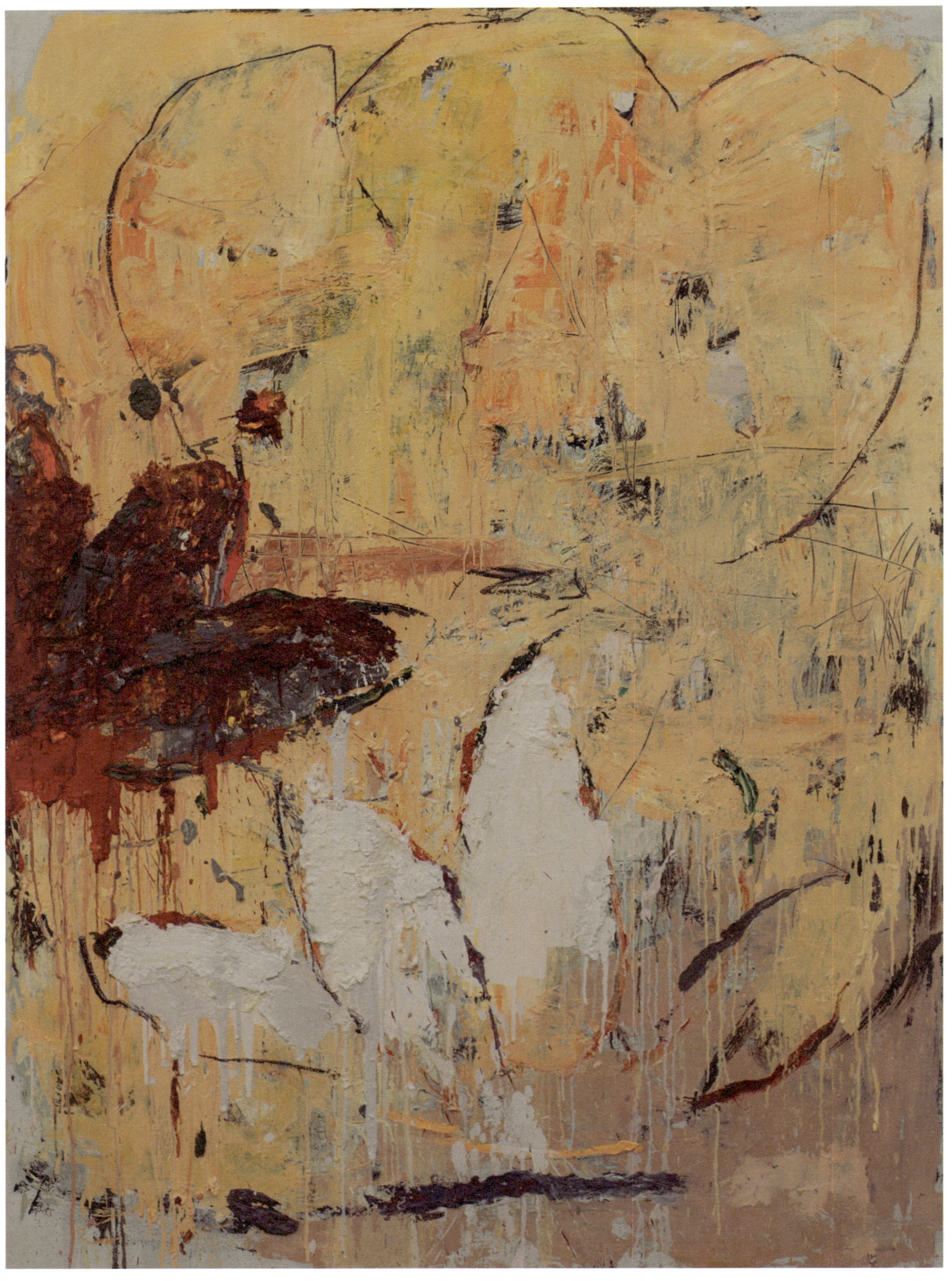

Lotus 05, 2016, oil on canvas, 182.9 × 137.2 cm

Carcass Series 06, 2004–16, mixed media, 61 × 45.7 cm

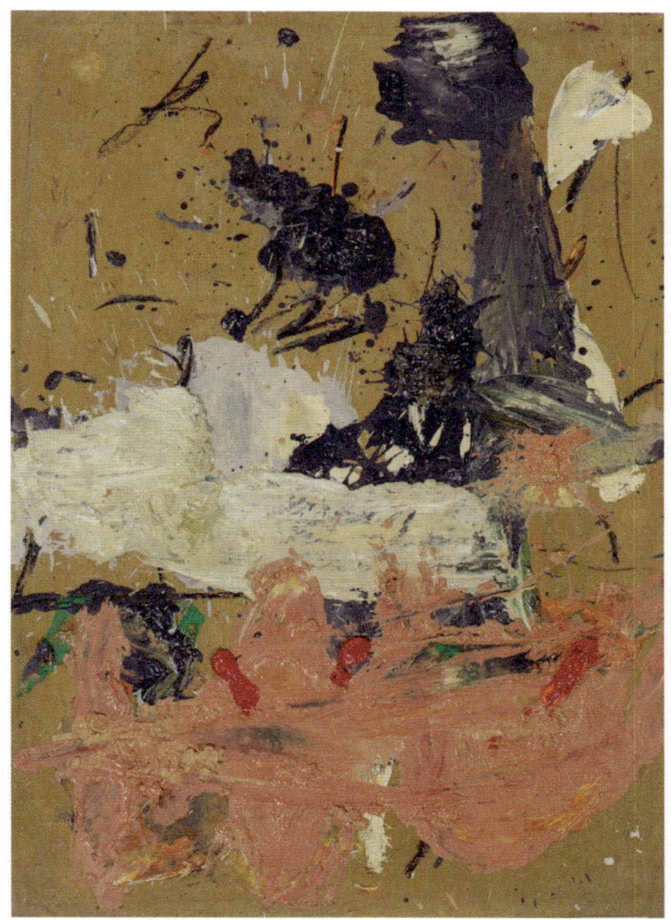

Carcass Series 02, 2004–16, mixed media, 61 × 45.7 cm

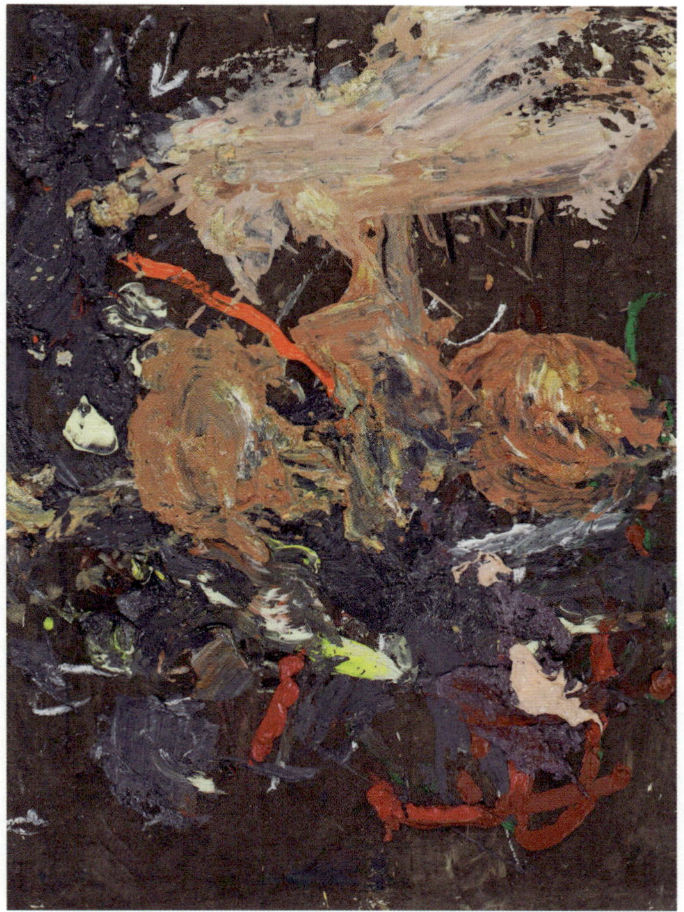

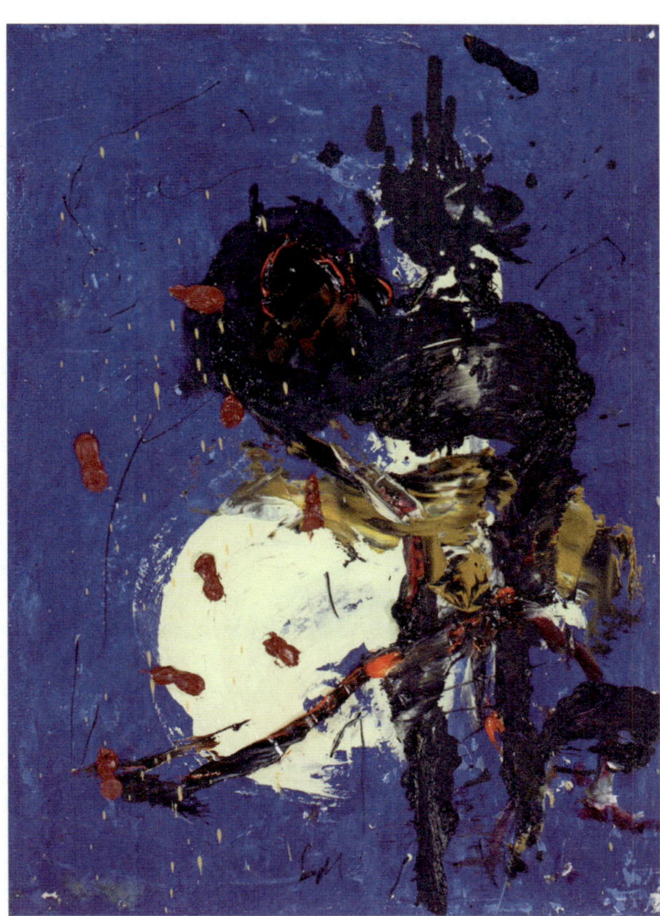

Carcass Series 05, 2004–16, mixed media, 61 × 45.7 cm

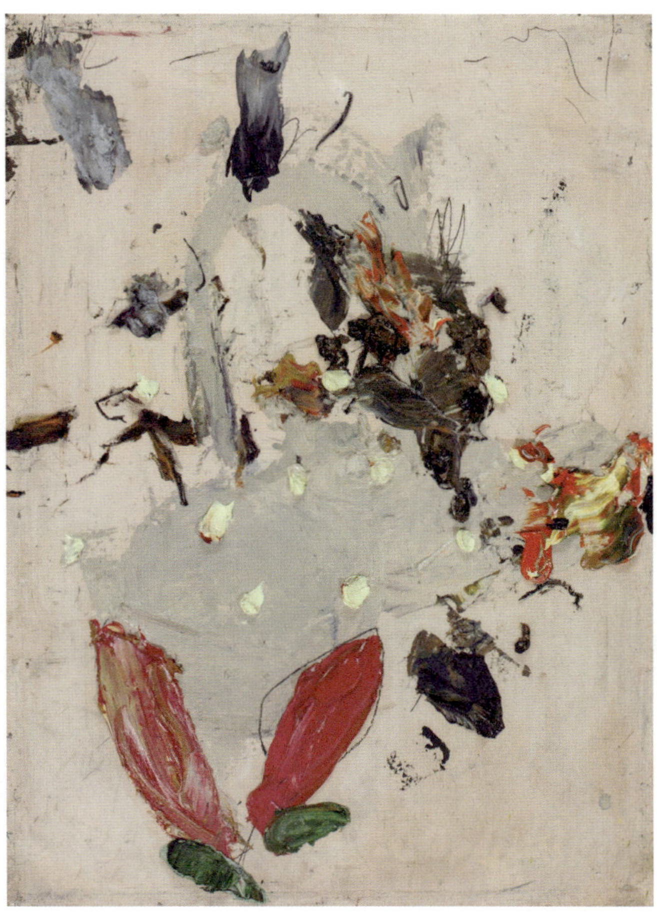

Carcass Series 07, 2004–16, mixed media, 61 × 45.7 cm

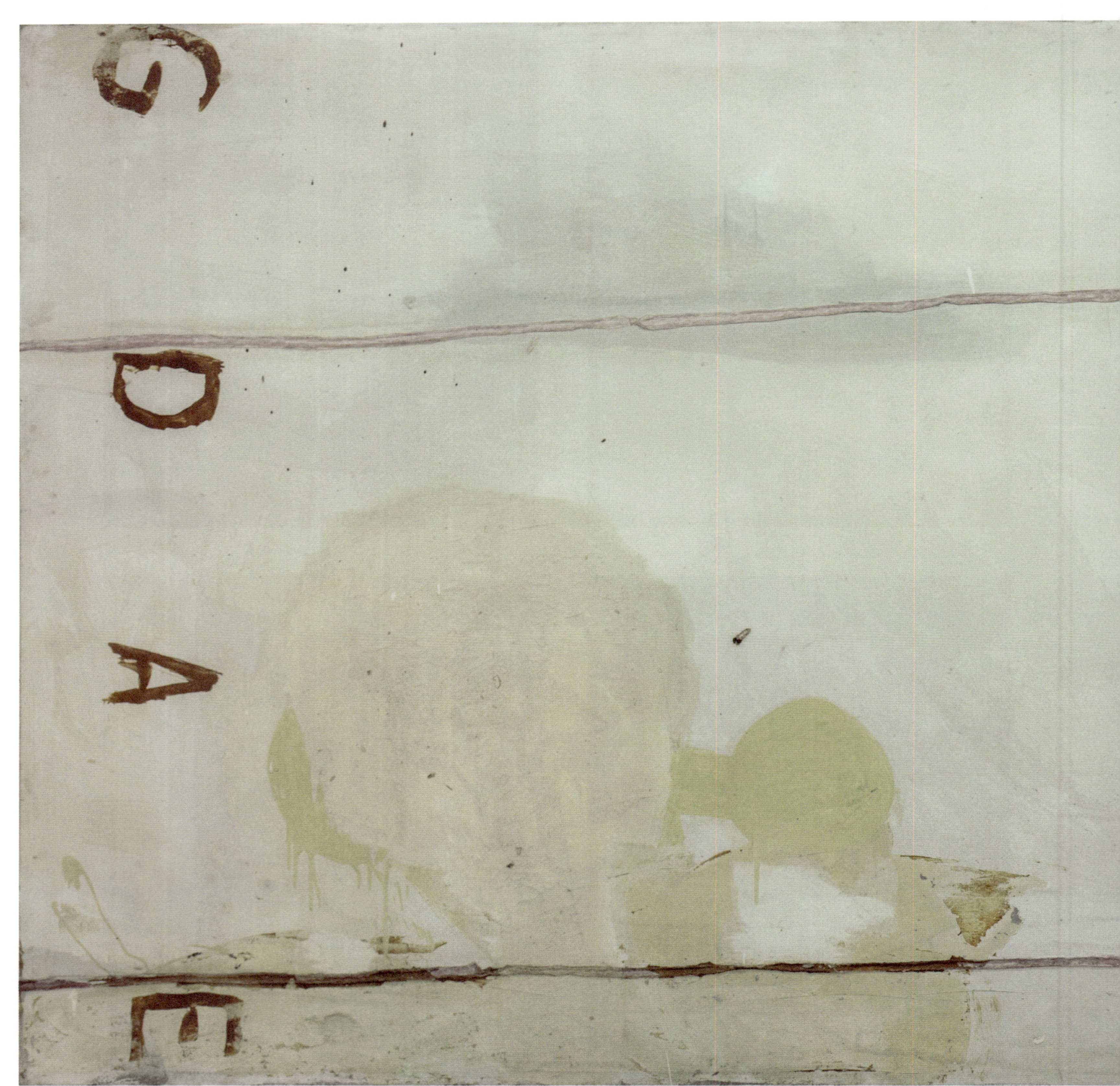

Untitled, 2009, contact cement, oil on canvas, 152.4 × 304.8 cm

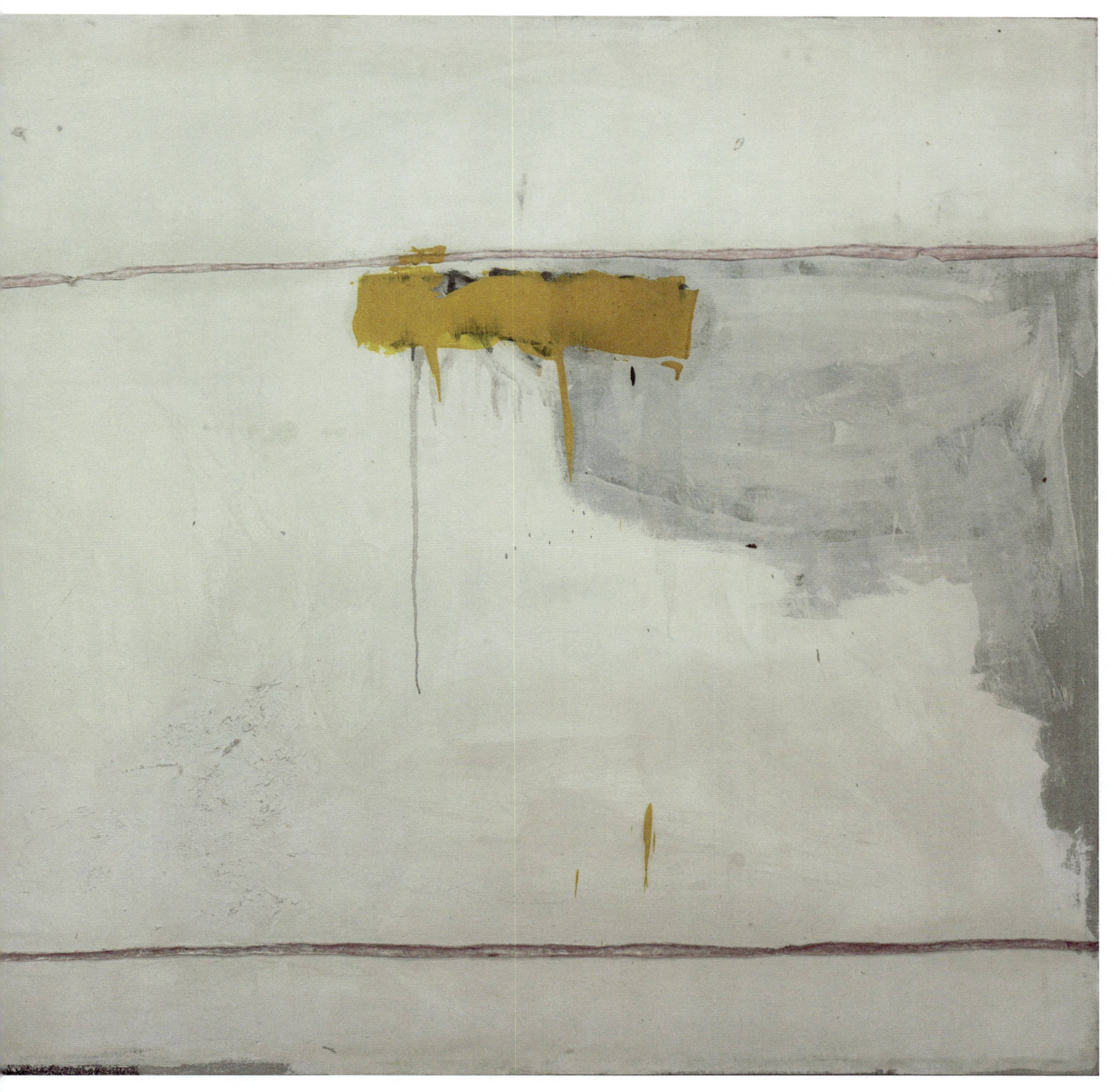

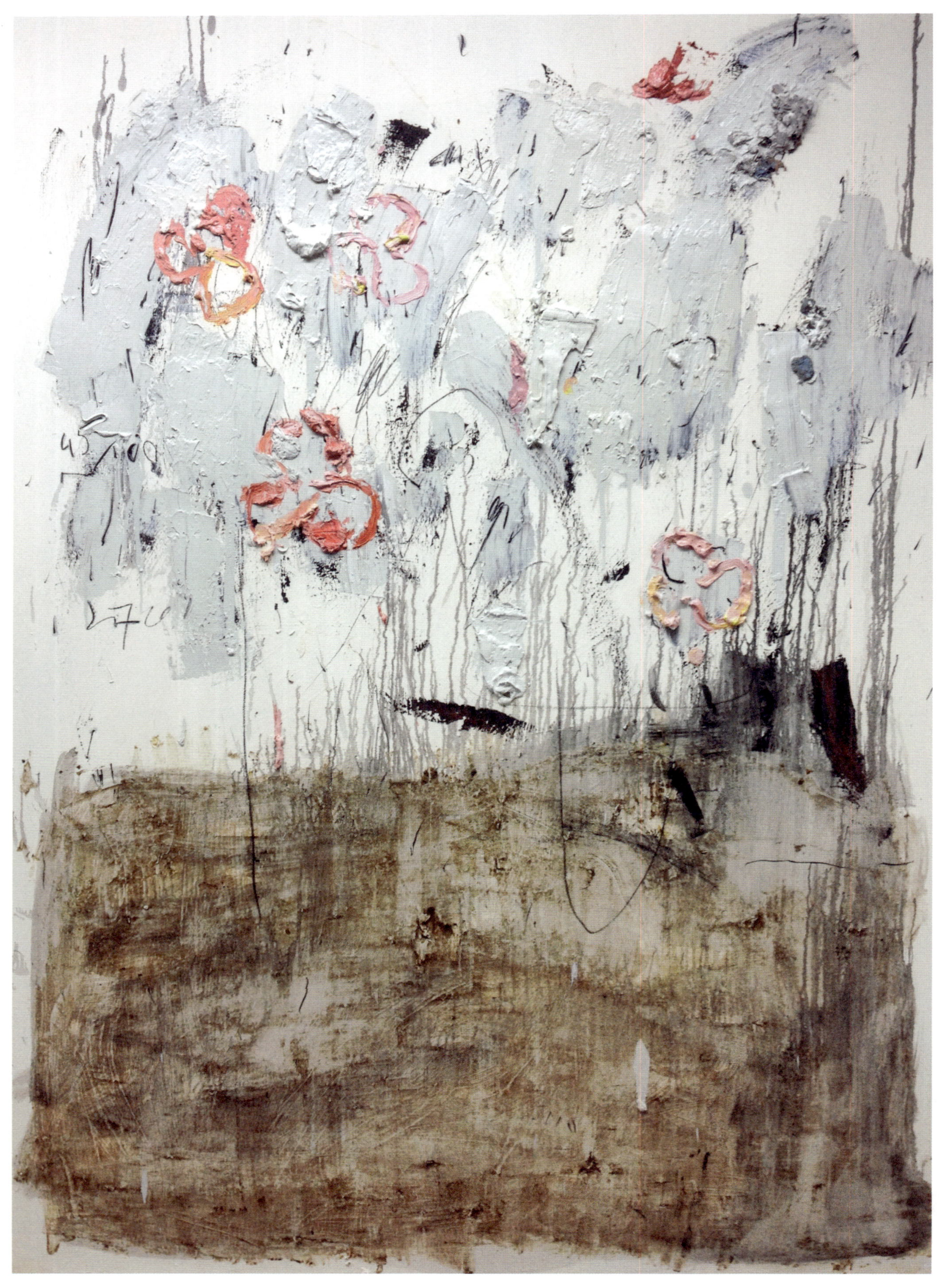

Untitled 1401, 2014, oil on canvas, 182.9 × 137.2 cm

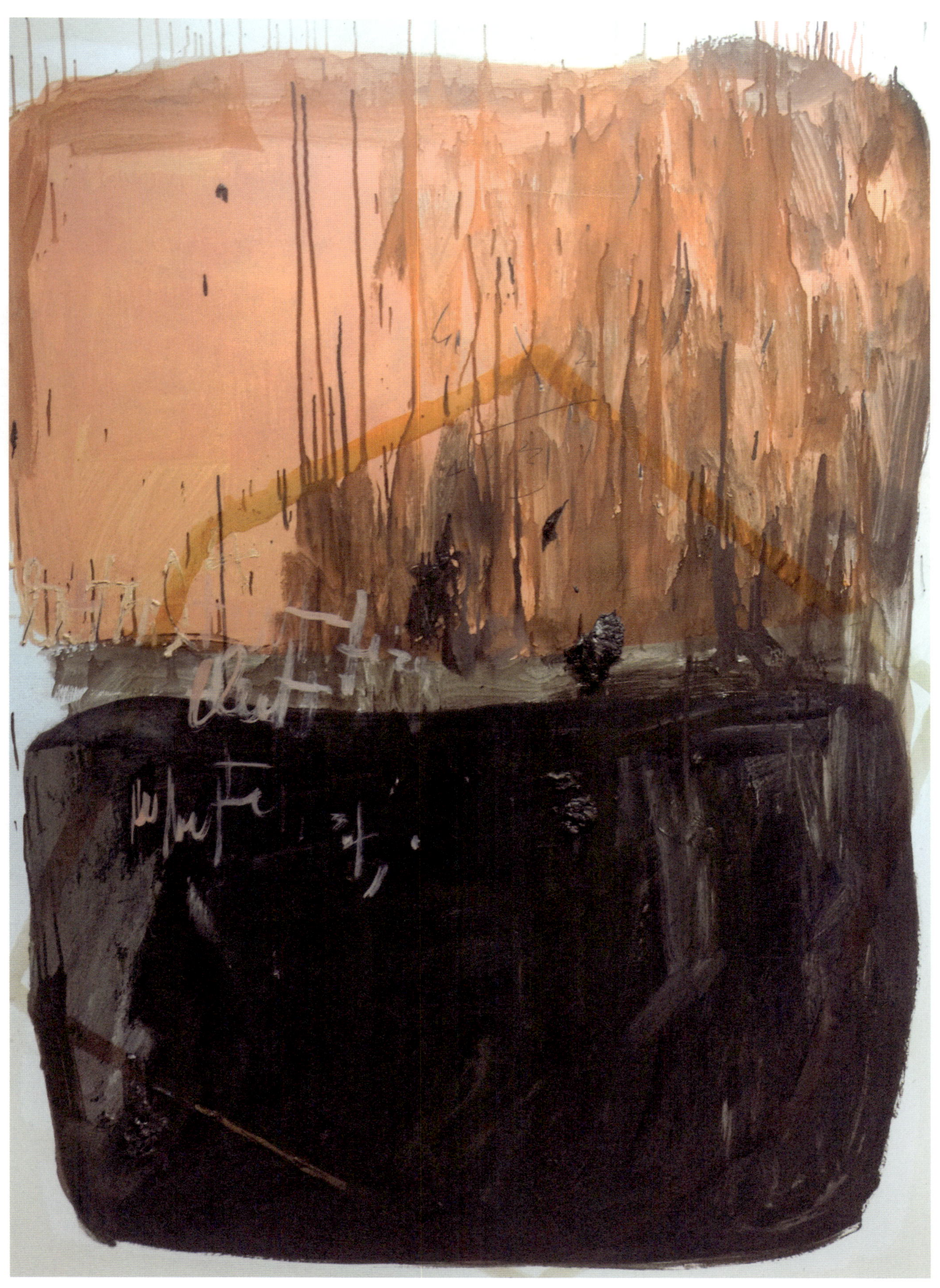

Untitled 1402, 2014, oil on canvas, 182.9 × 137.2 cm

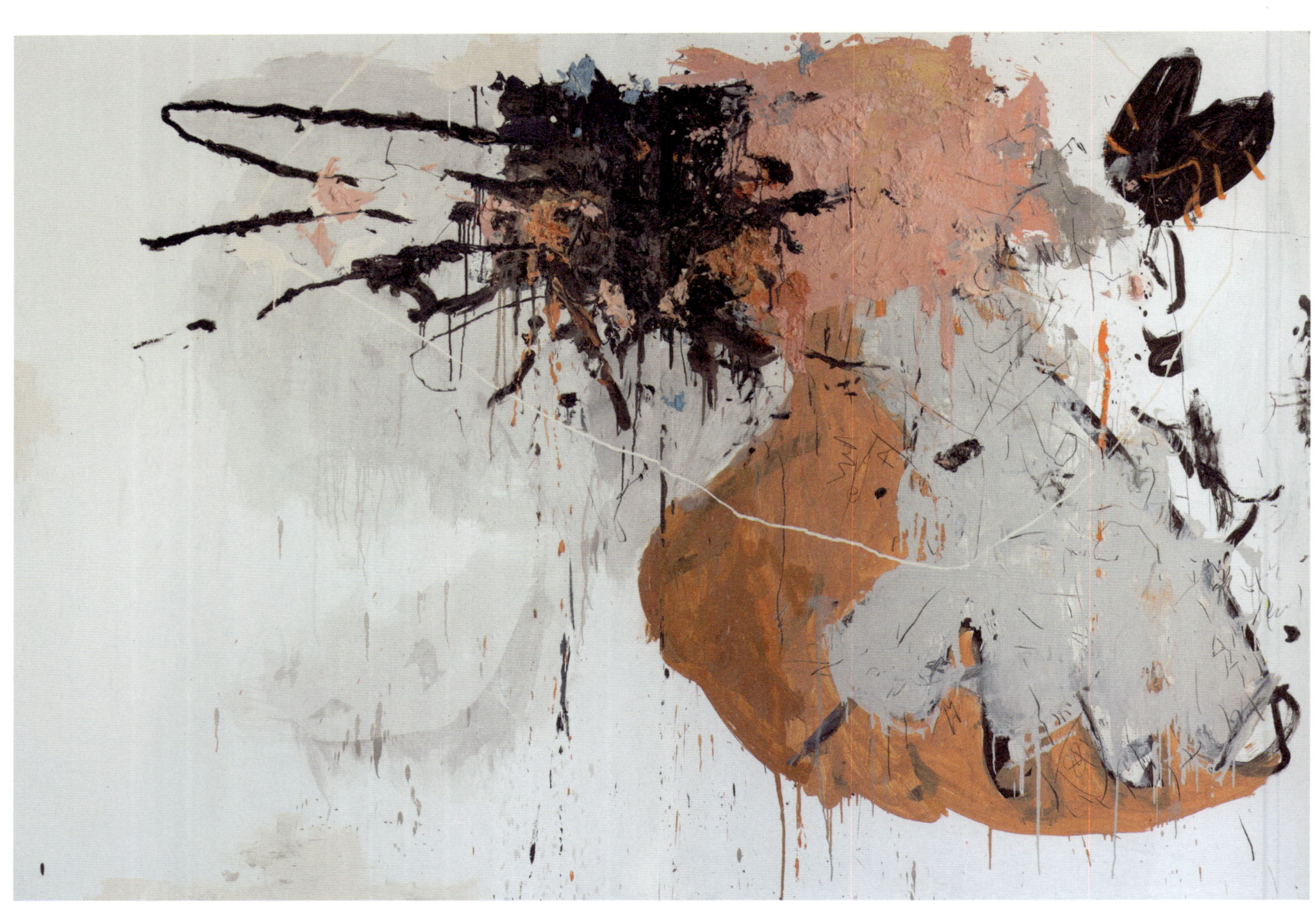

Who Hunts in the Middle of the Crowd?, 2014,
oil on canvas, 182.9 × 274.3 cm

The House on Dos Castillas Street

Josephine V. Roque

Bernardo Pedro Pacquing arrived at 1159 Dos Castillas Street in Sampaloc, Manila, from Mindanao when he was 15 years old (Fig. 1). The district had been named after the tamarind trees that grew there before it became known for its universities. After three colonizers, a world war, and a dictator, the area was a place that had become "elsewhere." The house at the address had belonged to the Pacquing family since the 1920s, a time when the neighborhood was popular with Manila's emerging merchant-class families. During American colonial rule, *tramvias* (electrical coaches) had plied the major roads instead of automobiles. Bernardo's father, Oscar, had grown up in and run away from the wooden house, with its cement base, iron-sheet roofing, and Art Deco flourishes. It was the tallest house on the street. During World War II, Oscar became a teen guerrilla in the resistance movement, fighting in the mountains while his three aunts remained in rooms in the basement. The house was then occupied by Japanese soldiers who used it as their headquarters, keeping the garden beautiful with flowers.

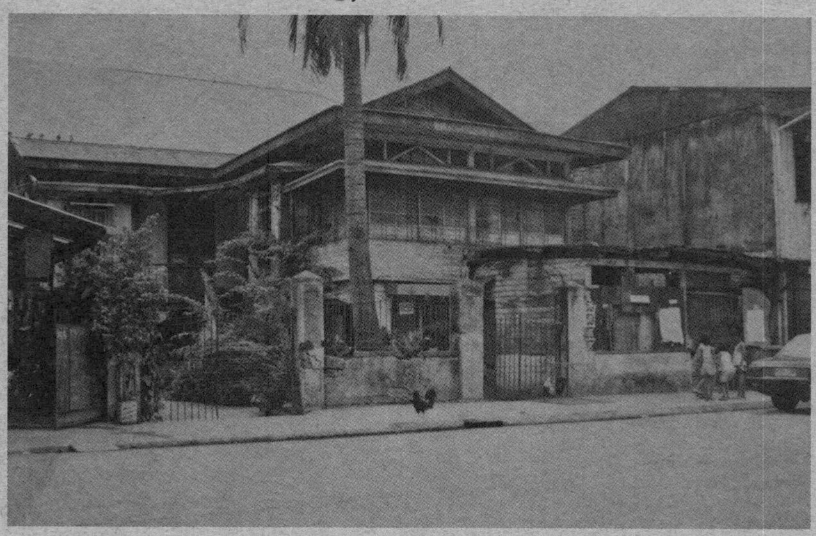

Fig. 1. Bernardo Pacquing's Dos Castillas Street (Manila) family residence, 1995

The 15-year-old Pacquing could not run away, even if he had wanted to. While his brothers and father had gone back to the Manila house, he remained with his mother and grandmother in Misamis Occidental in Mindanao, where life was more stable. Upon his return to Manila in 1982, the bucolic life in which he had grown up in Mindanao, then his entire universe, vanished. Nothing could have prepared him for the shock of downtown Manila. He went from knowing everyone to knowing no one. Ramon Magsaysay High School was a public institution down the street, overcrowded with students, where one could get stabbed. It was a West Side Story sort of place, even in 1982. Pacquing remembers how people were hungry and unemployed on the streets.[1] This was the height of the martial law years, when the Marcos dictatorship took in debts it could not repay. There was the nuclear terror of the Cold War, and the American proxy war in Vietnam, during which the Philippines served as a pit stop. Writing about this now, with the Ukraine war still raging, it seems that the world has not stopped burning.

1. The author's interview with Bernardo Pacquing, Makati, June 24, 2023.

The house on Dos Castillas became an elsewhere place to which Pacquing could retreat when the world was too much. He was bullied for not knowing Tagalog and for having a thick Visayan accent, which resulted in his keeping quiet and lacking the confidence to speak. The house became a bolt-hole where, like Oscar Jr., or Sonny Boy, his eldest brother, he could go to draw. He looked up to Sonny Boy and did whatever he did. His *kuya* (brother) had the knack of knowing when the teasing was bad, telling him to draw, to let it out and draw. In the family, he was the most supportive of Pacquing's interests and served as an inspiration later on. Sonny Boy abandoned an engineering degree for music, even though it broke their parents' hearts. In fact, one of the hardest things about being an artist is to persevere, despite the opposition of one's family. Parents should be protected from children's ambitions that will only disappoint them. In the Pacquing household, all of the children pursued atypical professions, despite the parents having practical jobs: their mother, Maria Luisa, was a dance teacher and serial entrepreneur, while Oscar was an analyst for the Philippine Board of Investments. Their eldest child, Maria Theresa, became a ballerina; Oscar Jr. was a concert violinist; Luis Antonio became a football coach; José Mari was also in ballet; and the youngest, Oscar Ian, joined the US Army. The fifth of six children, Bernie was the only one in the visual arts.

Growing up, his aspiration to be a painter became a point of tension with his parents. Oscar Sr. called painting a profession *para sa mga mayaman* (for the rich). He believed that a fine arts degree was vocational rather than collegiate. And he did not want his child attending the University of the Philippines (UP), a state university with a proclivity for student activism. But Pacquing got his way, even if it meant lying by omission. He did not tell his father that he had received a scholarship from the University of Santo Tomas to study fine arts near their home, for fear that he would be forced to study there instead of UP. And, as a concession to his father, at UP, he majored in visual communications, within the fine arts program, since it was more practical than painting.

Beginning in 1984, Pacquing studied fine arts at UP for eight years, completing a documentary thesis about indigenous instruments; however, he did not complete his degree because, as he explains: "I lacked a math subject to graduate, which I was bad at."[2] It was a time when students either stayed too long at a university or not long enough. The 1980s battle cry was "revolution." There were secret bomb-making classes, and students took to the mountains. The economy was unraveling as the Marcos cronyism bled the country dry. Companies collapsed. The best and the brightest could not find employment. Artists also began to question concepts received from abroad and Western claims about universal truths. Pacquing was a member of the UP Artists' Circle fraternity (AC), where he made friends, met mentors,

2. Ibid.

and developed connections that would serve him for the rest of his life. It was through this organization that he met his future wife, Maria Leah Peachy, and lifetime peers Johnny Alcazaren, Felix Bacolor, and Nilo Ilarde. Not much has been written about his artistic friendships during this period, perhaps because they were not seen as formal engagements; however, as collaborative and symbiotic relations, they are an important source of artistic influence. Pacquing painted with friends who encouraged each other to compete in art contests. He learned to shed his shyness and fashion his own artistic education. As he puts it, "I made sure to attend the painting classes, even if it wasn't my major."[3] To keep on studying, Pacquing cobbled together an income from projects at the AC, while also doing stints as a dishwasher, working at a printing press, and making posters for the university cafeteria.

3. Ibid.

Pacquing met one of his future mentors, Rock Drilon, through the AC; he was a more senior member who sometimes visited the UP Diliman campus. "Rock was already showing in Paris shows then, and we looked up to him," Pacquing recalls in an interview.[4] Drilon had begun his career as a figurative expressionist, but by the time he met Pacquing, he had already shifted to abstraction, and as a practitioner of automatism, he created art as a means of accessing the unconscious mind. In his work, he freely applied paint to a canvas, creating unfettered figures with colors. Pacquing also tried this method in his work later on. When Drilon opened the art space Mag:net in Quezon City in the 2000s, Pacquing also did solo shows there. He recalls, "Rock took good care of the shows and gave me good advice."[5] In 2004, he curated a show for Drilon at Galleria Duemila called, "When You Lose, Don't Lose the Lesson." The renowned Filipino conceptual artist Roberto Chabet was another strong, though informal, influence during that time. Although he was never Chabet's student, Pacquing encountered him in social settings. Once, at a party, Chabet told the artist about rubber patterns left over from making slippers. Rubber slippers are ubiquitous footwear in the Philippines, laden with class and cultural meanings; they are even used by politicians as free giveaways during visits.

4. Ibid.

5. Ibid.

Maybe this conversation or his experience on the streets inspired Pacquing to start using rubber slippers rather than paintbrushes while he was doing his DIY renovation of the family house on Dos Castillas Street. The house had previously survived the Battle of Manila as a medical base for American doctors; but after two fires in the ensuing years, the home was in awful shape. As the rest of his family had already migrated to the United States, Pacquing was in charge of fixing up the structure. In this post-dictatorship world, there were those who stayed and those who left. With the help of the Americans, the Marcoses fled in 1986 during the EDSA Revolution I, a historical juncture that should be done and over with, but whose ramifications continue to be felt.

Pacquing considers the house to be his first canvas, his initial attempt as an artist presented with a problem to solve. He made canvases from the extra plywood, recovered objects, and scraps from the construction site and used house paint to cover them. Cheap Chinese oil paints were not available then, making painting expensive. During the 1980s, Filipino artists began to incorporate easily obtainable found objects into their works. Writer and visual artist Jeannie Javelosa wrote in a 1992 *Chronicle* article: "This became one of the preoccupations of local mainstream art. Such a move proved economical because materials did not have to be imported. It also answered the need for a uniquely Filipino, if not Asian, identity in the arts."[6] Peachy, his wife, remembers how she saw him painting the walls of the house using a rubber slipper. This detail would become an inside joke between the couple later on, when younger artists, in turn, tried to imitate Pacquing's style. "They don't use *tsinelas* [rubber slippers] like you do," Peachy would say.[7] The house provided him with a basic visual grammar, which he used, abandoned, and then returned to in his work.

6. Jeannie Javelosa, "Junyee Makes Waves in Havana," *The Manila Chronicle*, January 11, 1992, 32.

7. The author's interview with Bernardo Pacquing.

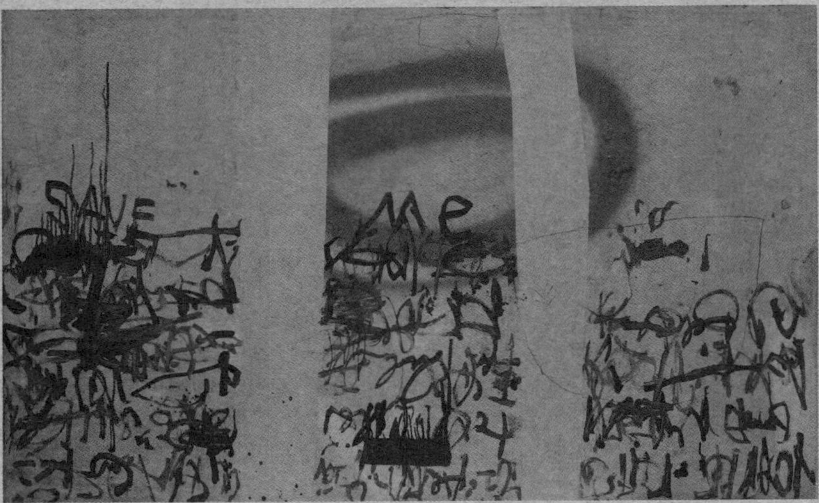

Fig. 2. *Untitled No. 11*, 2007, oil on canvas, 91.4 × 152.4 cm

No canvas remains from when Pacquing was living in the house, but works from the early 2000s show painterly beginnings. One untitled canvas is a textured white wall that looks aged and unwashed, with indecipherable scrawls smeared at the bottom (Fig. 2). Pacquing is known for his use of underpainting to give canvases depth and dimension, a method he stumbled upon while fixing the ancestral house. He says, "The house was so old, there were so many underpaintings, so many layers."[8] Another work shows an abstract figure in black with a scribbled form, which could be a whale flipping its tail or a tractor (Fig. 3). *Pink Painting III* has a white box at the rightmost corner and circles, which to an imaginative child could look like eyes, and it is full of lead marks (Fig. 4). When talking about his work, Pacquing often refers to his Sampaloc surroundings: the patterns and textures of layered paint and grime found on the steps of a pedestrian bridge; the fast and loose way that underpasses were painted, then abandoned; and how neighborhood kids with colored chalk in their

8. Ibid.

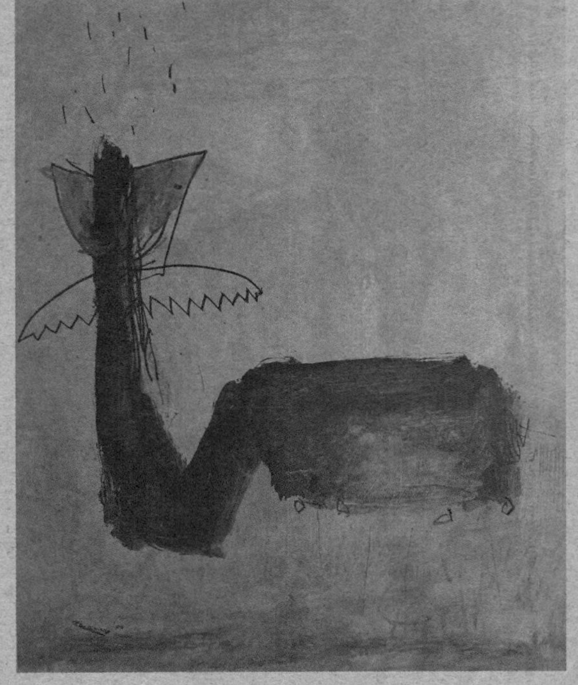
Fig. 3. *Untitled III*, 1998, oil and graphite pencil on paper, 40.6 × 30.5 cm

Fig. 4. *Pink Painting III*, 2005, oil on canvas, 61 × 61 cm

hands would draw lines on the walls and roads. Most people not only ignored these parts of the contemporary urban landscape, but also considered them unpleasant. This is what the artist wishes one to see – he paints until one sees what he sees.

Of course, one cannot reduce Pacquing's work to a reflection of the cultural elements of his time, place, or ethnicity; this is not what he wished to achieve in an individual creative act. *Damp Mortar* (2003), for instance, is a series of five panels representing an asphalt wall, shown as if one were walking by it, with uneven and translucent parts done in gradations of gray, white, and black (Fig. 5). The work mixes old, dirty house paint and oil paint, resulting in an imperfect, finished surface. It thus marks the development of what the younger artist knew by instinct, but only the older one could articulate during an interview: "What I've always longed for is to do something with material that is not normal."[9]

9. Ibid.

Fig. 5. *Damp Mortar*, 2003, oil and house paint on canvas, 182.9 × 457.2 cm

Other works from this same period also display irregularly shaped figures on paper with paint smeared or scrawled over them (Fig. 6). One sees there remnants of the rigor of his graphic design training, with an attention to color, shape, balance of visual weight, and abstraction of forms (Fig. 7). After eight years at UP Diliman, Pacquing's first (and probably only) desk job was as graphic designer, for three years, at the Cultural Center of the Philippines (CCP). He recalls designing exhibition posters, which the then-artistic director and film critic Nicanor Tiongson criticized, complaining that they were too artsy and broke too many design rules.

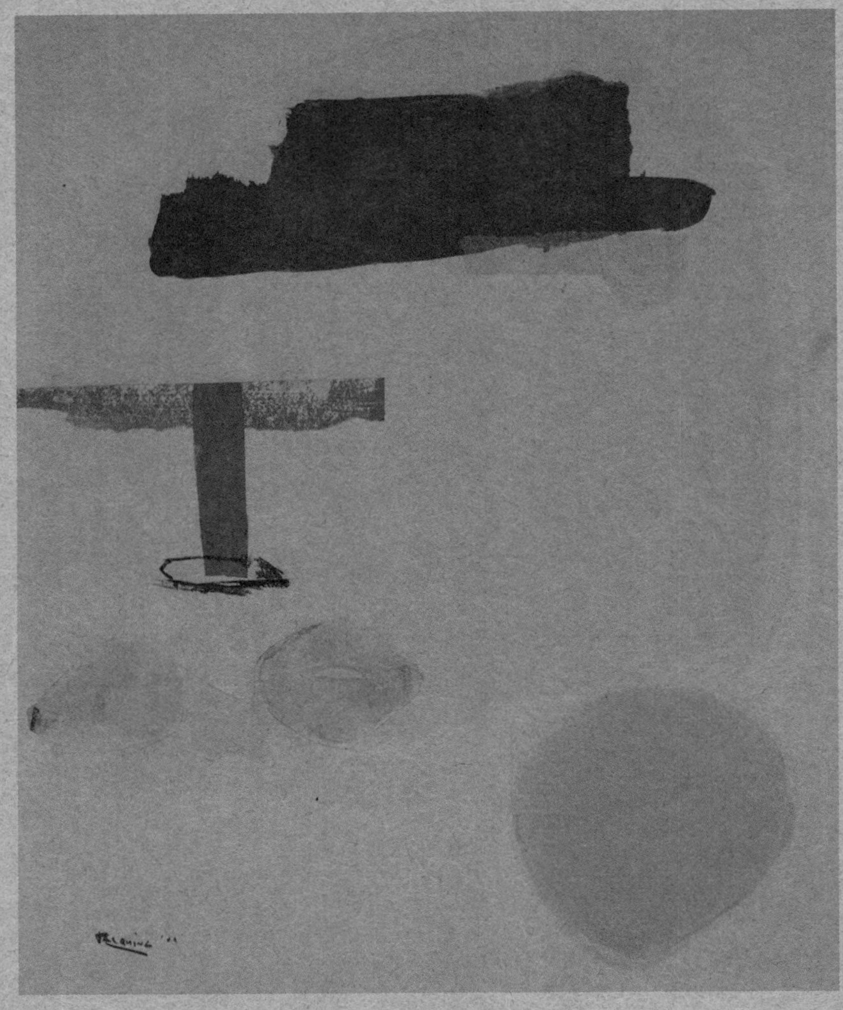

Fig. 6. *Drawing #149*, 2000, oil and graphite pencil on paper, 43.2 × 35.6 cm

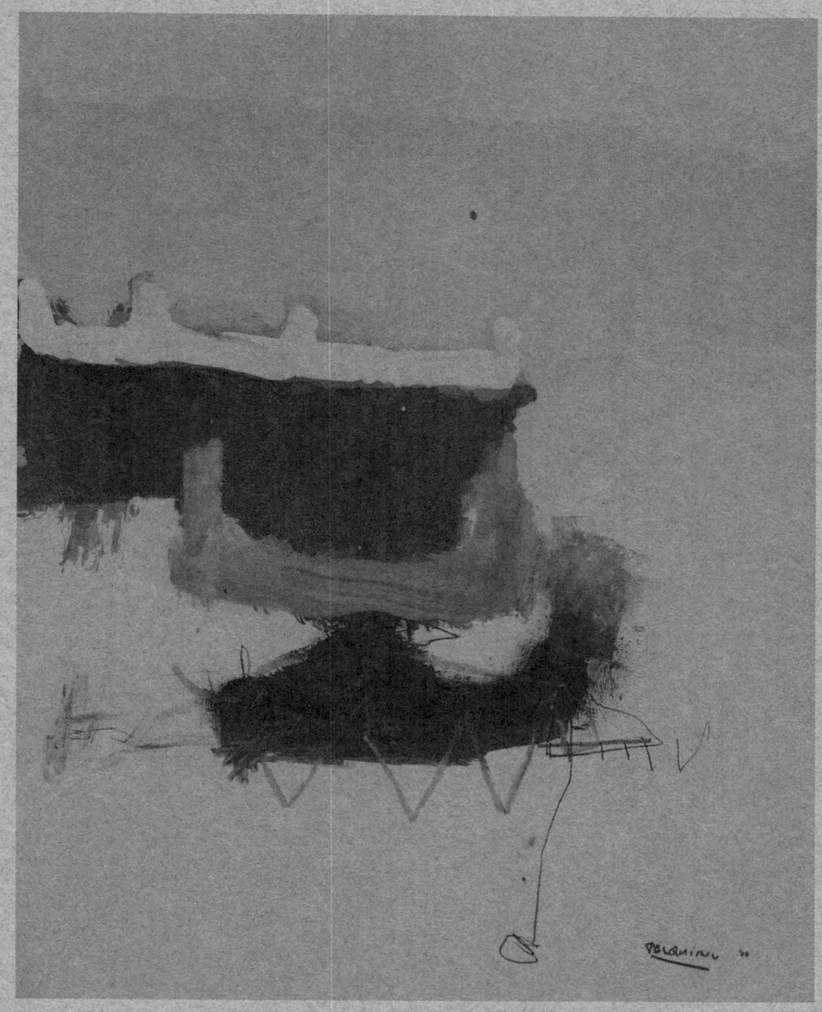

Fig. 7. *Drawing #151*, 2000, oil and graphite pencil on paper, 43.2 × 35.6 cm

He eventually quit the CCP to paint full time, while also working for Alcazaren Bros., the animation company that pioneered non-computer-graphic-generated animation in the country. During the ten years that Pacquing worked with them, they won several awards. In a capitalist system, advertising provided the financial stability he needed to pursue painting as a profession. At the time, Pacquing was also already married to Peachy, who was herself building her own successful career at the advertising agency Ogilvy & Mather. Perhaps, after all, his father, Oscar Sr., was not completely wrong in suggesting that Pacquing study something more practical than fine arts. "It was not only hard to be a visual artist in the 1990s, but it was hard to be an artist period," says Soler Santos of West Gallery.[10]

10. The author's phone interview with Soler Santos, June 26, 2023.

Pacquing was initially known more as a graphic designer than as an artist. So it was difficult for him to convince a Manila gallery to include him, an unknown artist, in a group show – more challenging still to convince them to give him a solo one. His first shows occurred through Source: Manila, a group of artists he knew from his university days. Together, they approached galleries in Iloilo, Cebu, and Bacolod on their own, convincing them to exhibit their work, then transporting their rolled-up canvases themselves from Manila to the various sites via Ro-Ro vessels to save on shipping costs.

Only with external validation did the art world come to believe that Pacquing was a painter. His break came when he won the grand prize in the painting category in the 1992 Art Association of the Philippines Open Art Competition. The recognition was even more significant then because the competition's founder, Purita Kalaw Ledesma, was an art critic and writer who was still alive. Soler Santos of West Gallery remembers how surprised he was to learn that Pacquing painted. "There was no Facebook, so I found out he painted when he won," Santos said.[11] After seeing a photo of his winning work in the association's brochure, which he thought was good, Pacquing was invited by Santos to do a solo show. This led to ten more solo shows at West Gallery from the early 1990s to the early 2000s. Pacquing remembers being well taken care of there, and he praises Santos for being one of the few who took a chance on his early work. In 1999, seven years later, he won the award again.

11. Ibid.

Pacquing showed his work from the 1990s on, but it was only in the mid-aughts that his paintings received serious attention. He says that at the time, "Only one or two paintings would get sold or none."[12] Some galleries would ask an artist to lower their price so a painting could sell, he explained; they would tell you to give a discount because they had already done so. There were also other factors making success difficult. Art-making is very different from the art market. During those years, abstract art was generally ignored, and only social realists and hyperrealists were successful artists. Their works sold for the same reason more realistic art still sells well today: their subject matter was recognizable. In general, abstraction is harder to understand, and the public feels less comfortable viewing abstract works. Abstraction seems to question what you know or what you understand. However, just because one can identify a form does not mean that one can understand it. In addition, Pacquing's works were not only abstract, but – as he puts it – they were less appealing and "ugly" abstractions, rather than "pretty" ones that exhibited traditional painterly features of fine art, such as a glossy sheen and smooth finish.

12. The author's interview with Bernardo Pacquing.

Talent is the easiest part of becoming an artist. The harder part is to endure, believing that one has something so important to say that it is worth the effort to remain true to oneself. In 2012, Jonathan Olazo curated a group show with fellow painters Argie Badoy and Johnny Alcazaren, called "Abstraction Is Homeless," at Manila Contemporary. For this exhibition, Pacquing made his largest painting to date, a 32-foot canvas, with yellow and black shapes and what looked like a half-drawn horse. No one came to the opening except for the artists' families, and nothing was sold. One of the installations was recycled into Halloween decoration. A painter half-jokingly told Pacquing, "*Bernie konting konti na lang mag-hyperrealism na ako. Ang hirap kumita ng pera* [I am this close to doing hyperrealism; it is so hard to earn money]."[13]

13. Ibid.

Awards helped to motivate the artist when financial earnings were slim. In 2000, Pacquing won the Cultural Center of the Philippines (CCP) 13 Artists Award, a prize given to exemplary Filipino artists in contemporary visual art. In the accompanying CCP brochure, there is a blurry, black-and-white photo of Pacquing looking much the same as he does today in his 50s, but with the bewildered look of a 1970s rock guitarist with feathered hair. Apparently, he would cut his hair whenever he felt agitated about a new work. "I am always anxious every time I paint," Pacquing says, referring to how the process never became easier.[14] Paloma, who grew up watching her father paint before he had his own studio on the floor of their one-car-garage home, would say in jest that his paintings were "suicidal," referring to how restless he would become when preparing for a show. The youngest child of three, along with Miguel and Sancho, Paloma shared her father's artistic sensibilities, looking for unusual ways to present ordinary things. In a 2016 show at Underground Gallery at Makati Cinema Square called "Smalls," he exhibited collages inspired by Paloma and the color pink. The collages stand out because they seem to be a detour from previous works, with their thick paint either squiggled on like toothpaste, or spread on thickly like jam (Fig. 8). There are also cut-out photos of balloons, tables, hearts, and girlish paraphernalia, all mixed up with scraps of weathered material.

14. Ibid.

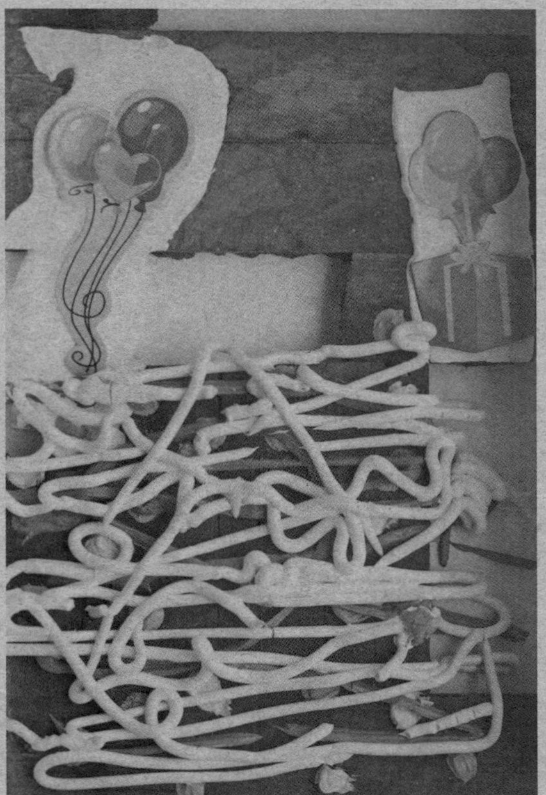

Fig. 8. *Untitled #001 (After Paloma's Pink)*, 2016, assemblage on wooden parquet, 19.1 × 14 cm

In 2014, he signed up as one of the represented artists at Silverlens in Makati. Isa Lorenzo recalls how she was warned that Pacquing and Peachy were "difficult" to deal with, something she found untrue when the time came to talk to them herself. Isa says that they were straightforward and professional, but not difficult.[15] Difficult can mean many things, including: ambitious and bold, determined and badass. At Silverlens, Pacquing explored other media, venturing into land art and public commissions with *Domes Village* (2019) in New Clark City, *Cracks and Crevices* (2018) at the NEX Tower, and *Earth Mounds* (2018) at Lubi Art Island Project in Davao. In particular, *Domes Village* and *Earth Mounds* reveal the artist's knowledge of and interest in materials with patinas of past lives (Figs. 9a, 9b).

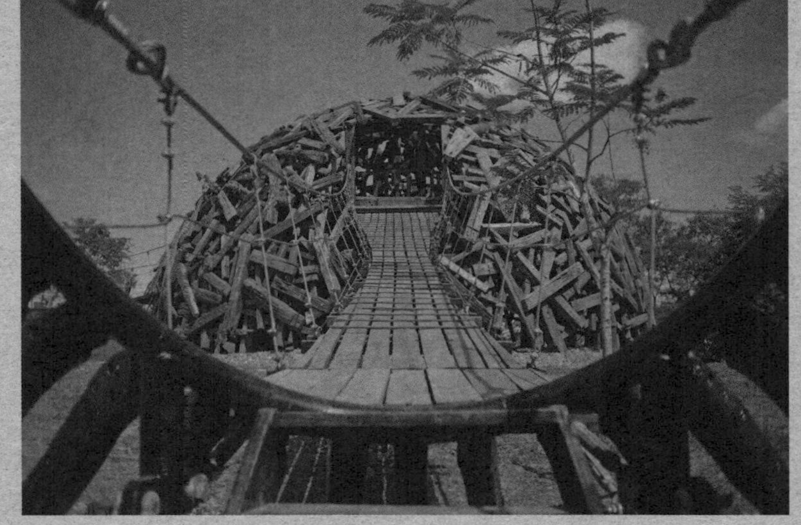

Fig. 9a. *Domes Village* (Detail), reclaimed endemic hardwood, 2019

15. The author's discussion with Isa Lorenzo, *Parañaque*, April 3, 2023.

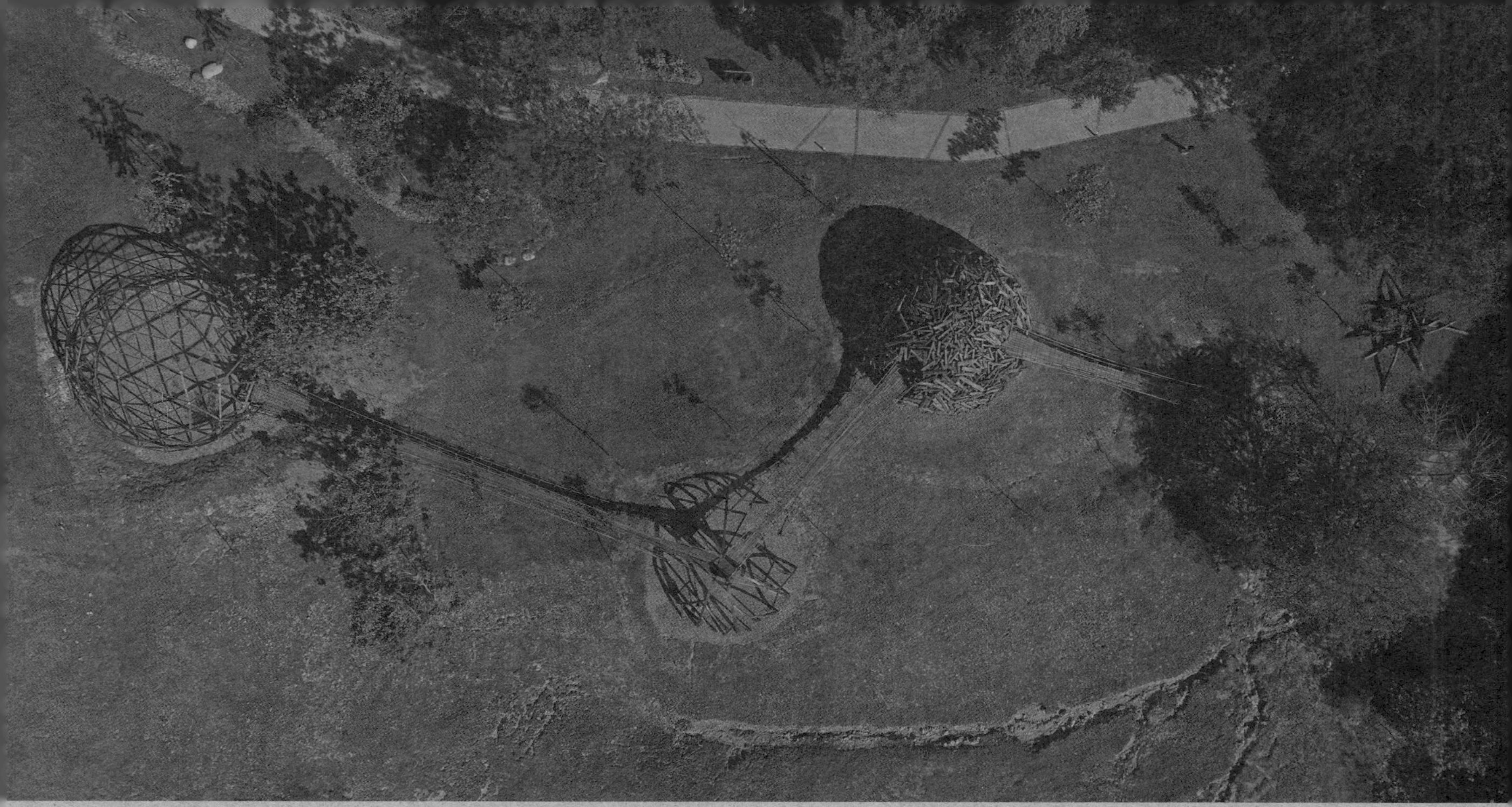

Fig. 9b. *Domes Village*, reclaimed endemic hardwood, 2019

German musicologist Ulrich Konrad writes about "departure points" during the creative process, which involve stockpiling ideas and then returning to them again later on.[16] In a similar way, Pacquing cycles through departure points in his oeuvre, marking a territory, leaving it, and returning to it later. His studio is filled with piles of studies and materials gathered and kept for years. The domes are an important departure point for him, to which he returns every few years, as are collages made from cardboard scraps and wooden sculptures.

At Silverlens, his first show was a duo exhibition with Max Balatbat. The paintings offered messy abstractions in muted colors with raw, translucent surfaces for which he was then known; however, they also marked a change in his creative methods, incorporating other materials along with the paint. For instance, in *Drill Press* (2014),

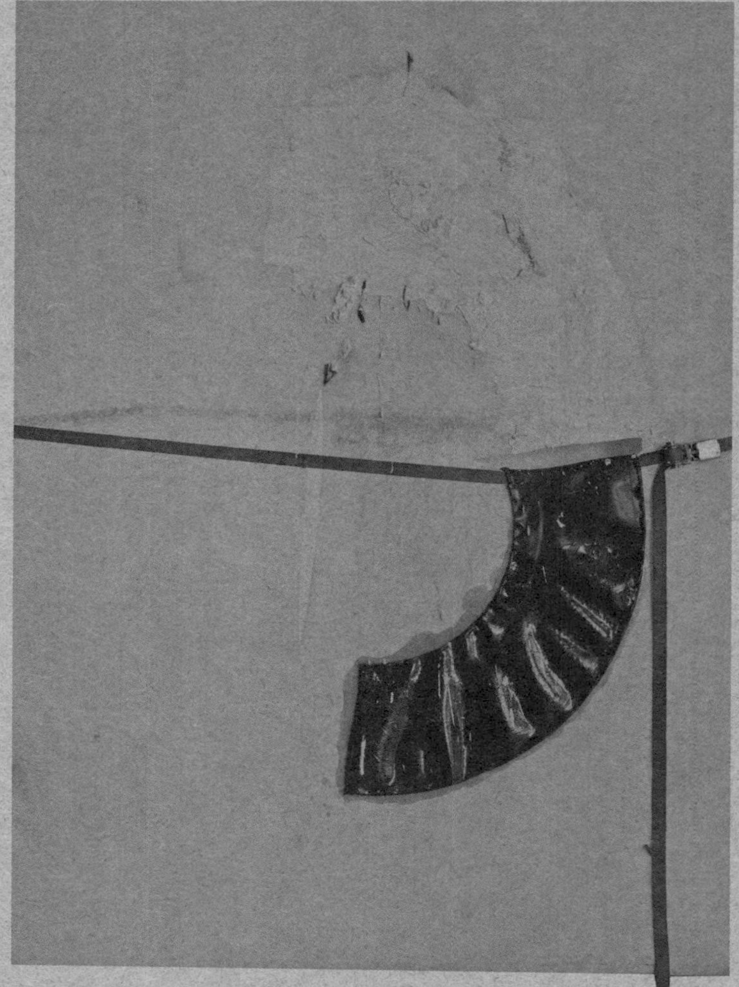

Fig. 10. *Drill Press*, 2014, tire tube, ratchet, resin, oil on canvas, 182.9 × 137.2 cm

16. Alex Ross, "The Storm of Style," *The New Yorker*, July 24, 2006, www.newyorker.com/magazine/2006/07/24/the-storm-of-style.

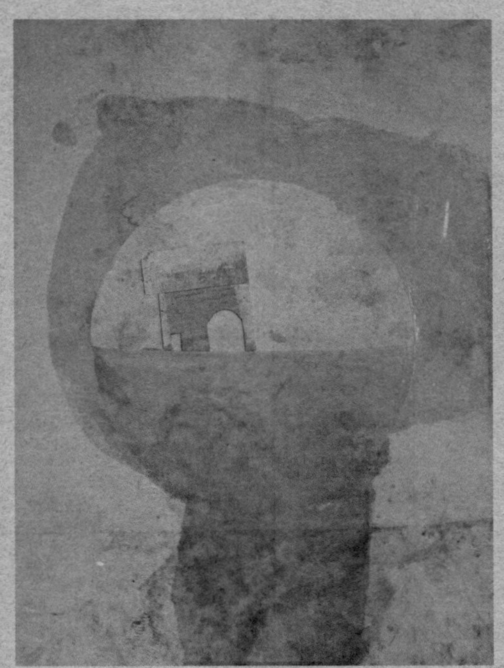

Fig. 11. *Focus Pocus*, 2014, scrap wood, resin, oil on canvas, 182.9 × 137.2 cm

a painting in shades of white and beige, a blue cord is anchored in the middle, from which, on the right, hangs a black rubber object shaped like an elbow macaroni, threatening to fall off (Fig. 10). Another, called *Focus Pocus* (2014), resembles a mushroom-shaped brown abstraction with a layer of plywood sheet, perhaps in the shape of a house (Fig. 11). Pacquing explains that since he began including different media and elements, the creative process had become more complicated.[17]

17. The author's interview with Bernardo Pacquing.

For the show "Half-Full," the artist was inspired by hydroponics, which pushed him even further toward abstraction and the inclusion of other unusual materials. He discovered that the more varied and unexpected the material was, the more technical his treatment of it was. There, for the first time, he used unprimed canvas exposed to the sun and rain (Fig. 12). Another work consists of a sculpture made from a fat, folded mattress drenched in white epoxy paint and crowned with a pile of nails also covered in white epoxy paint (Fig. 13). Other totem-like wood sculptures are hemmed in by unexpected objects, such as a baluster, slivers of corrugated cardboard, and an old paintbrush (Fig. 14). Pacquing mixes his own colors, experimenting with aged industrial paints and resins, both oil and water based. Under the intense heat of the Philippines, these colors change, adding an unpredictable aspect to the work.

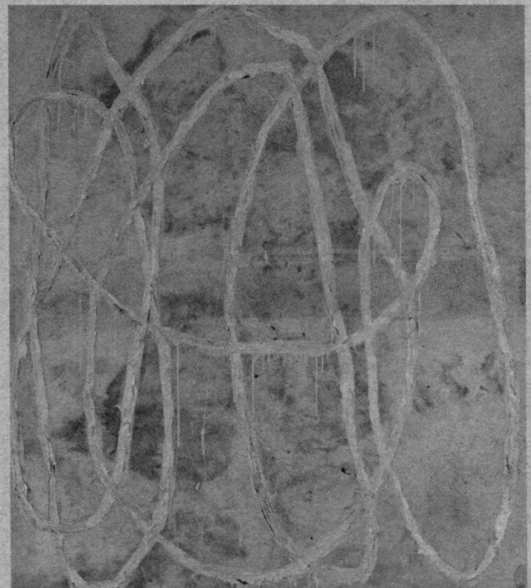

Fig. 12. *Ampalaya*, 2015, acrylic emulsion, oil on canvas, 152.4 × 133.4 cm

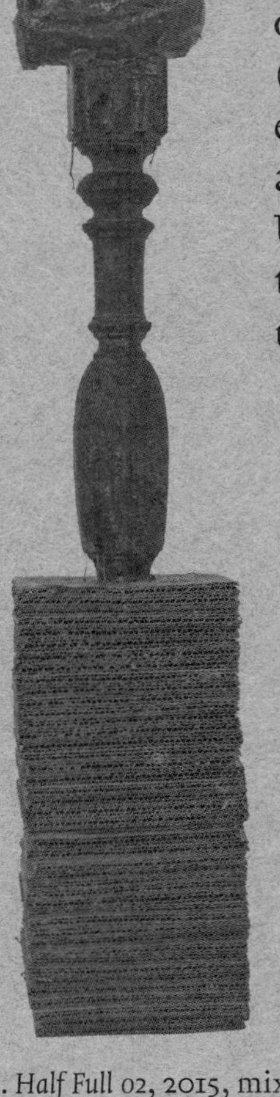

Fig. 14. *Half Full 02*, 2015, mixed media, 102.1 × 18.5 × 12.5 cm

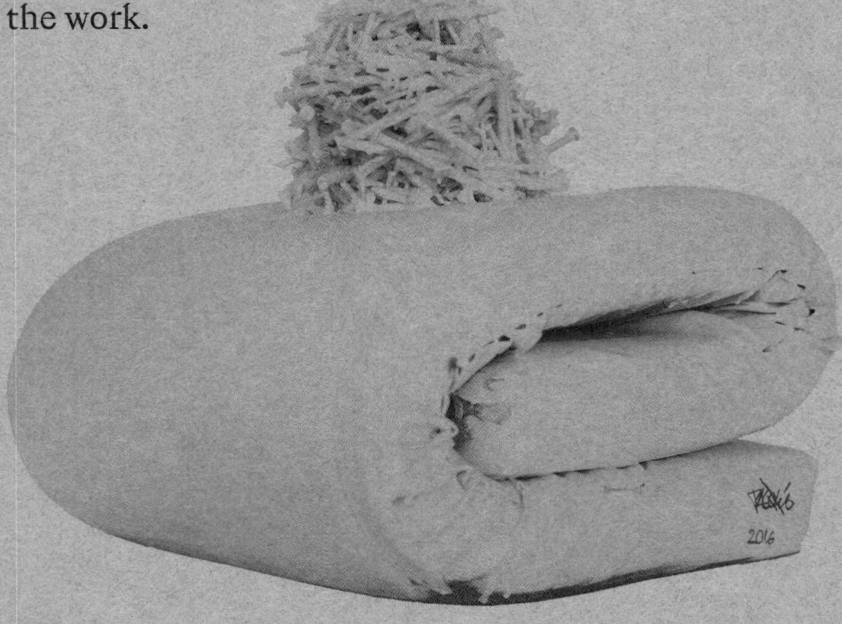

Fig. 13. *Cornerstone*, 2016, mixed media, 36.8 × 39.4 × 31.7 cm

Fig. 15. *Strata of Thought 02*, 2022, mixed media on canvas, 152.4 × 133.4 cm

Pacquing's artworks reveal his art-making process. For instance, for one of his most recent works, shown during the COVID-19 pandemic at FOST Gallery, Singapore, he boiled tar, which he then poured over the canvas, playing with the dualism of concealment and revelation. Black on black on black is layered over the folded canvas (Fig. 15). He also does not believe in destroying bad paintings because it is not part of the process: "The point is to make something out of it; you don't stop, you correct it. You forfeit the process if you destroy it."[18] For him, it is easy to spot a mistake, but very difficult to correct one. It would be akin to changing direction midstream and then improvising, based on the current shape of the work.

18. Ibid.

He admires artists committed to creating by following the natural, internal transformations of a given material. This is what Pacquing likes about the works of Richard Serra, who, for instance, is seen in a video throwing molten lead with Philip Glass. Other artists he admires are Cy Twombly, Robert Rauschenberg, Richard Tuttle, Antoni Tàpies, El Lissitzky, and Kazimir Malevich. They are a varied group and come from different backgrounds, but they share an affinity for everyday materials used both as residue and resource. Pacquing does not hide his admiration for their work and has named paintings after them. In *Homage to Cy* (2011), a huge flower in a state of melting or disintegration dominates the canvas. Another series called *"Untitled" After Malevich's Black Square* (2019) shows two discarded bed springs painted black, inserted inside a canvas frame with a roughly drawn square (Fig. 16). There is a quality to the work that can only be described by the Tagalog word *gigil* (the urge to pinch or squeeze hard). The material is manipulated in unusual ways to arrive at the final composition. *Untitled (After Tuttle #1)* and *Untitled (After Tuttle #2)*, paintings done in 2010, appropriate Tuttle's shapes, translating them into filled-in solid forms, some geometric, some with broken lines (Fig. 17).

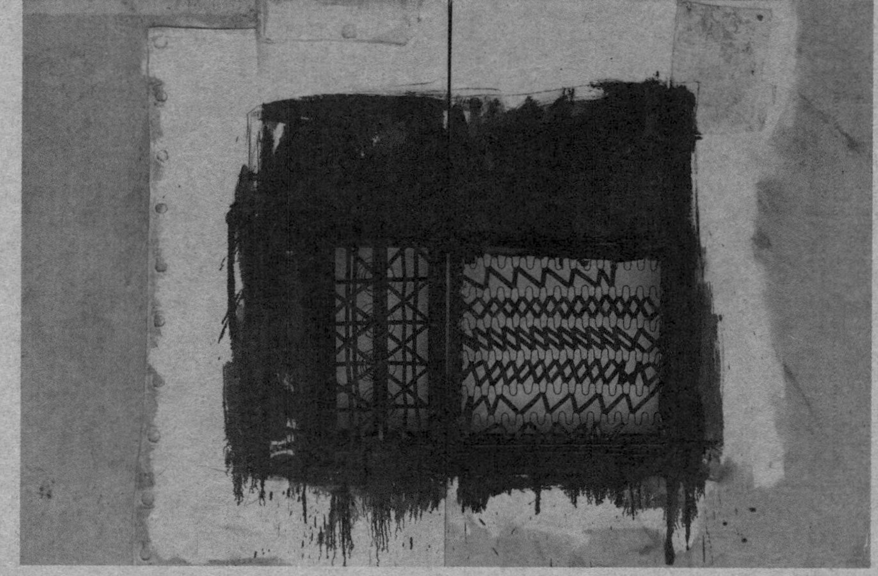

Fig. 16. *"Untitled" After Malevich's Black Square*, 2019, assemblage on canvas, house paint, 213.4 × 274.3 cm (diptych)

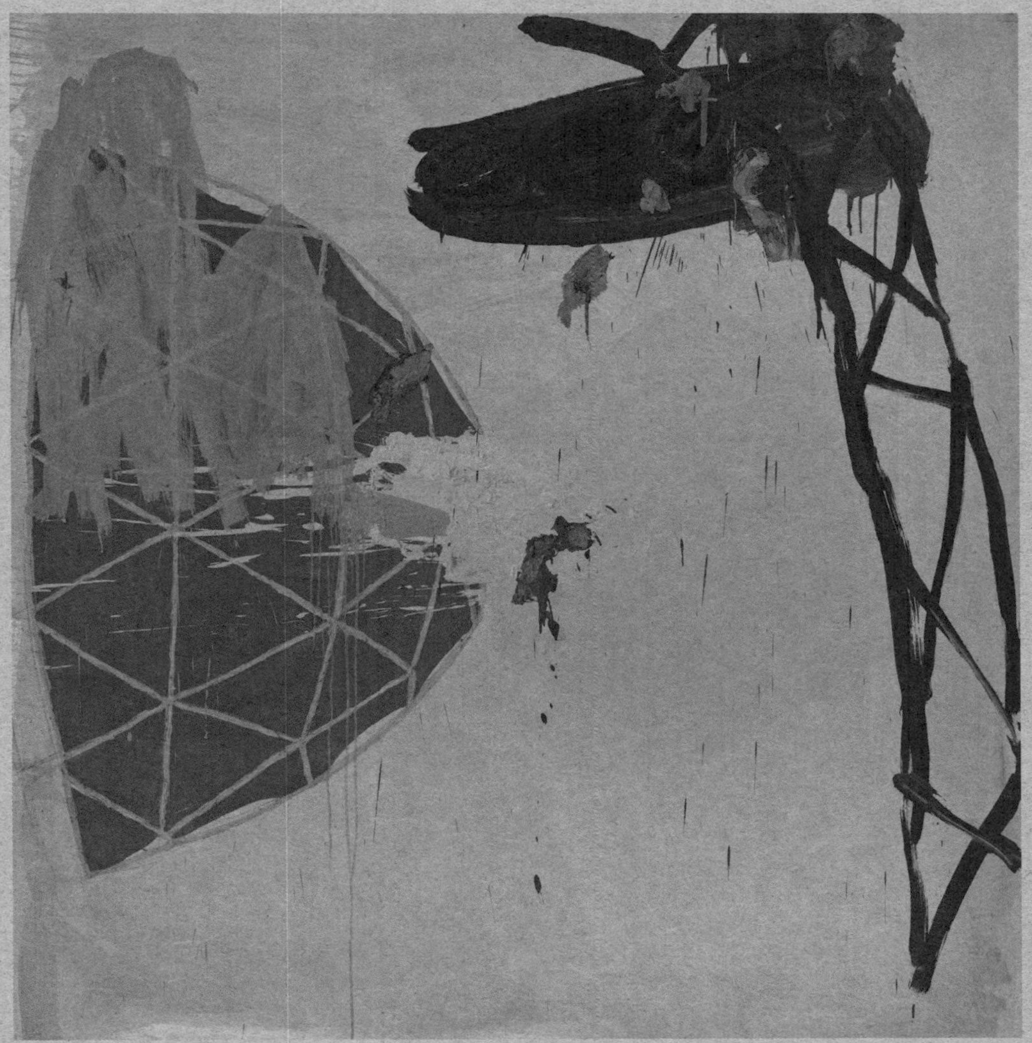

Fig. 17. *Untitled (After Tuttle #2)*, 2010, oil on canvas, 203.2 × 203.2 cm

The fact that Pacquing did not stop working during the strange, scary years of the pandemic is nothing short of a miracle. He describes how he coped with the uncertainty and hopelessness of lockdown after lockdown. When the virus began to spread, he was caught in Singapore with Peachy. They were separated from their children and the rest of the family. He wrote, "Months went by and my works kept adding up... I noticed my colors were getting darker... For sanity's sake, I kept going."[19] A photo from Singapore in 2020 shows him standing in an apartment making do with a corner table for painting and a makeshift clothesline hung on a loft railing as a drying area. The space was smaller than a hawker's stall, a huge contrast with his Manila studio (Fig. 18).

19. Bernardo Pacquing, artist's personal notes submitted to Silverlens Gallery for "Disquietude," December 2021.

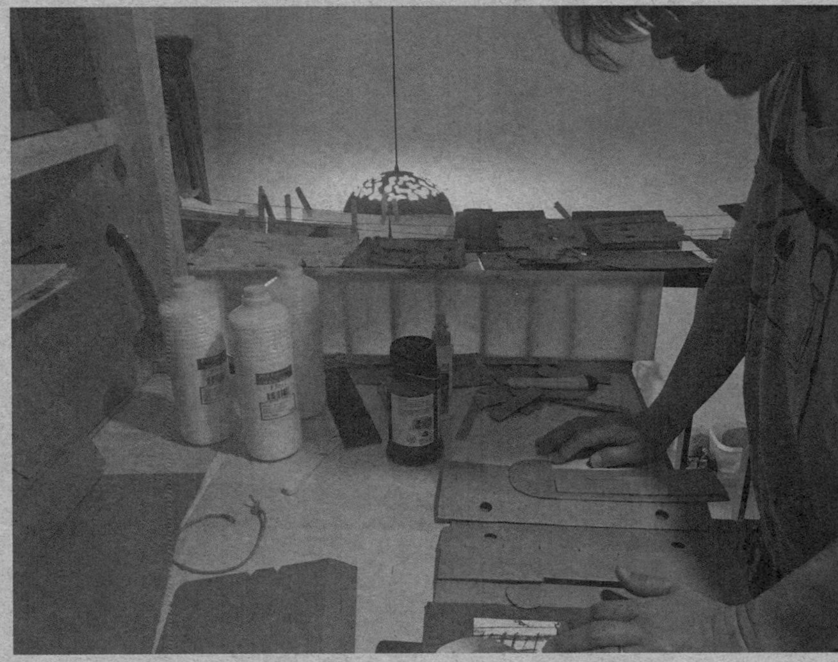

Fig. 18. Bernardo Pacquing in his Singapore studio, 2021

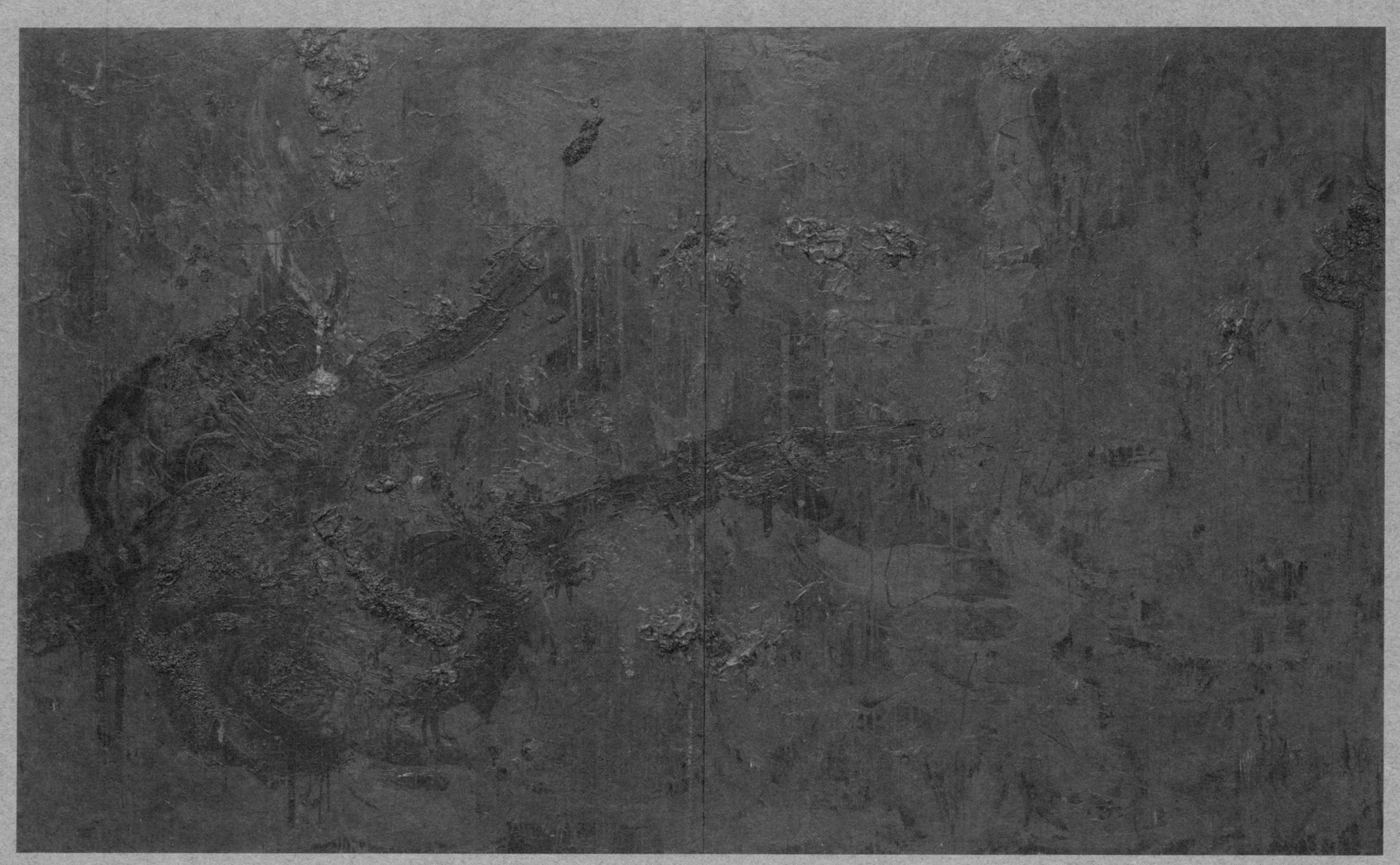

Fig. 19. *Red Object #02*, 2021, oil on canvas, 182.9 × 304.8 cm (diptych)

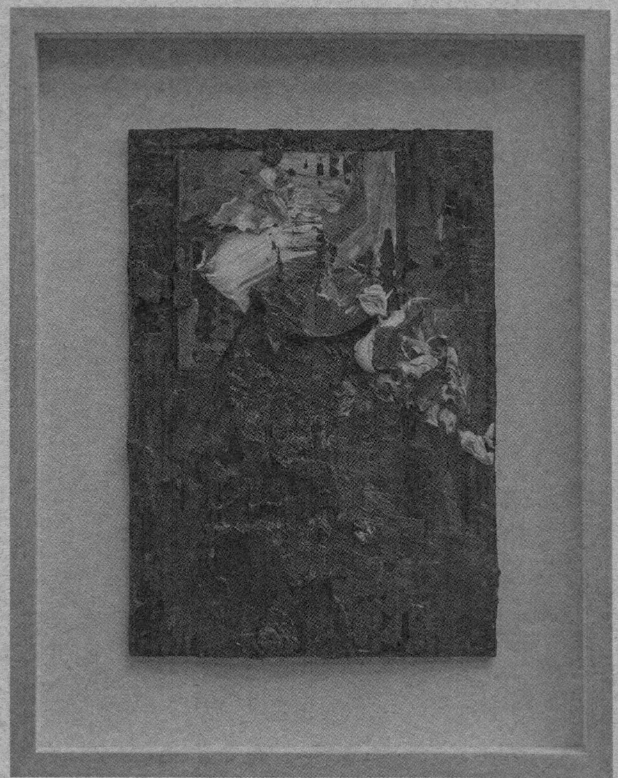

Fig. 20. *1-Beta Chain 23*, 2020, oil on cut cardboard, 29.7 × 21.1 cm

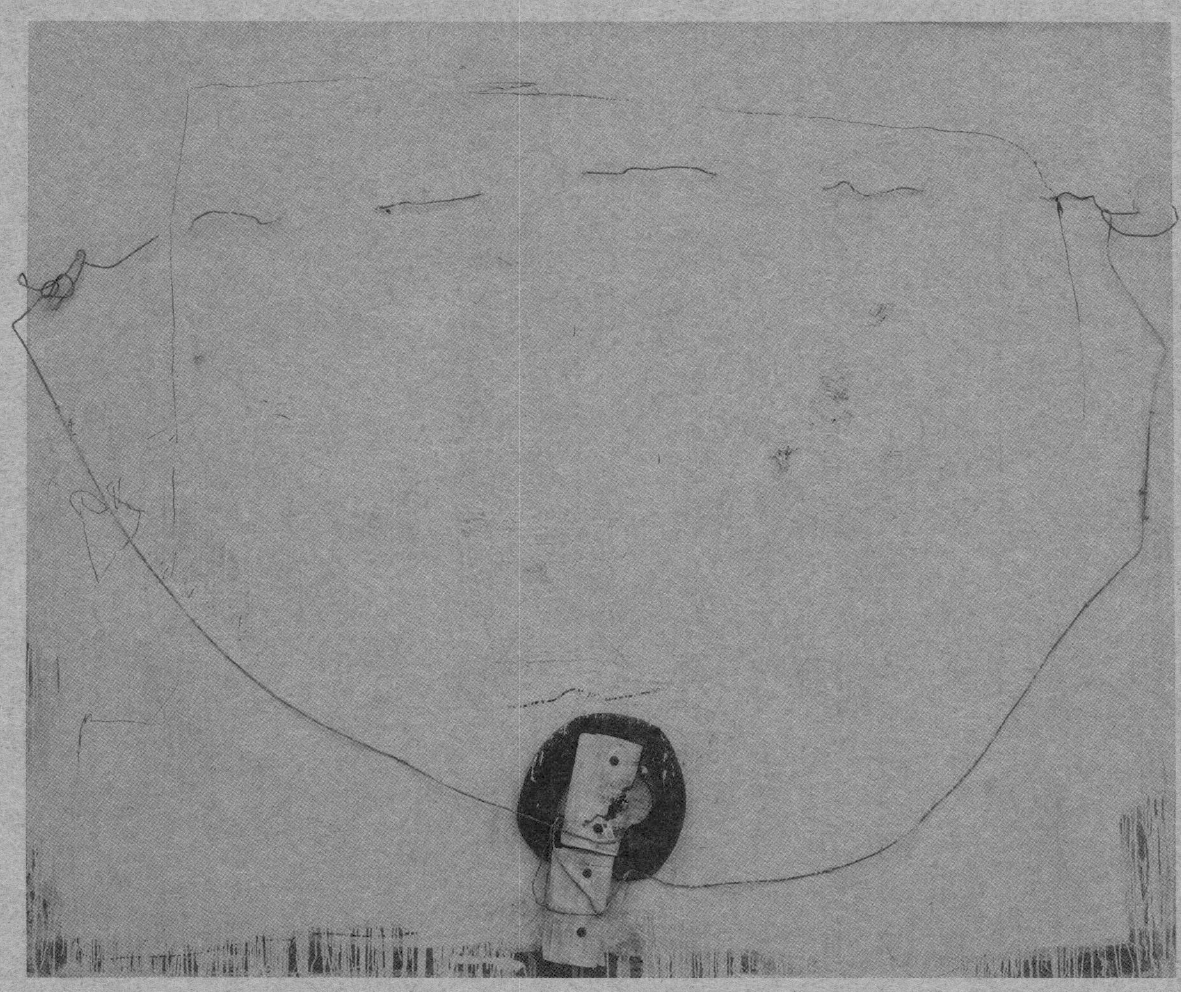

Fig. 21. *Convergence of Conditions and Culprits*, 2017, assemblage, house paint on canvas, 182.9 × 243.8 cm

Despite Singapore's strict lockdown codes, Pacquing was somehow able to paint the huge six-by-ten-foot canvases for the series *Red Object* (2021) in this cramped space. He transgressed his own creative principles by resorting to store-bought oil paints, giving these paintings the shiny gloss of a sports car. For texture, he used layers of thickly smeared-on red, orange, yellow, and black, making the canvases look like open flesh wounds or crusted-over scars (Fig. 19). Not being able to insert found objects into his works, he instead tried to compensate through oil paint. And because one was not allowed to collect discarded cardboard in Singapore, he gathered takeout food boxes for his small collage series *Beta Chain* (2020) (Fig. 20). This work was sent to Manila, and its difference from his other works, as well as its angry, emotional affect, surprised collectors and critics.

Pacquing's artworks are frequently described as having a stillness, a minimalist Zen quality, because of their luminous colors, symmetry, and matted texture. This is not incorrect, but it is incomplete. Abstract art can be a source of opposition. Abstract art wishes the viewer to take a different point of entry into the infinite crises possible in our ordinary lives. In *Convergence of Conditions and Culprits* (2017), one contemplates house paint, lead, and exposed wires applied to a canvas, seeing the materials not only from the vantage point of everyday life, but also as a step toward a transformation (Fig. 21). Just as the 15-year-old boy living on Dos Castillas Street did not think that a house was just a house, here, construction wire is not just construction wire. It would be arrogant for an artist to presume that he could change the world or even one's mind. But that is beside the point; the point is to try.

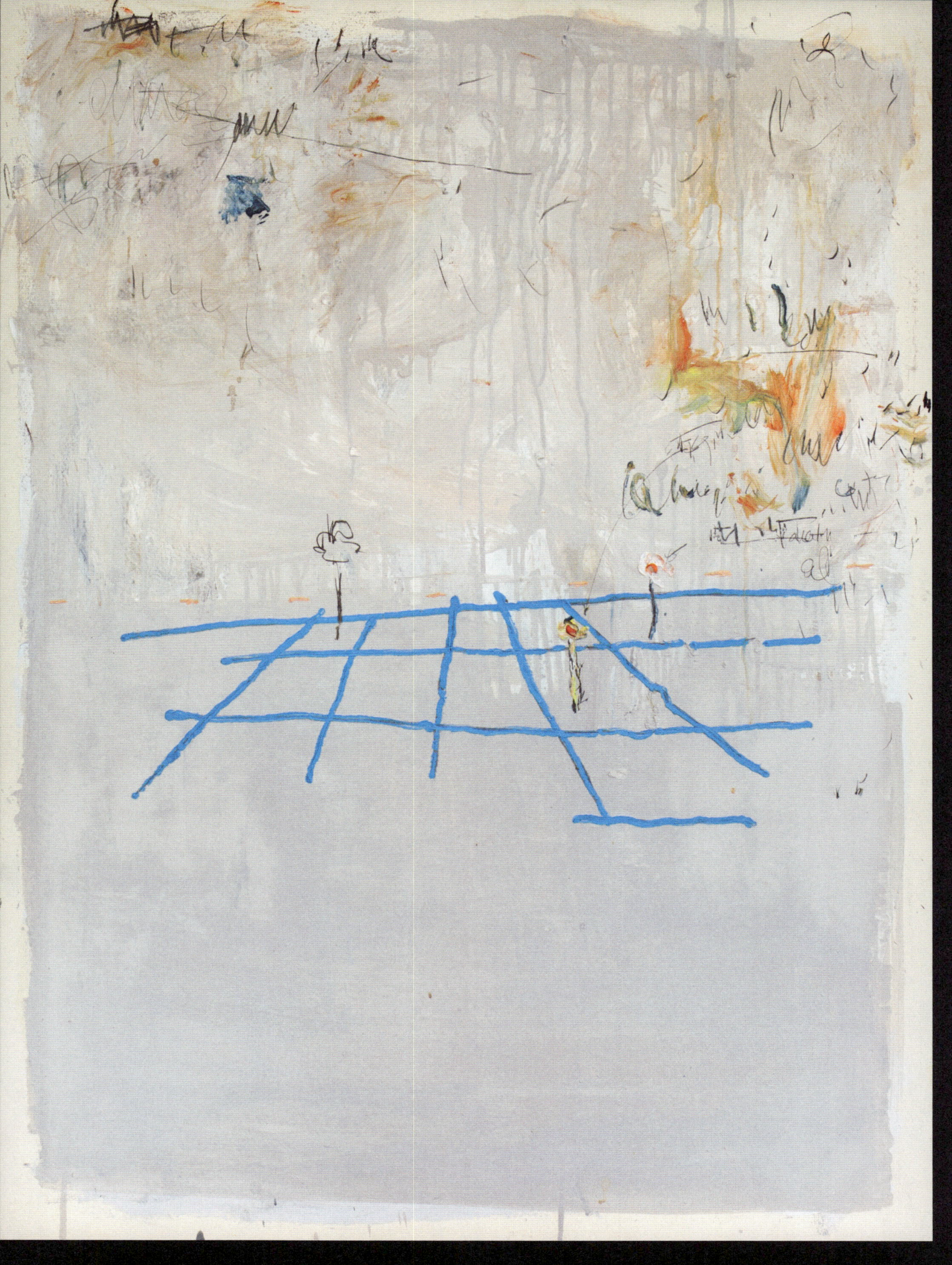

Hydroponics Series 2, 2014, oil on canvas, 122 × 91.4 cm

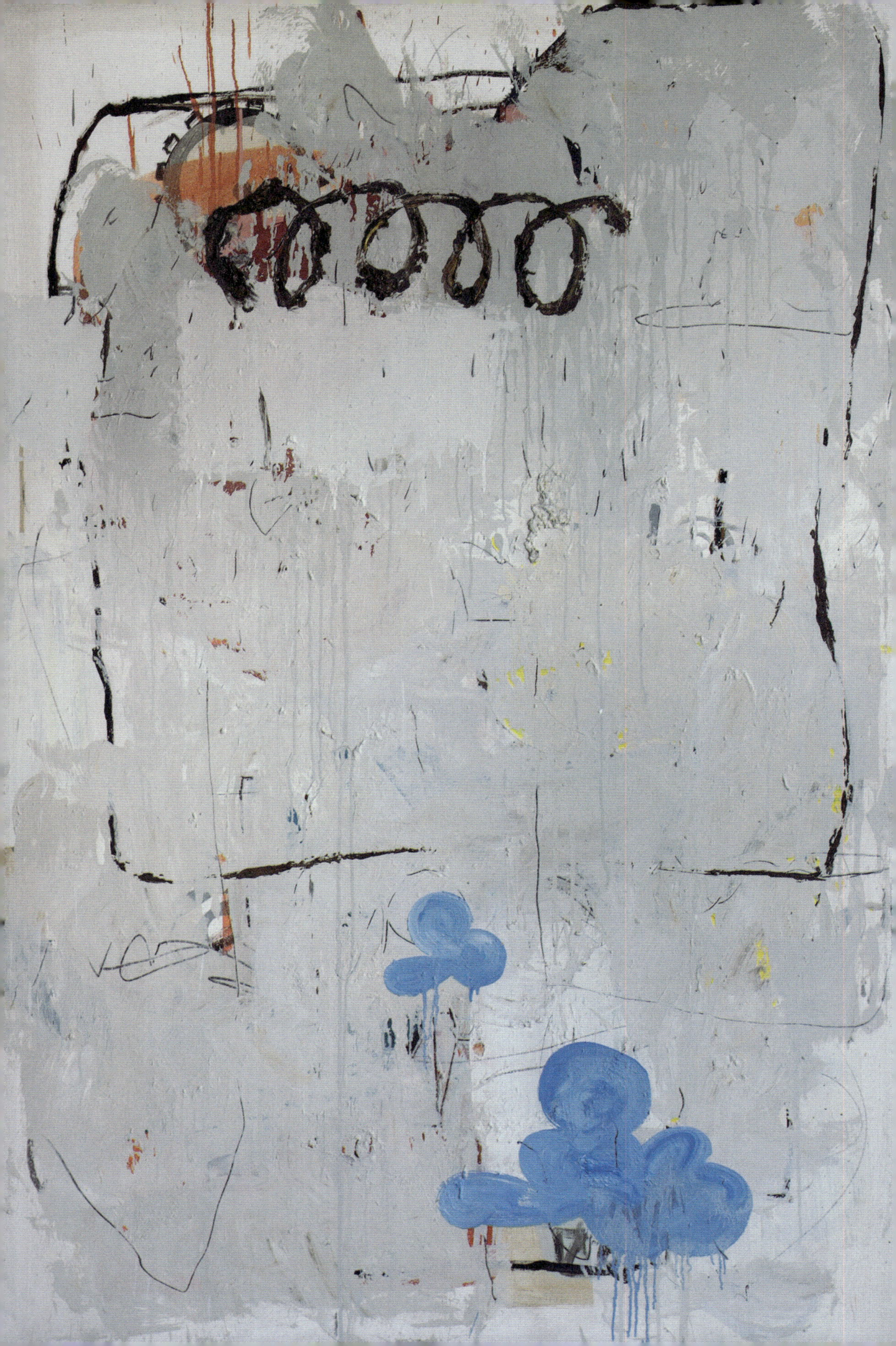

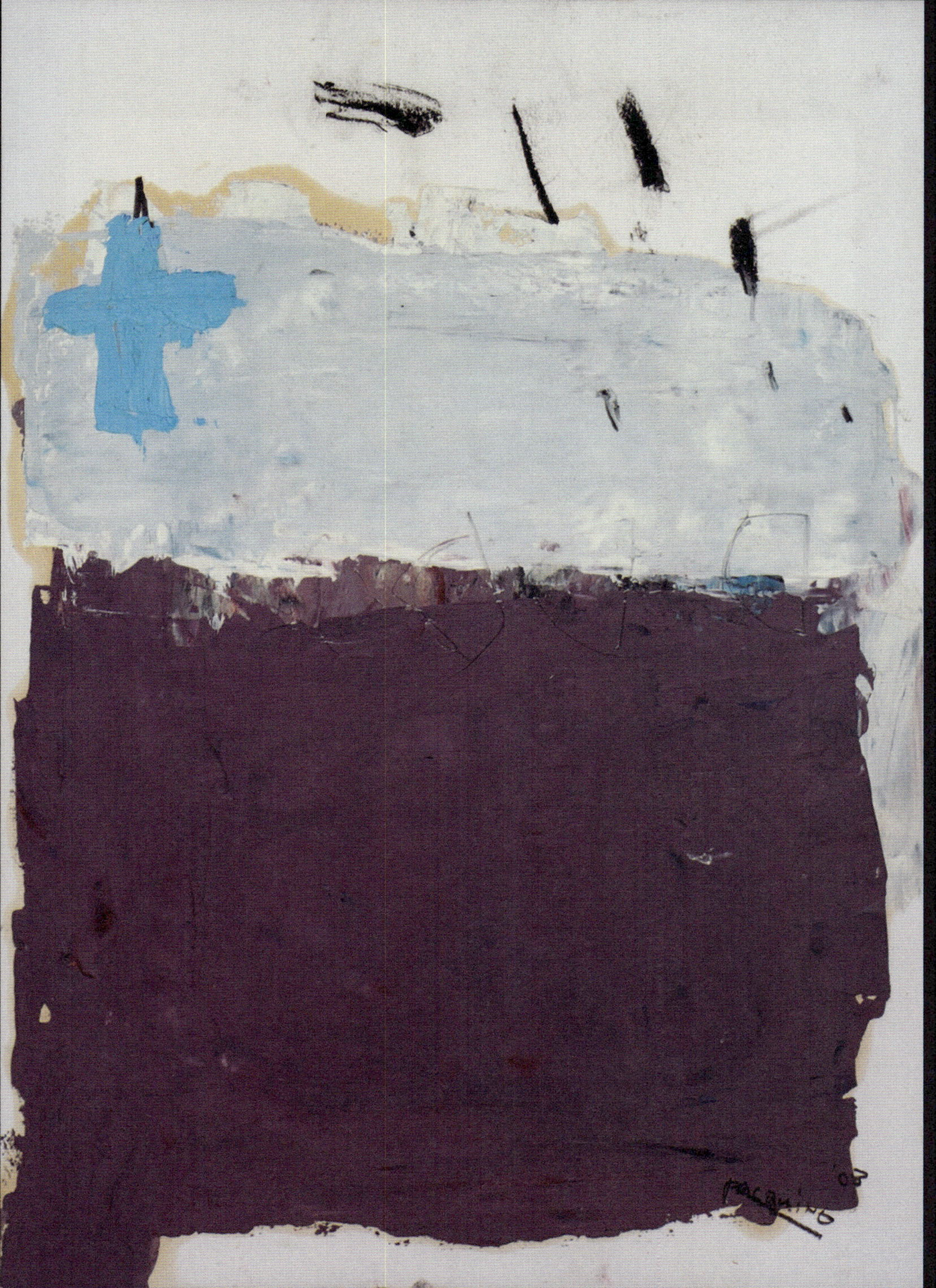

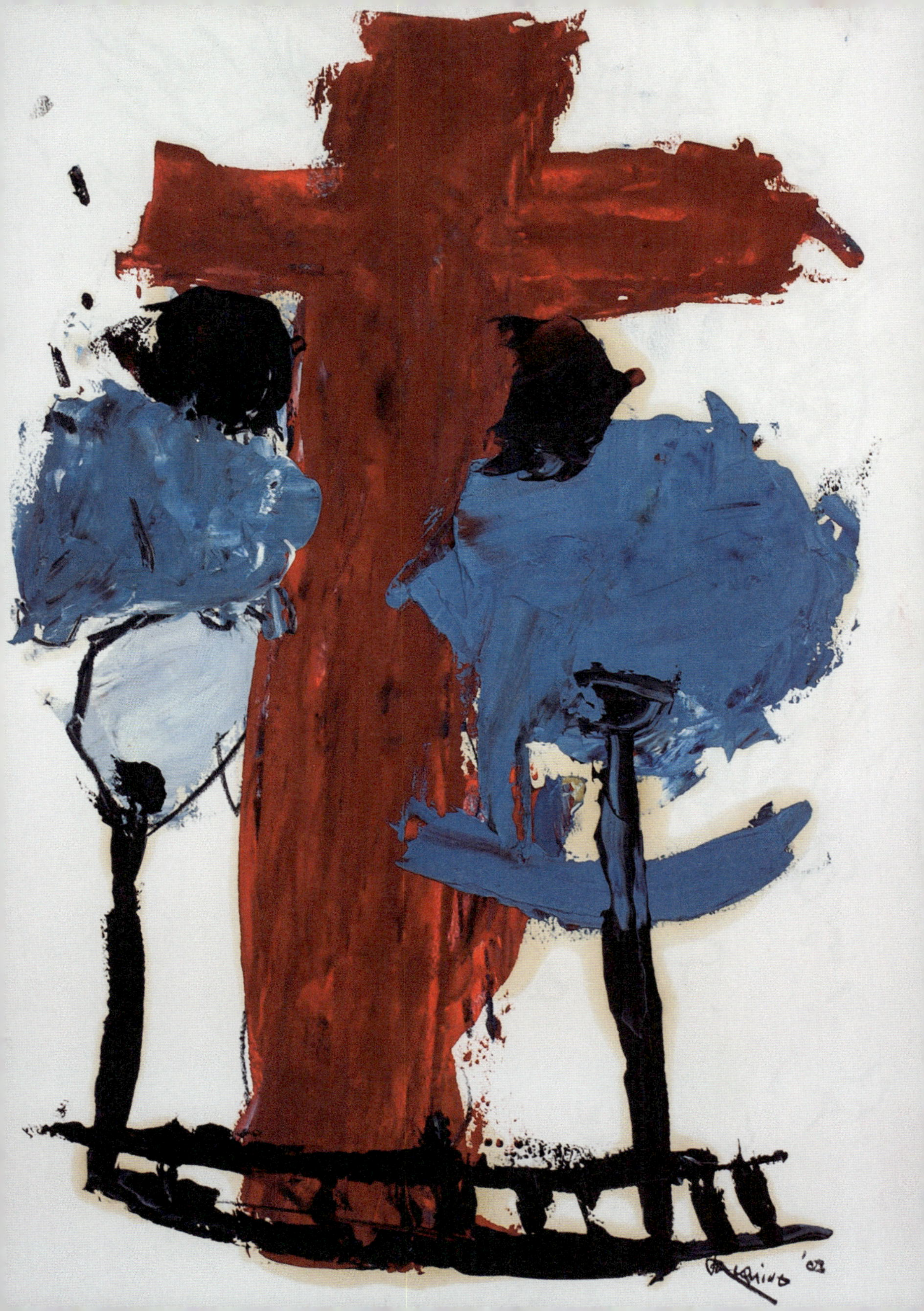

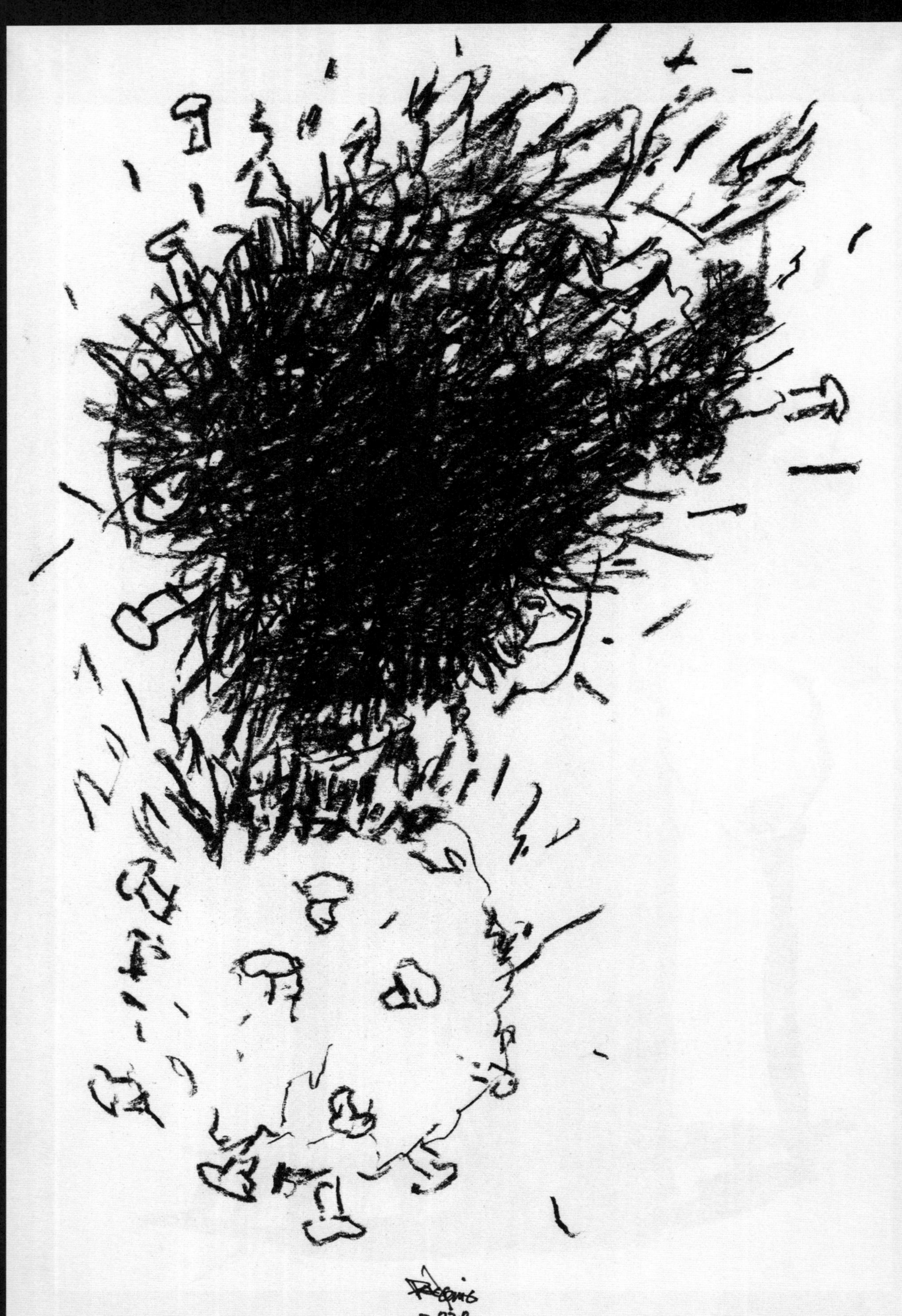

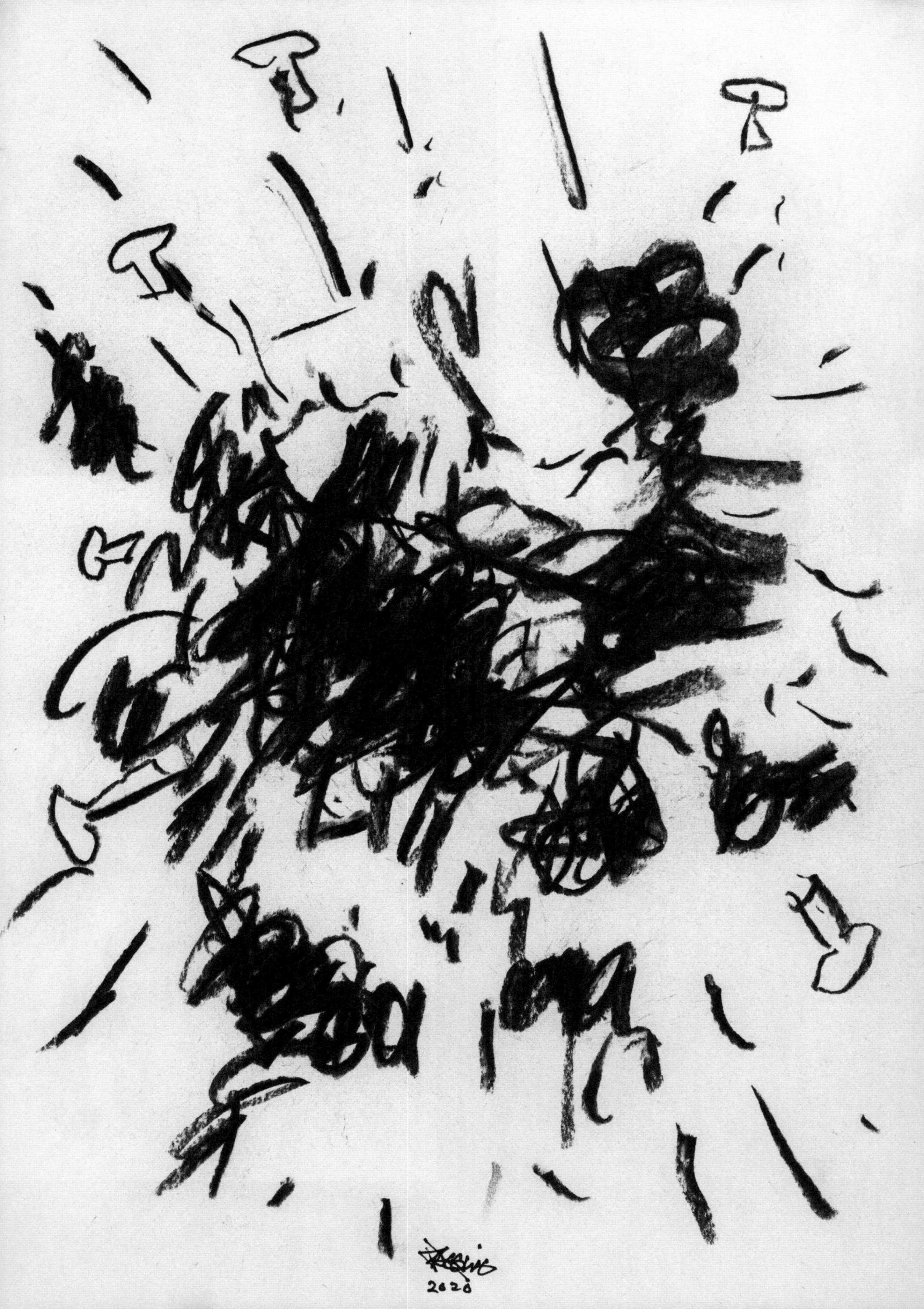
2020

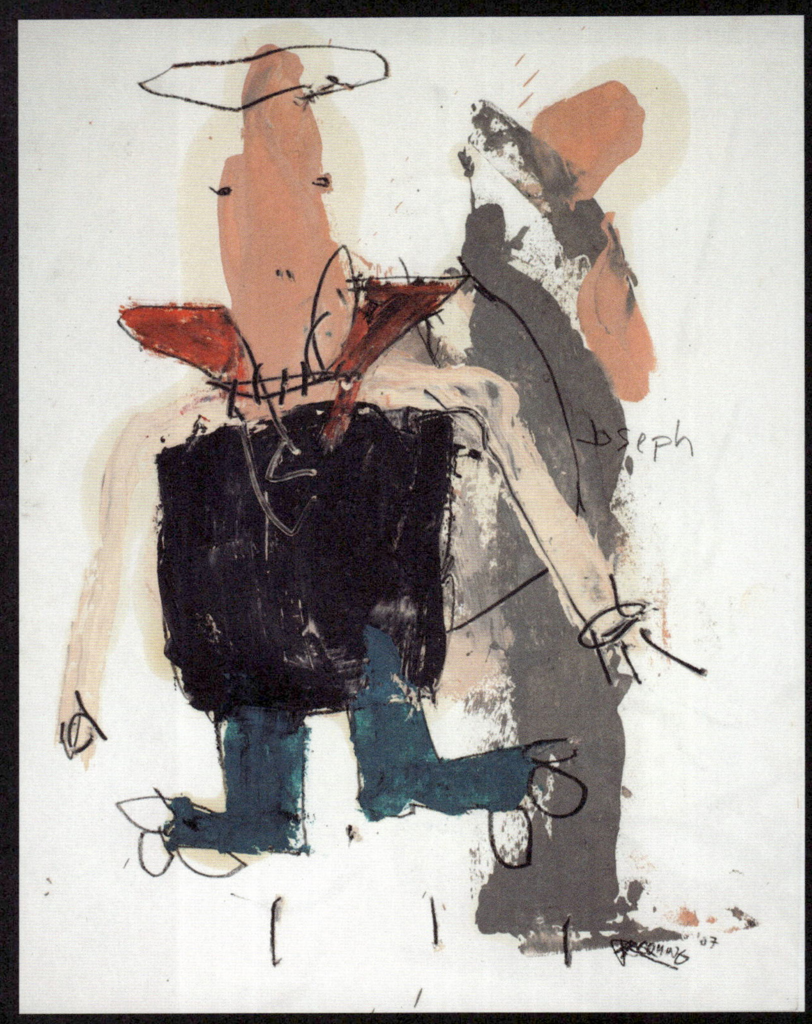

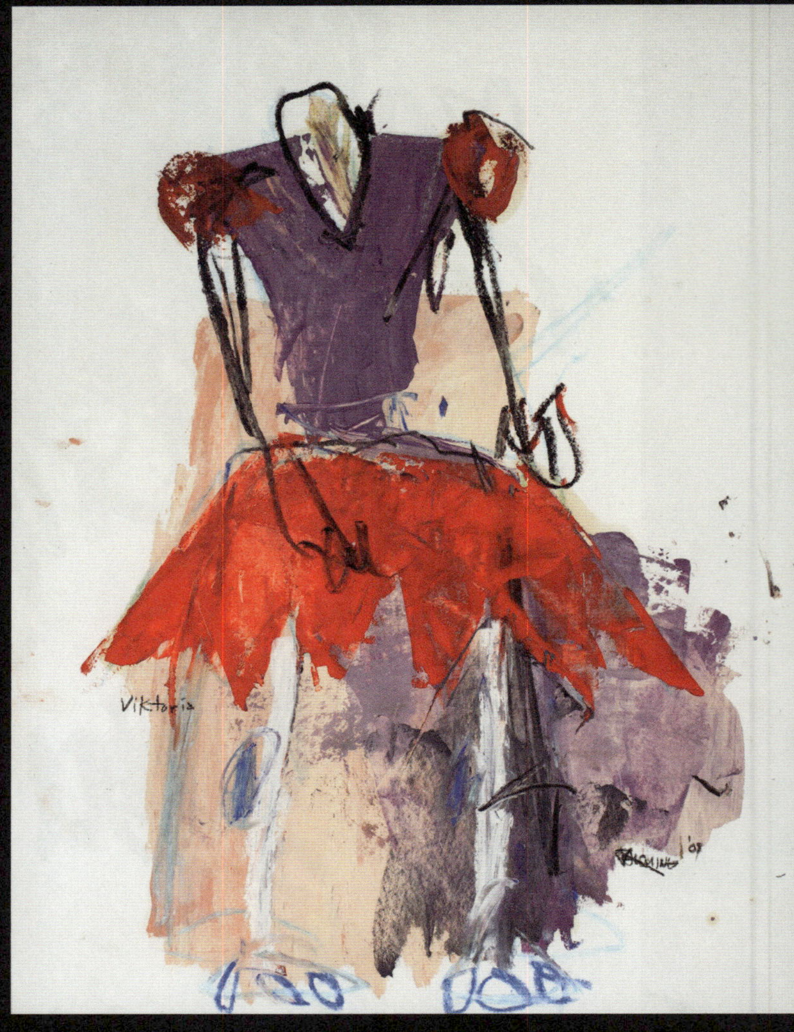

Joseph, 2007, acrylic on paper, 43.2 × 33.7 cm

Viktoria, 2007, acrylic on paper, 43.2 × 33.7 cm

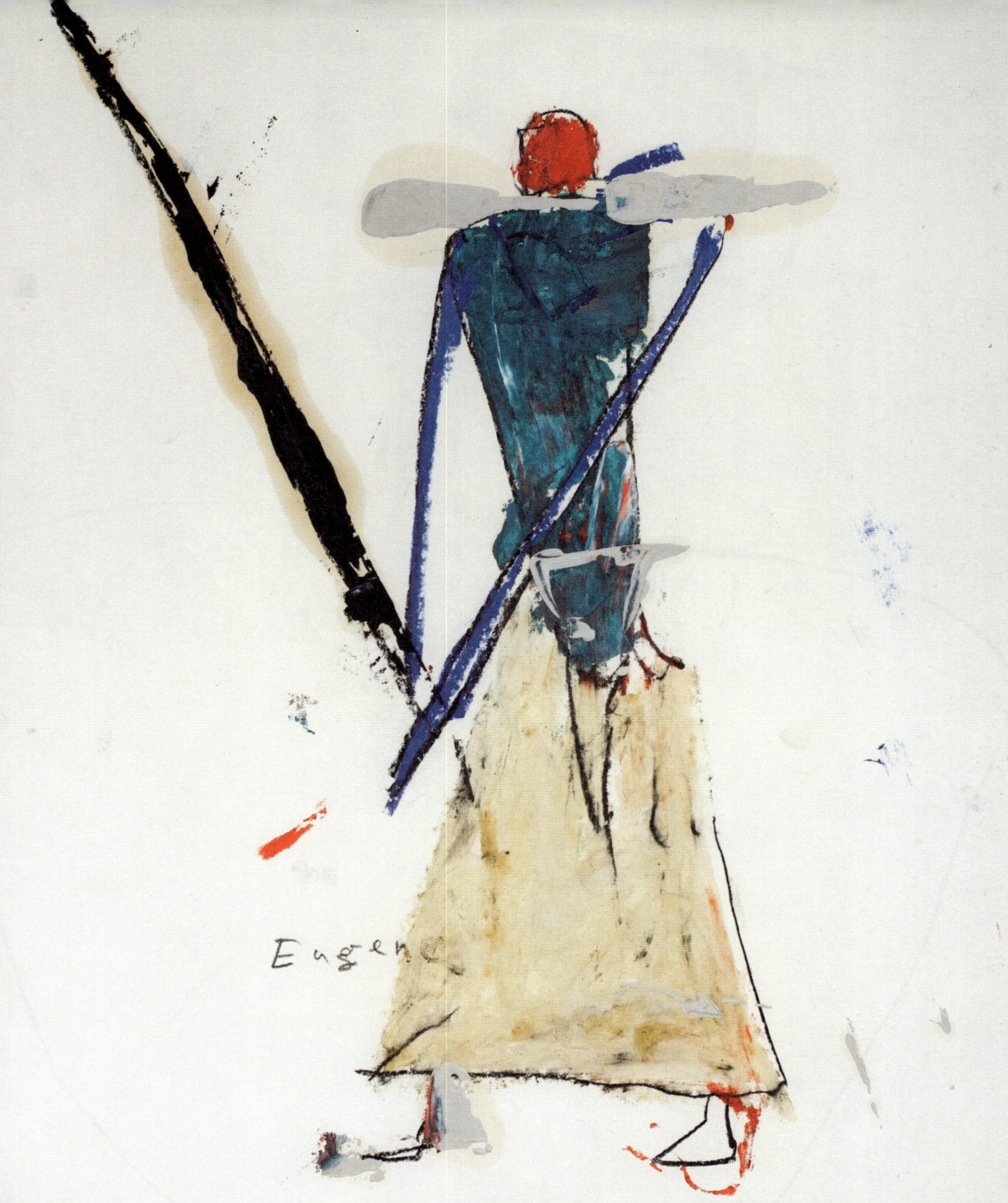
Eugene

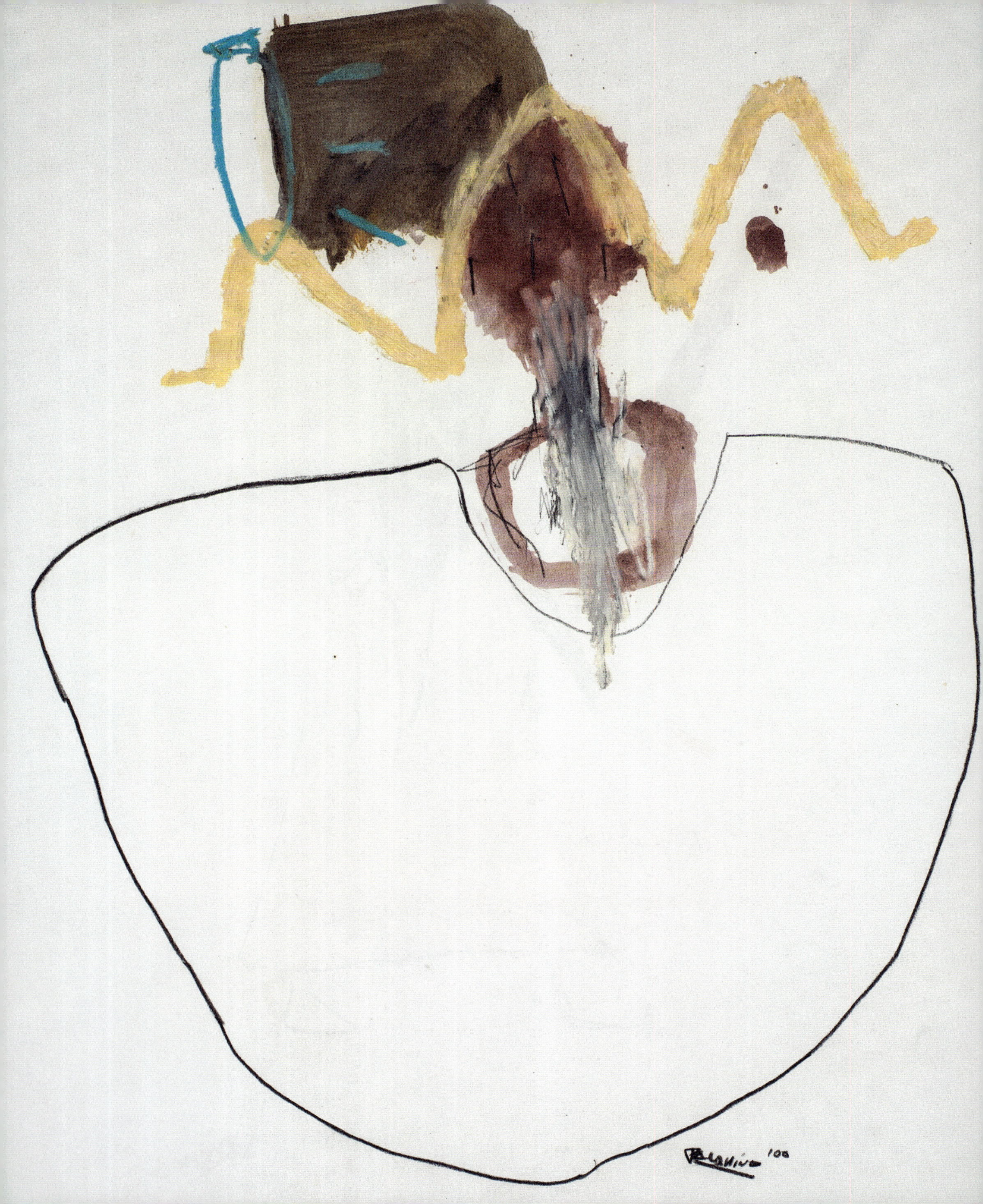

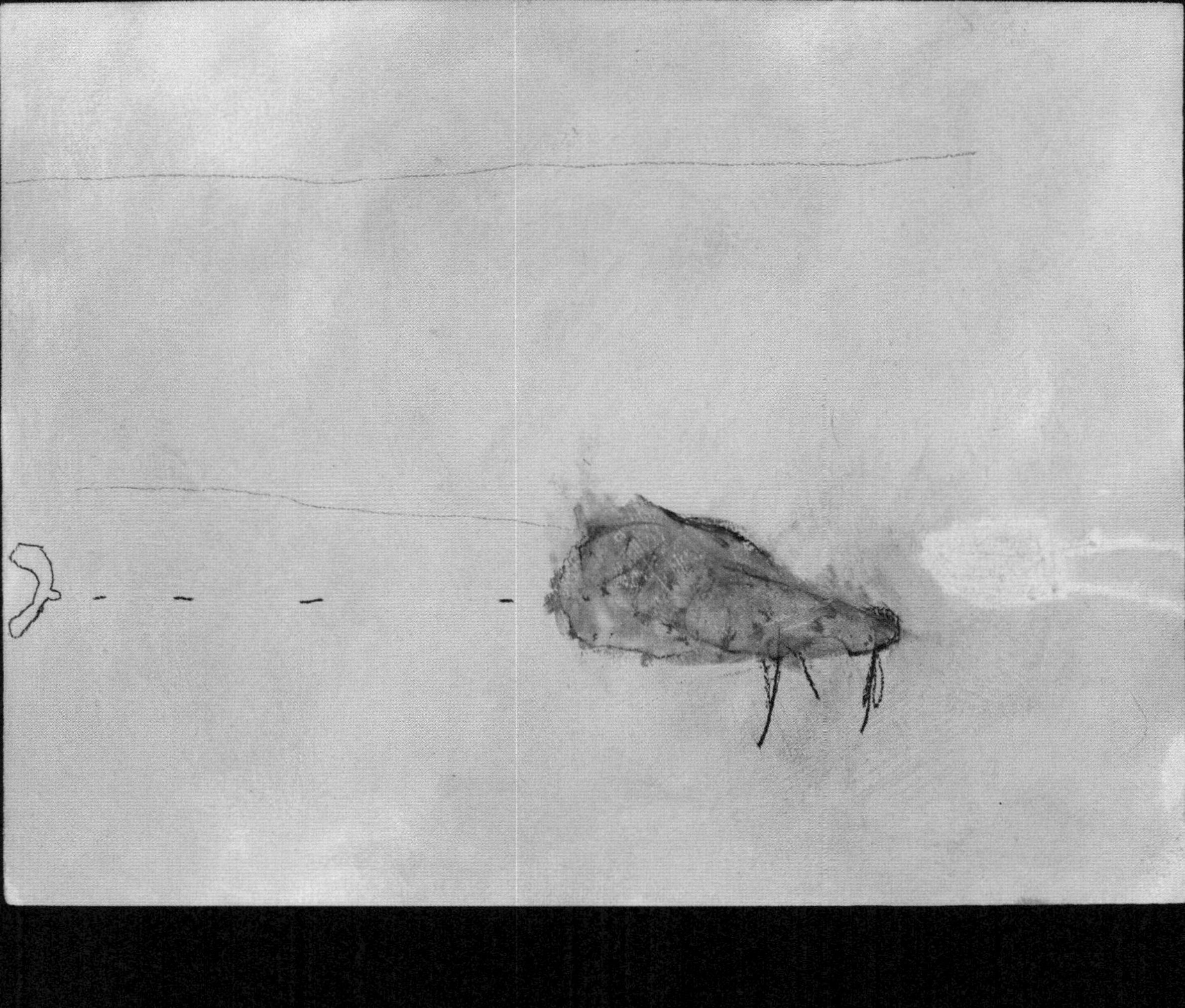

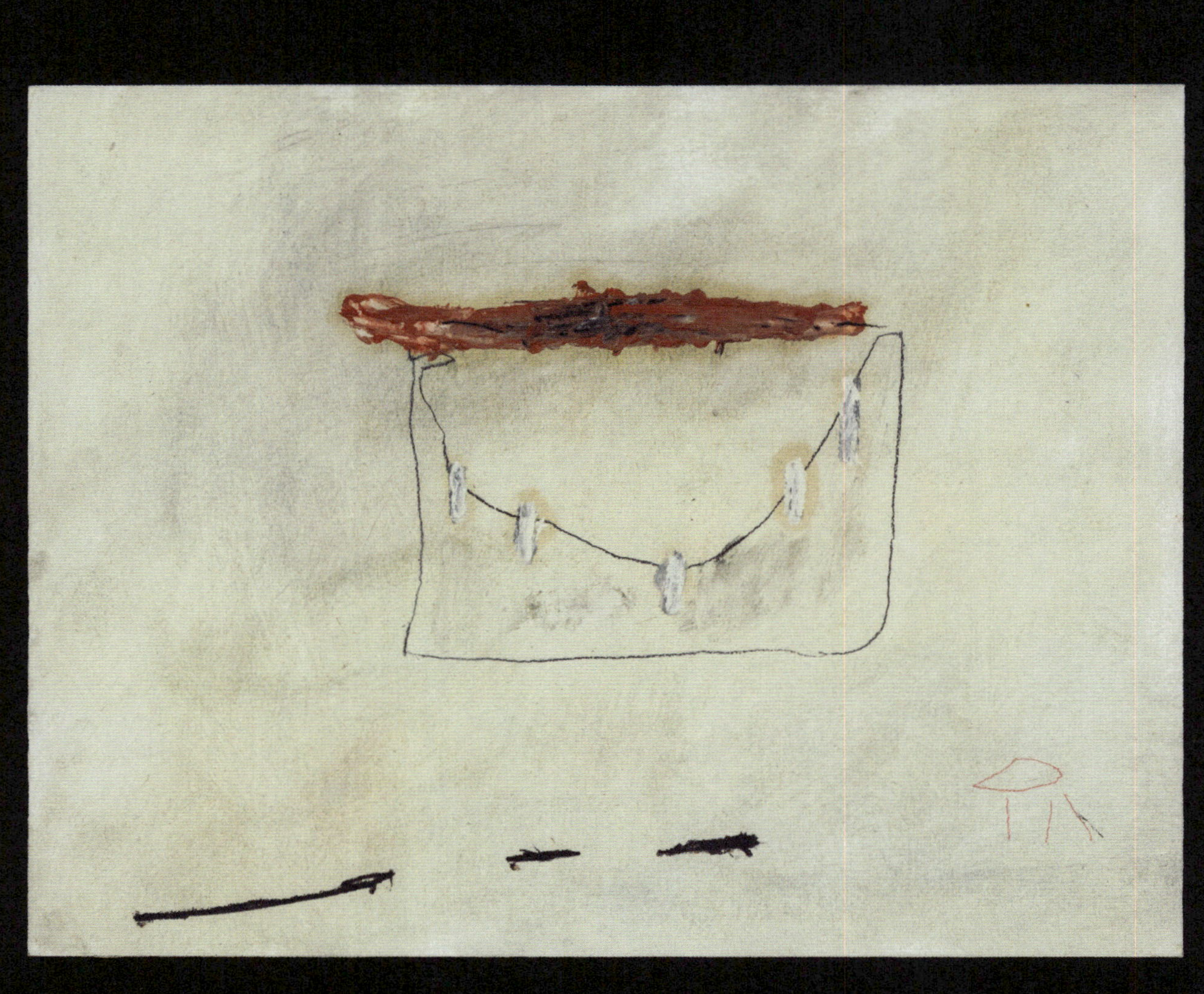

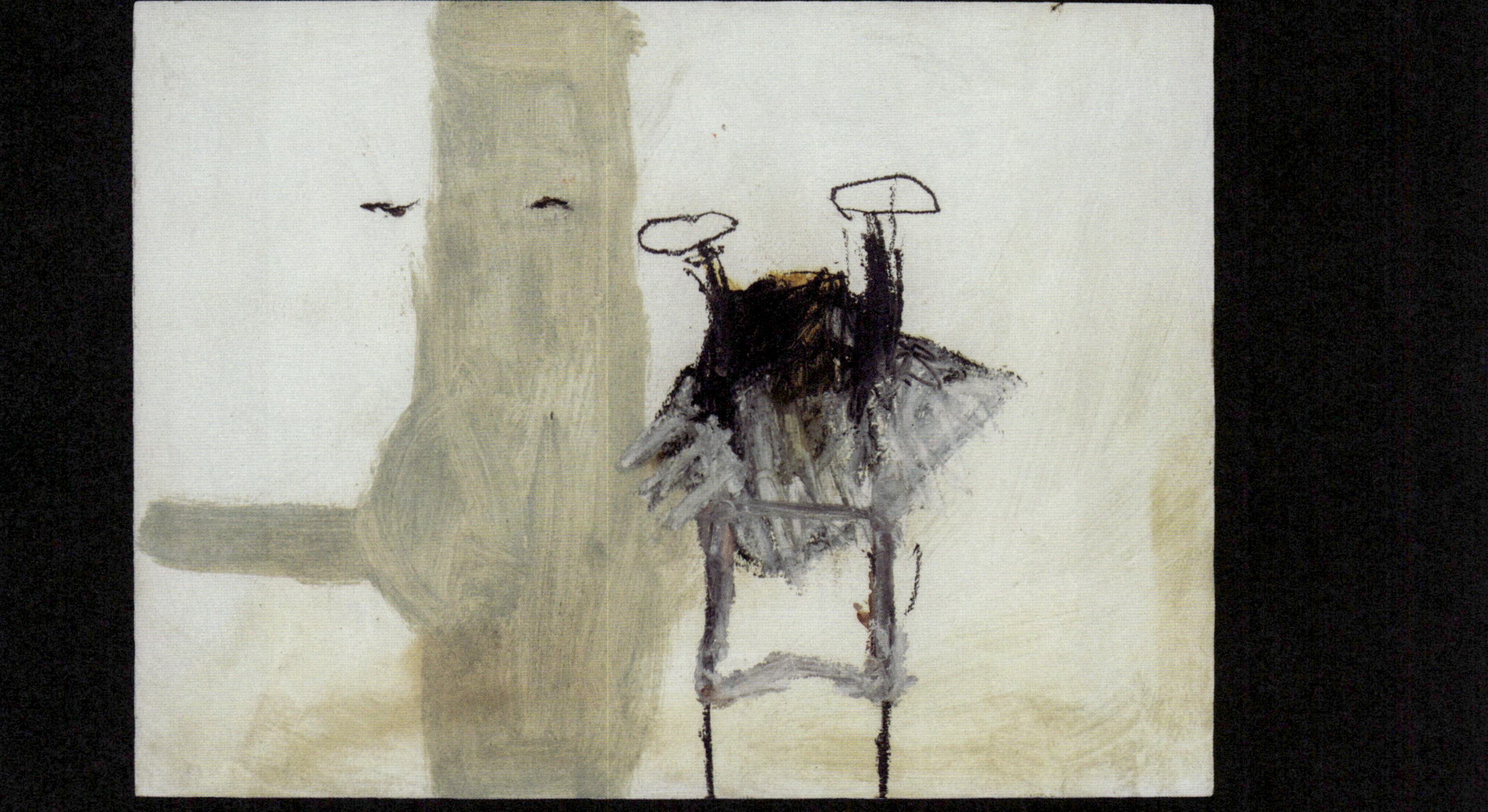

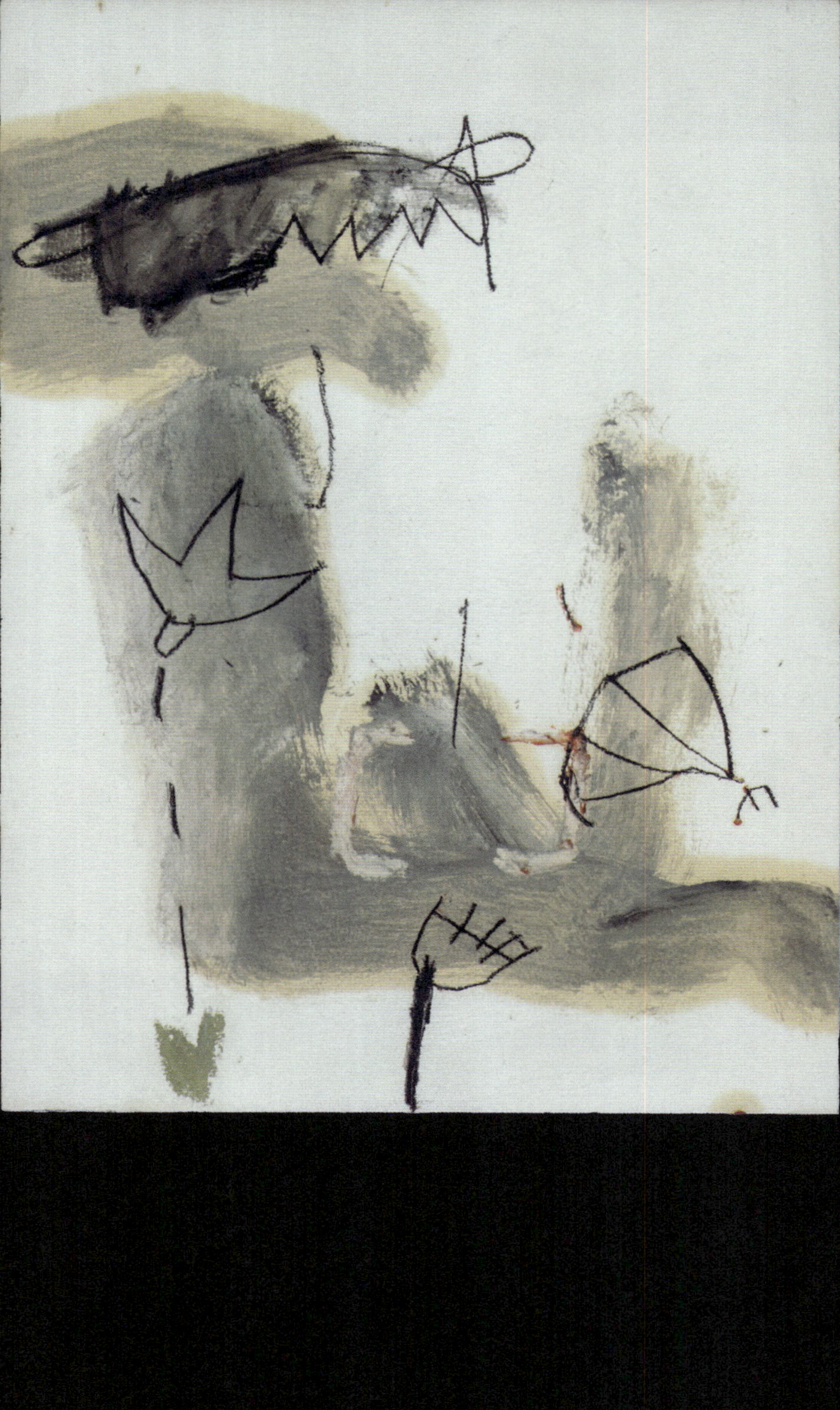

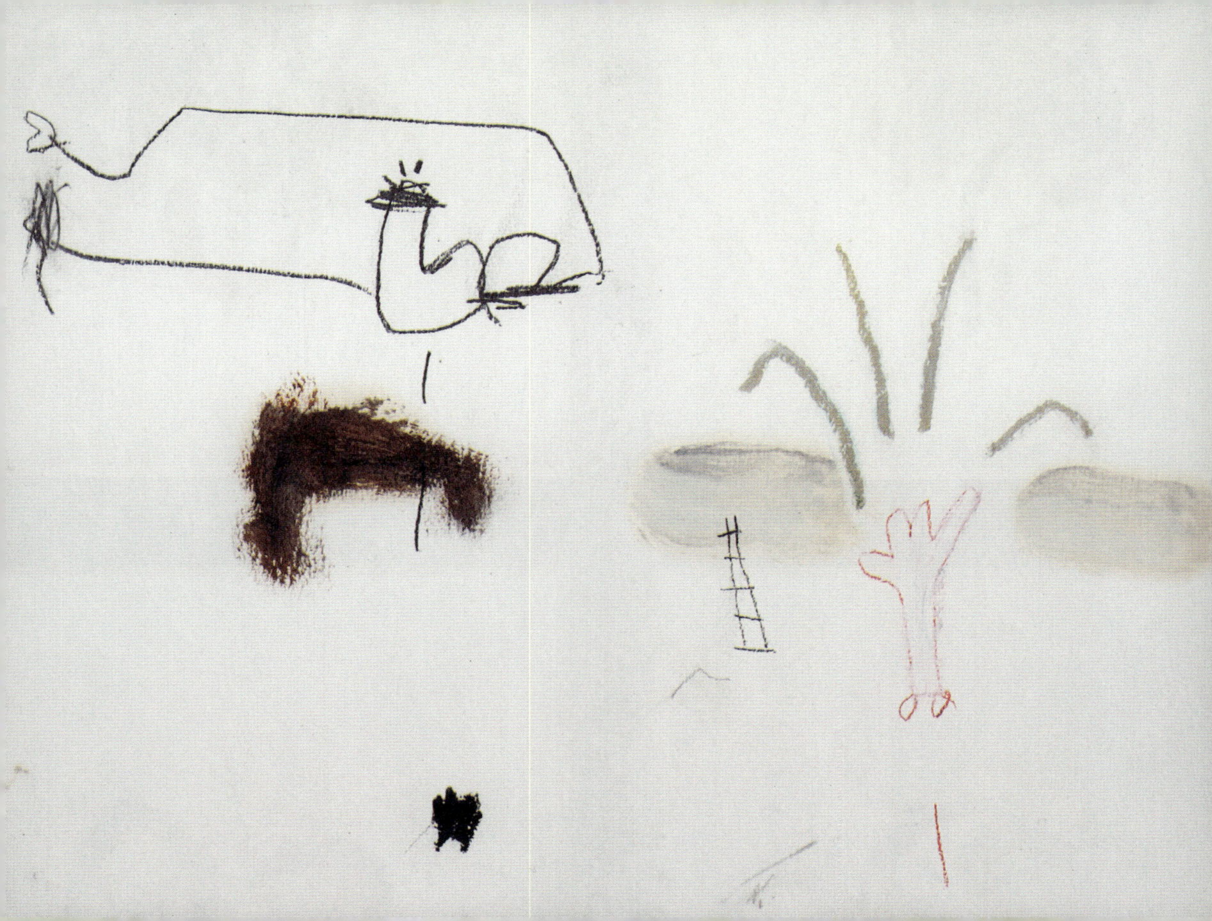

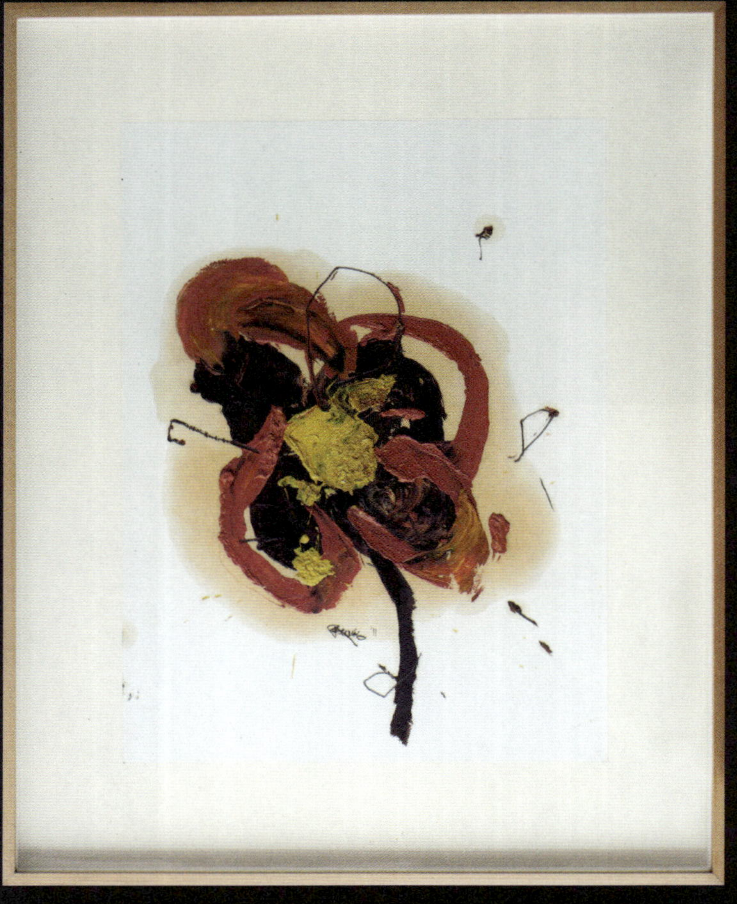

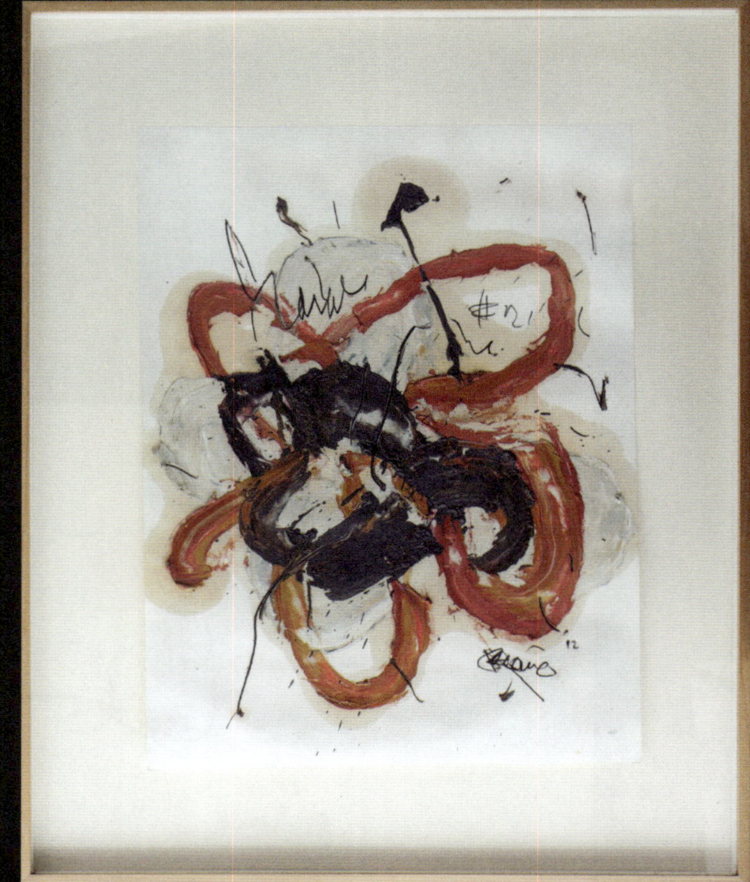

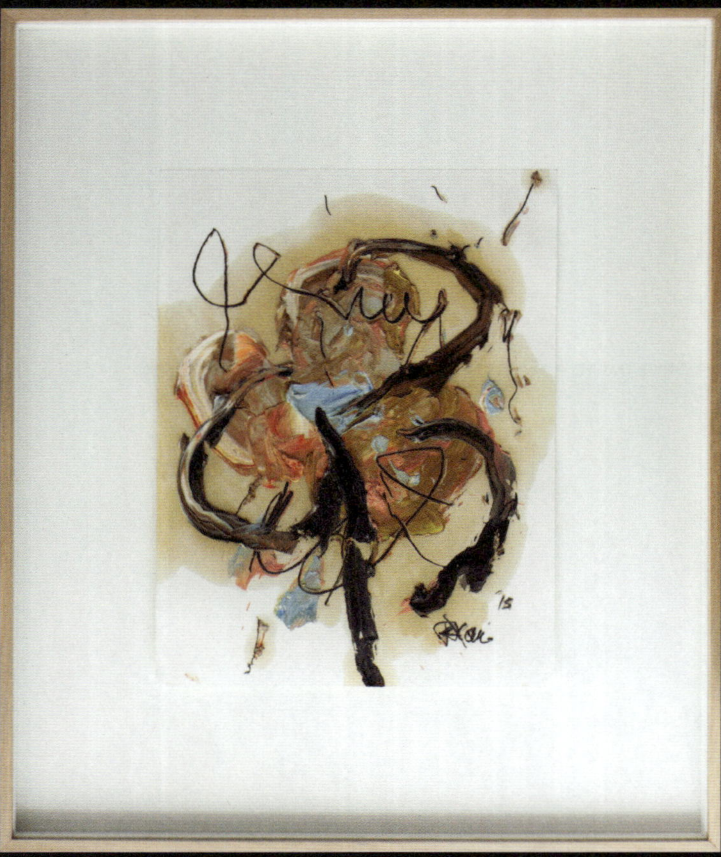

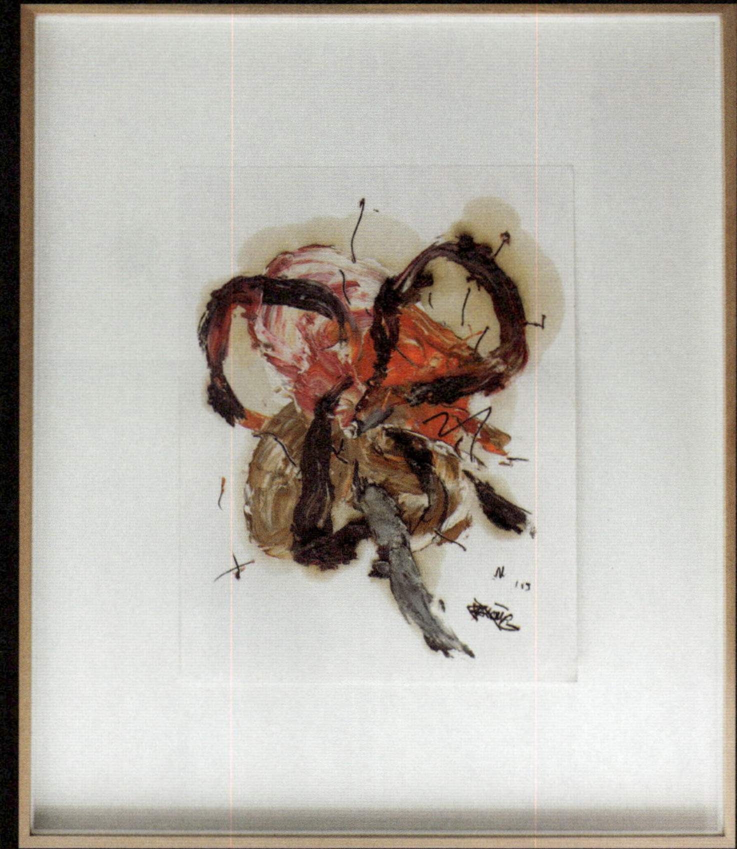

d, 2013, mixed media on paper, 43 × 34 cm

Untitled, 2013, mixed media on paper, 43 × 34 cm

Salvaged Armor, Concrete Flesh: On Bernie

Gary Ross-Pastrana

I.

I count twenty-one hand planes, four spokeshaves, six vintage back saws (three European-style dovetail saws, three Japanese double-blade pull saws), three hand-cranked drills, four carpenter's marking gauges, a pair of wooden mallets, and a set of eleven chisels. (Fig. 1) Under the stairs hang a collection of F- and C-clamps that I did not even dare to count. Other implements are scattered around, in use among the various ongoing projects within the studio. I am sure a few more are hidden elsewhere and out of sight, stored in the array of toolboxes and metal drawers waiting to be cleaned and honed before being added to the current roster. It is not just hand tools; move around and you come across contractor-grade impact drills and angle grinders, a jackhammer, a welding machine, a drill press, a compound sliding miter saw, and a handsome-looking, possibly collectible, vintage lathe.

I have never asked Bernie about these tools, why he has so many of them, or why he collects them. I somehow understand the compulsion, as someone who admittedly shares the same impulse to mend and, sometimes, break things. It may also be that I recognize a similar attraction toward used and older things in other artists whom my contemporaries and I looked up to when we were in art school. (Alfredo Aquilizan, Juan Alcazaren, and Romeo Lee come to mind.) This was the time when trips to antique shops, surplus stores, and hardware outlets became part of our art-making process: hunting for materials, tools, or inspiration among cheap yet deeply interesting objects, with their distinct characters and past lives.

As a young kid, I remember spending several afternoons watching a carpenter, working by himself, build this wall-to-wall wooden wardrobe for my cousins from scratch. In Manila's pre-IKEA times, Mang Benito was the man: hard of hearing, with slick, perfectly parted hair, pencil shooting out of slightly overgrown sideburns, and a familiar white towel around his neck.

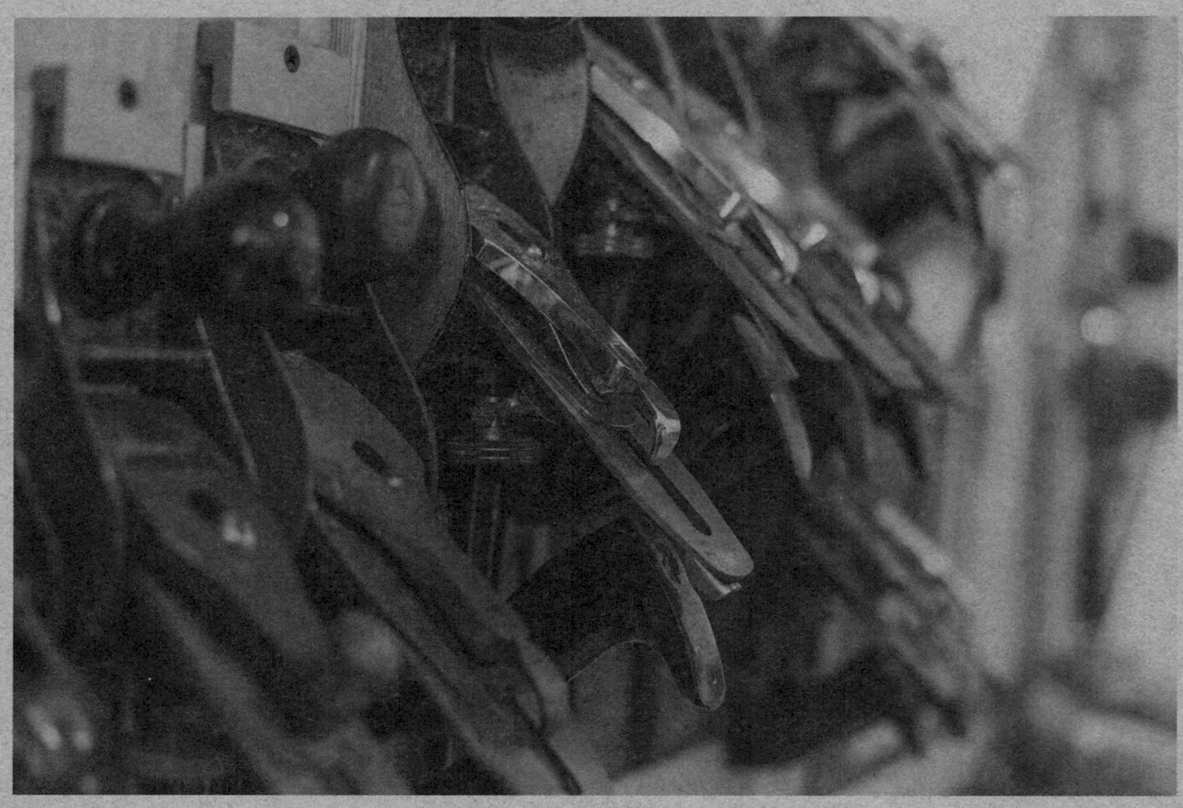

Fig. 1. The artist's tools

He had a serious demeanor as he worked silently — I never heard him speak — but he allowed me to hang around as the job continued to take shape. I distinctly remember being puzzled by this piece of solid wood he was shaping with a chisel; I just couldn't figure out where it would fit, structurally. It later turned out to be a small corner detail on the cabinet's doors. I remember feeling happy to see him again when he came by for the housewarming, in a lighter mood, having drinks with the other guests.

It never occurred to me that this was a core memory until I began to think about how I felt about tools, making things, and "keeping house." Now I see that the countless hours I spent as a kid watching how things were made has allowed me to appreciate this special bond between a carpenter, indeed any maker, and his tools. How even the meekest ones can suddenly become visibly irked when their hammer or saw goes missing, worried it might be misused by a less conscientious workmate. *(I often joke that I may stop making collages altogether if I lose or break this one pair of scissors that I have used for a while.)*

Arriving at his studio, one sees Bernie's tools, which should be a visitor's first clue that more things, larger things, things beyond painting, are being hewn, negotiated with, tirelessly worked on (Fig. 2).

Overleaf: Fig. 2. Bernardo's Manila studio, 2024

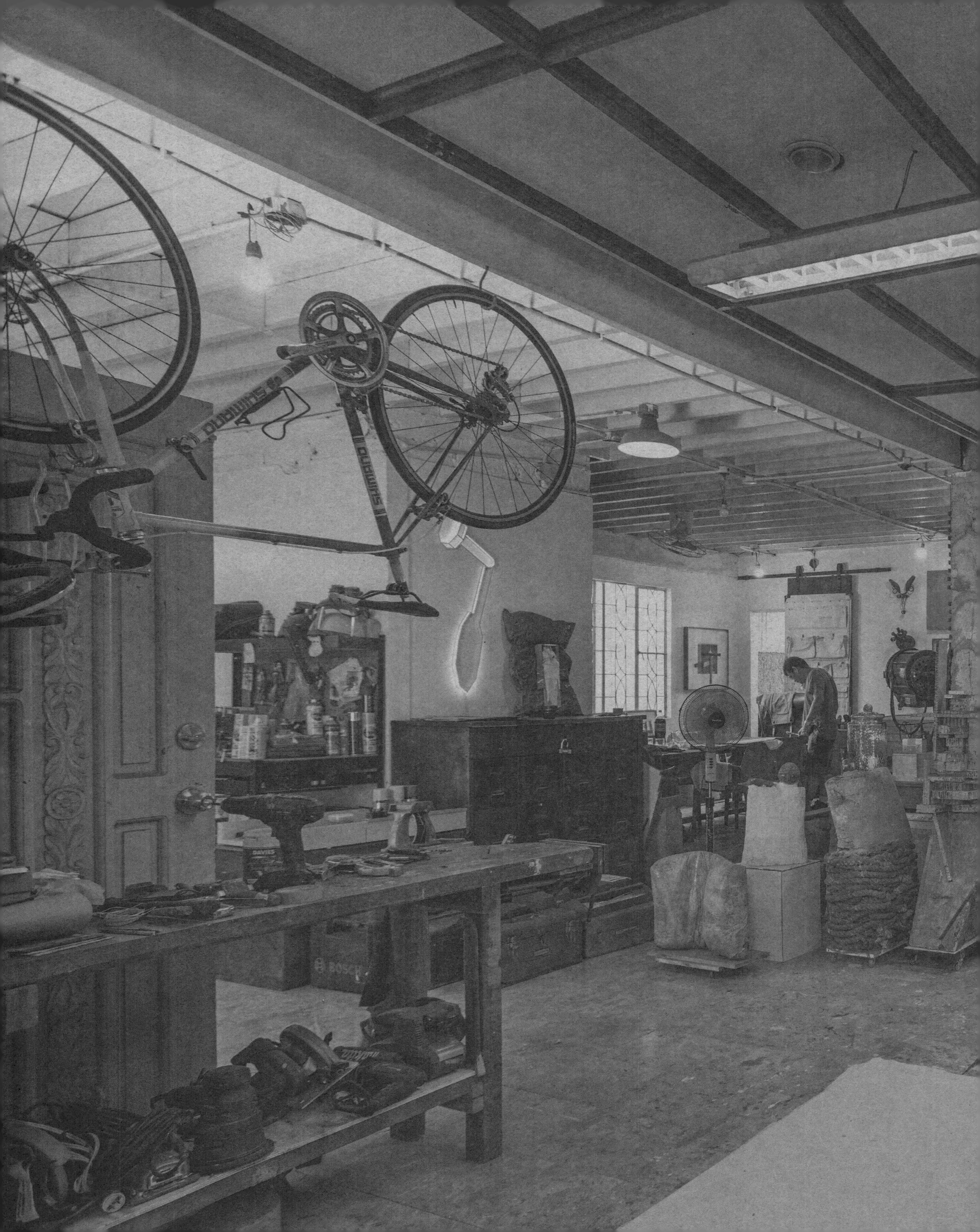

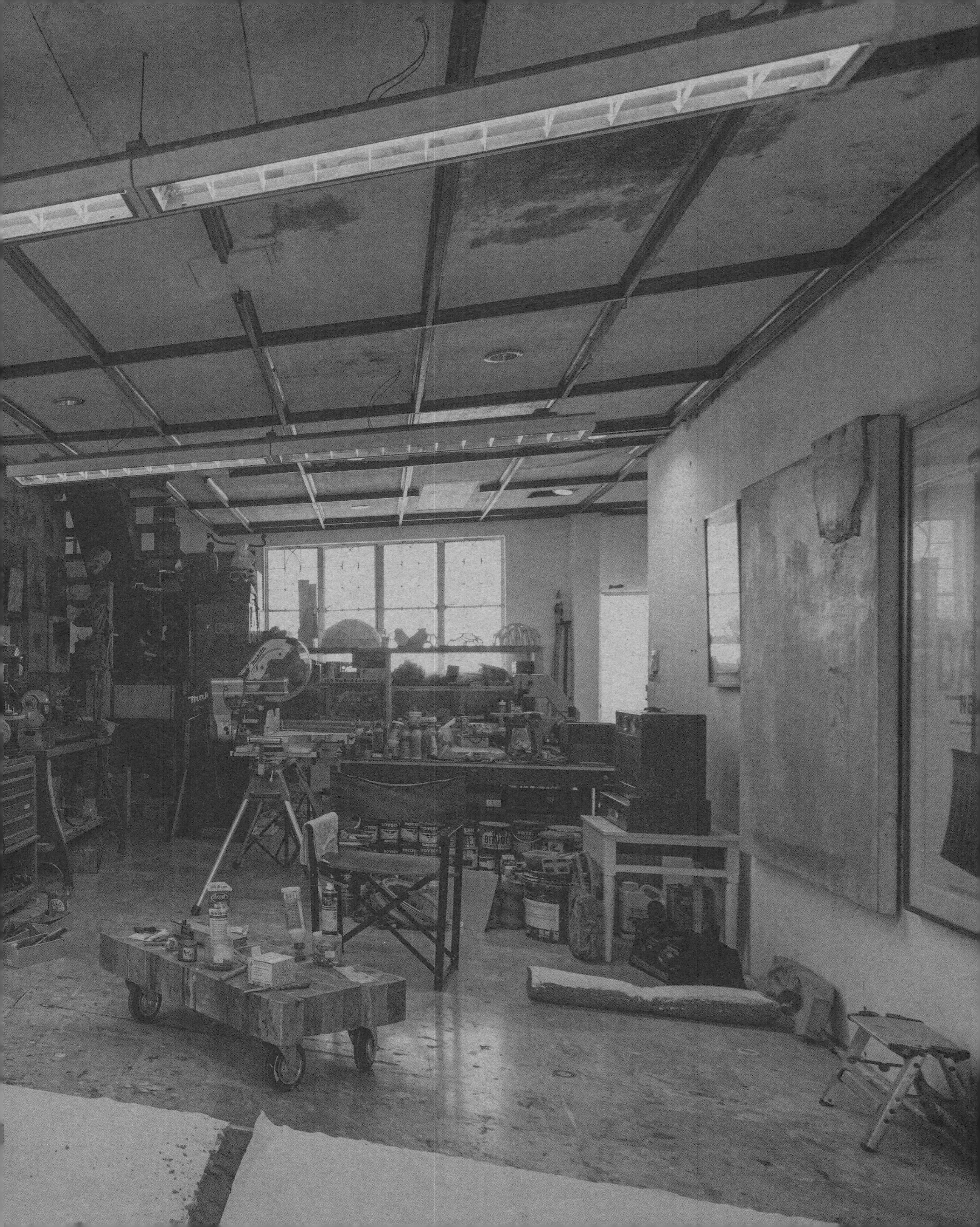

(I imagine it begins with a short drive to the neighborhood hardware store.) Of course, they must know him by now—or at least someone who has worked there long enough does, since he has gone to this preferred shop for years, save for that stretch when he was abroad. He puts in a bulk order of 1 by 2s, perhaps further specified as "good lumber," "s4s," preferably "kiln-dried," along with other workshop consumables, such as a gallon or two of white latex paint, half a kilo of finishing nails, and several sheets of 120- and 240-grit sandpaper.

With the order placed, the store helper begins to pull out the wood pieces with red markings from a large stack and lays them on the ground. As if aiming a terribly long rifle, he (our hero) inspects each piece of lumber, checking for a straight edge, weeding out those that are uneven, peppered with knots, or too bent out of shape. The ones that make the cut are moved to one side and tied together with plastic straw before being hauled to his truck, chosen not just for its rugged demeanor or famed history but also for how it comfortably allows lengths of around ten feet to fit easily, perhaps with some negotiation, through the backrests. If the need arises, even longer ones can still be hauled away with a foot or so peeking out of a cracked window or perhaps tied onto the roof rack, where whole sheets of 4 × 8 foot plywood can likewise be easily secured, without much overhang drooping over the windshield.

Back home, the studio assumes its workshop persona, essentially becoming a de facto assembly line for canvases. Before work begins, there must be an overall idea of the finished dimensions of the stretchers to be made, say ten units of six-by-four feet, selected to fit either the "assigned" exhibition space or a current theme being explored.

After the necessary lengths are marked, each piece of wood is fed into the waiting, agile circular saw that has been calibrated to a 45-degree miter, making swift work of a show's worth of stretchers. *(The power tool may have been a later addition, an addendum to a process long carried on solely by hand.)* Suddenly, the smell of slightly burnt wood, with a hint of heated Singer oil, fills the air. Soon after, the prepared parts are nailed together, but perhaps not before adding a tiny dab of tacky, nougatlike wood parquet glue squeezed out of a slit snipped from a corner of that familiar yellow sachet. (*In certain circles, this glue is reputed to hold wood so well that, under duress, a correctly prepared frame may break, with the wood giving away and splitting in other places while the glued corners remain willfully intact.*)

The completed stretchers now lean against a wall, waiting for further instructions. Some go the more traditional route and are tasked to hold up raw canvas.

Remember to begin from the middle of one length, *tack*. Pull the canvas across the opposite side, *tack*. Now eyeball the center on the adjacent sides, *tack*, *tack*. Pulling tightly, steadily work your way toward the edges, *tack*, *tack*, *tack*. The way one folds and trims the excess cloth on the corners reveals more than just a personal touch, but a kind of hidden signature that future authenticators can perhaps look into, especially for painters who still insist on preparing their own canvases.

It is late afternoon, and the offcuts and sawdust have been swept into a soft mound in a corner. Music, momentarily drowned out by the squeal of power tools, begins to be heard again. Instead of the smell of burnt wood, the space is now enveloped with a calming scent of cloth dust. (*Think of arriving at a fabric shop within the dry goods section of a public market, just before they are about to close for the day. Even in the afternoon heat, the surroundings remain somewhat cool, with strategically placed oscillating fans reinforcing the balmy, sleepy atmosphere. As the hefty scissors glide through the pre-measured cloth, tiny, invisible particles are released, mixing with the surrounding air and completing the mood.*)

As the sun sets, it is time for a cold beer.

Nothing is more pregnant with promise than a row of silent, neatly prepared canvases. Yet this is only the beginning, and more often than not, one must start here, at this jumping-off point, in this neutral state. Whether one of these ends up as a painting is totally up to chance. Some that came before were taken to task, brought to their limits: pinched by tensioned rope from the sides, bulging, almost splitting at the seams, on the verge of collapse. Like a lassoed, feral animal—corralled, broken, and tamed.

III. Cities

Bernie came of age at a time when young boys still made their own toys, cars fashioned from sardine cans, sticks, and old rubber slippers and pulled with strings, prompting endless racing sessions throughout breezy summer afternoons. It was also when stern fathers willed their sons to become doctors or lawyers, soldiers or priests.

His brief stint in Mindanao may have cultivated a feeling of being on the outside, looking in. His return to Sampaloc in the final year of high school further reinforced this uneasiness, the struggle to find his place in a changing city—a Manila becoming increasingly cosmopolitan.

Although he is too young to have actually seen it, Bernie would sometimes refer in casual conversations to the devastation of postwar Manila. Perhaps growing up in a house where the Japanese Army may have been stationed plays a part. He talks about this fateful event with genuine, palpable affection, a clear sense of regret (*panghihinayang*) for the loss of built structures, and with them, the loss of a vital chunk of the Filipino people's identity and, to a greater extent, of our nation's history.

With the same affection, he recalls the legendary tough guys of the streets of Manila, often with monikers linked to the hard and crazy stuff: Totoy Bakal, Nonoy Bato, Boy Toyo. They, who on rainy mornings would set up makeshift elevated walkways out of scavenged wood planks, hollow blocks, and rocks so that students and other commuters could navigate the flooded pavement with their shoes and socks relatively dry for a small "donation." The collected change would later be used to fund a group drinking session under the street lights, a regular gathering that would run from happy hour until past midnight. In these late hours, they would actually keep the streets safe, unless you were a petty thief or a troublemaker from a rival neighborhood, in which case you were better off taking a different route.

Bernie would later enroll in the advertising department of the University of the Philippines in Diliman, a good 12 kilometers away from Dos Castillas Street, where the storied University of Santo Tomas, the country's oldest institution of higher learning, is just across the next block. That he opted for UP, despite the longer commute, proved to be a life-defining choice. There, he became part of a brotherhood and made lifelong friends, some of the very people who gave him the necessary push to pursue painting over a tedious desk job.

That we ended up today as neighbors may not have been a complete accident. I had wanted to move further south ever since I started a family, when the yearning for more space within and outside of the house developed. A visit to Bernie's studio some years back perhaps planted a seed, introducing me to the neighborhood in which he had chosen to settle with his own family. As someone who also spent his early years in the heart, or maybe the guts, of Manila, we are now both far removed from the perennial flooding and tough guys of yore, living a less eventful, quiet suburban life.

IV. Heroes

As I am writing now, I am listening to (or watching on YouTube) a Sibelius violin concerto in D minor played by Isaac Stern (Fig. 3). I see him now as an older gentleman – stout, with piercing eyes and a grave demeanor – attacking the violin with long yet fluid strokes, wielding the bow like a *wushu* master's dancing blade.

I searched for this musical piece to learn more about the person behind the sole figurative painting by Bernie I have ever seen; he turned out to be this famed violinist and his musical hero. Stemming from a challenge by his son, who was tasked to draw local heroes for a school project, Bernie happily obliged and made a set of paintings of the people he truly admired.

As I continue to watch the renowned violinist, I get a sense of his immense skill and passion. Intense flurries are built up on top of each other, punctuated by delicate and sustained notes, all of which remain firmly under his control. Even members of the orchestra seem to be as transfixed by the master as the audience.

A quick glance at the comments reveals a similar reaction among viewers: "a force of nature," he plays "aggressively" with "reckless abandon," "raw and free," yet still able to produce the "most beautiful tone."

I suppose that the tool belts and working gloves in Bernie's studio track more in the direction of a Rolling Stones or Springsteen-type workingman ethos, far removed from the tailcoat suits we associate with classical musicians. While the clues may initially appear to be confusing, one must look beyond the obvious to map out an indirect route, a back-channel connection to the violin.

Here, I learn about Bernie's older brother, another hero, perhaps the strongest one, judging from the way he talks about him. Indeed, this is the person who inspired him to draw, paint, and even take up the violin and play music. He was also pivotal in Bernie's decision to enroll at UP. I opted not to dig deeper, but this was enough to paint an overall impression of a somewhat hidden, yet profoundly influential, figure in Bernie's life.

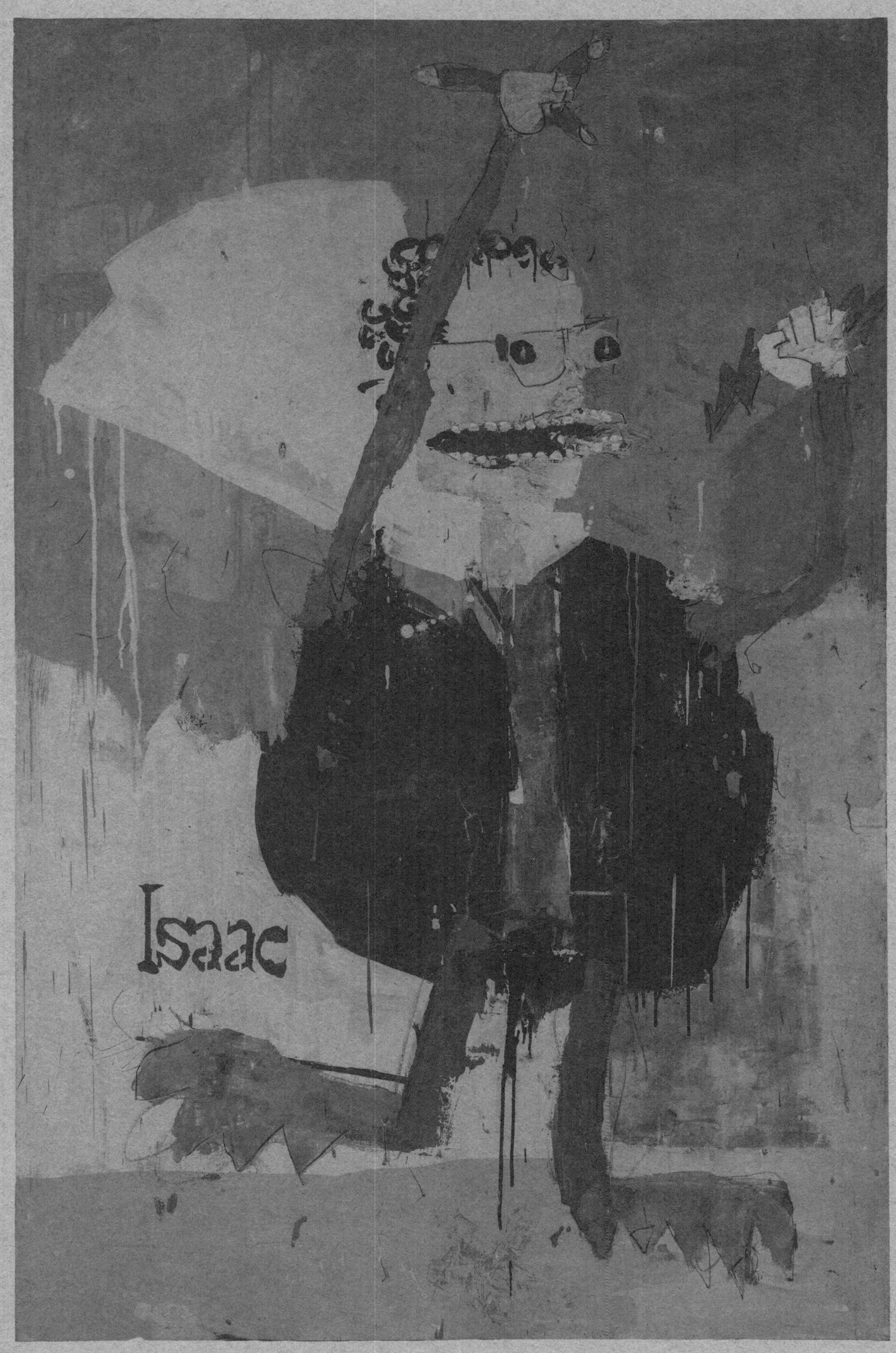

Fig. 3. *Isaac Stern*, 2008, oil and house paint on canvas, 182.9 × 121.9 cm

V.

In Bernie's work, things are allowed to age and receive what the world — indifferent and impartial — has in store for them. There is little effort to hide stains or scars; in fact, they are worn proudly, whenever possible. Perhaps there is also a belief that any damage can still be healed, salvaged, and repaired. (*I use "repair" here, not in the delicate way of restoring an heirloom watch, but in the way that a war mechanic keeps a battered tank running, ready to engage in the battlefield, under the circumstances, a scarred yet humming, behemoth.*)

Little premium is given to the spotless or the new; here, the time- and battle-tested are lionized. Things that have stood the test of time take on an air of mystique, acquiring mythical and heroic proportions. (*Say, a local hardwood tree that served as the main post or "mayor" of an old house.*) There is a reverence for honest materials and for lost or forgotten ways of doing things.

VI. WALLS

(One who is)
Versed in the language of walls:
Stained and lived-in,
Cracked and patched-up.
Peeling, splitting, abused.

Out in the open:
Tagged, sticker-bombed, vandalized.
Within a home:
A prepared canvas for an ambitious toddler's early masterpiece.
Height marks.
At the receiving end of a teenager's angsty fist.

Even further abuse—

Leaned on, pissed at, drilled into.
Marks from a territorial pet.
Rain splashes.
Sun-soaked and faded.
Water leaks.
Moss, mildew, and mold.
Chewed on by insects.
Inhabited by pests.

Hard water, oil spatter, fumes.

Even some attempts at repair fail;
Latex paint soon cracks over enamel.
Blame it on the uninitiated worker
Painting coats in the wrong order.

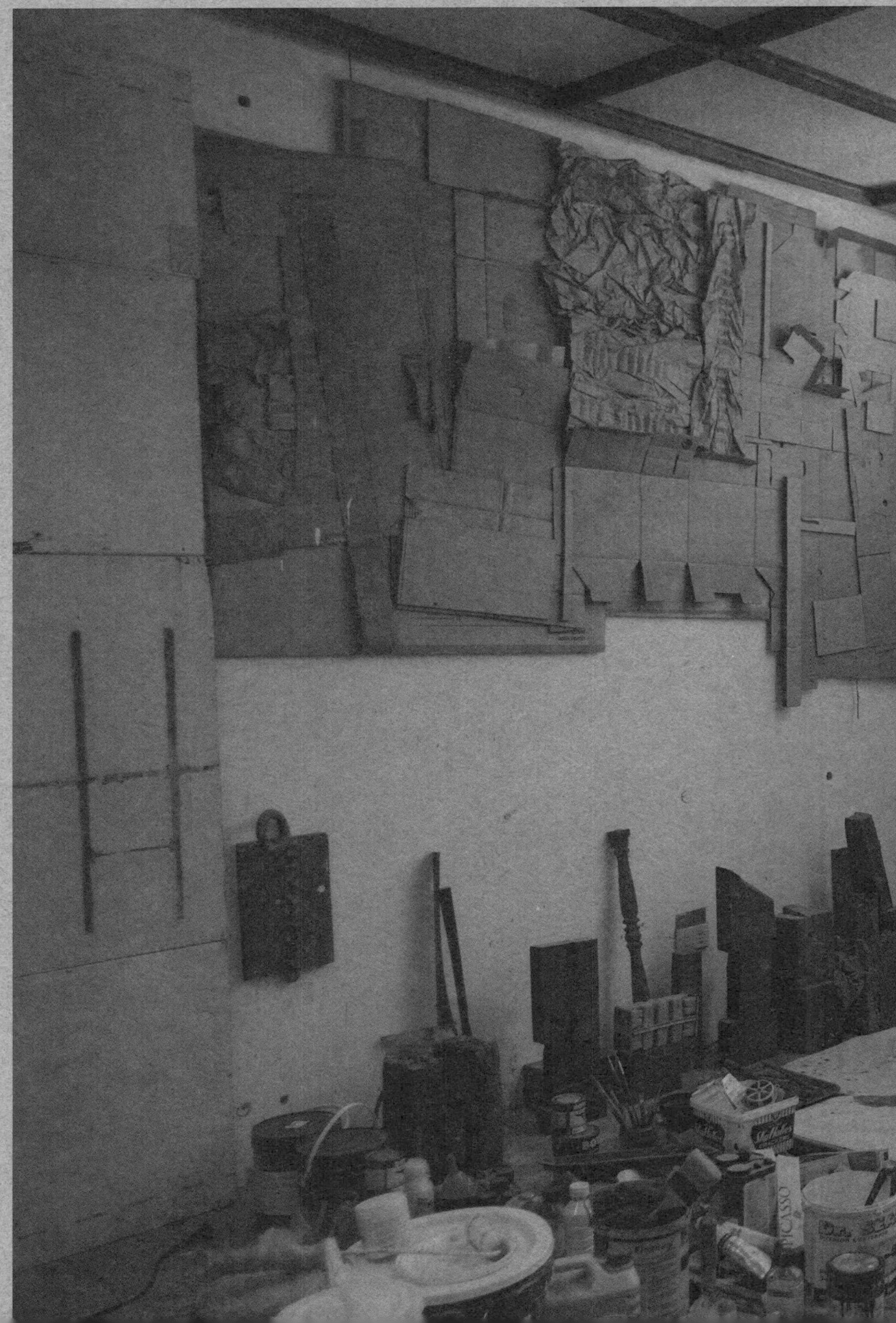

Or the same fall guy
hurriedly rolling paint over untreated, raw concrete.
(*"un-poisoned" or* "hindi nilason" *in local parlance*)

Years of holes drilled to hang the stuff
Of a serial hobbyist's changing whims.

Starchy from unwelcome election posters.

Thickened, with layers of paint from a proactive
Homeowner's yearly summer touch-up.

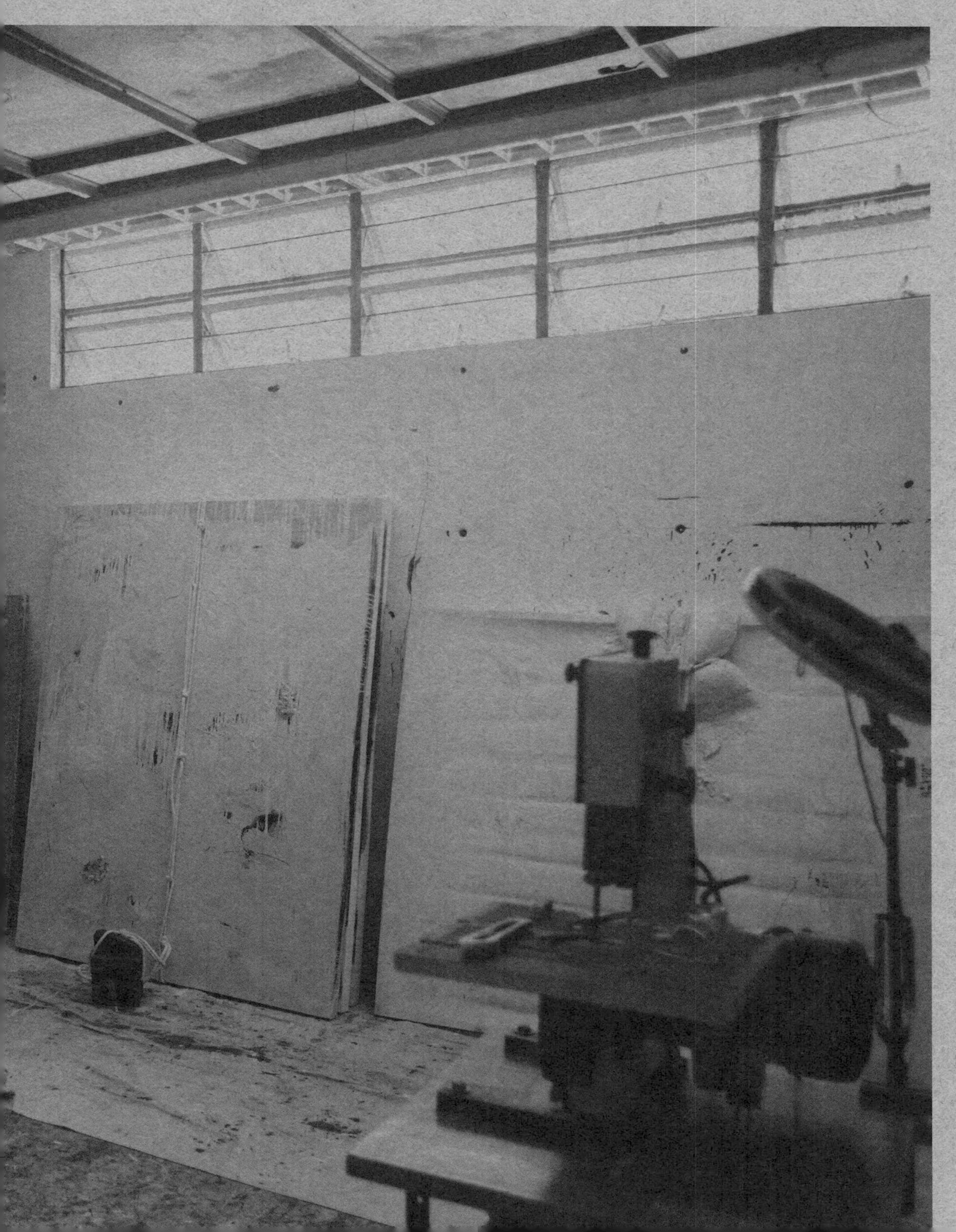

But all walls, even the best maintained,
Will age, acquire texture, and
Receive the incidental beauty of the unplanned.

Even nonporous walls absorb stories,
layers of encoded moments adding up.
Retelling them,
not in words, but as radiated mood.
Echoed, pictured, remembered.

1-Beta Chain 16, 2020, oil on cut cardboard, 30 × 21 cm

1-Beta Chain 17, 2020, oil on cut cardboard, 30 × 21 cm

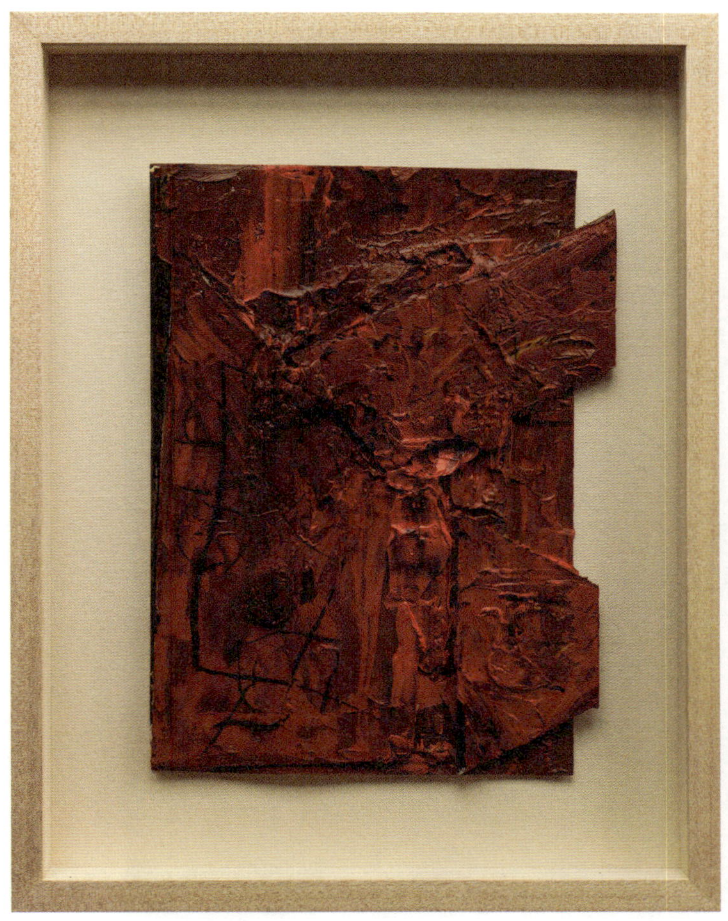

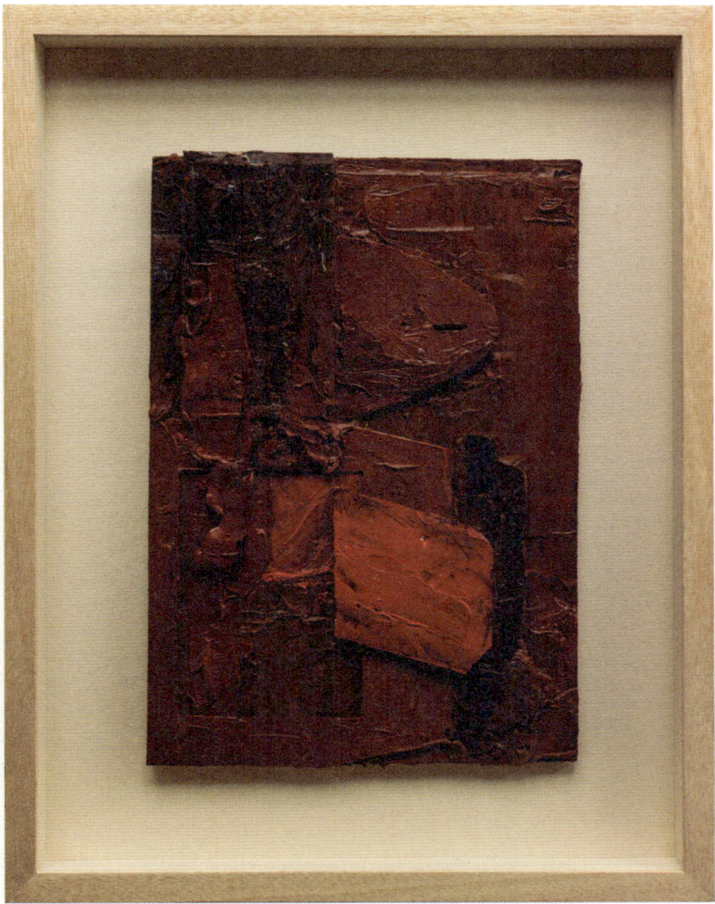

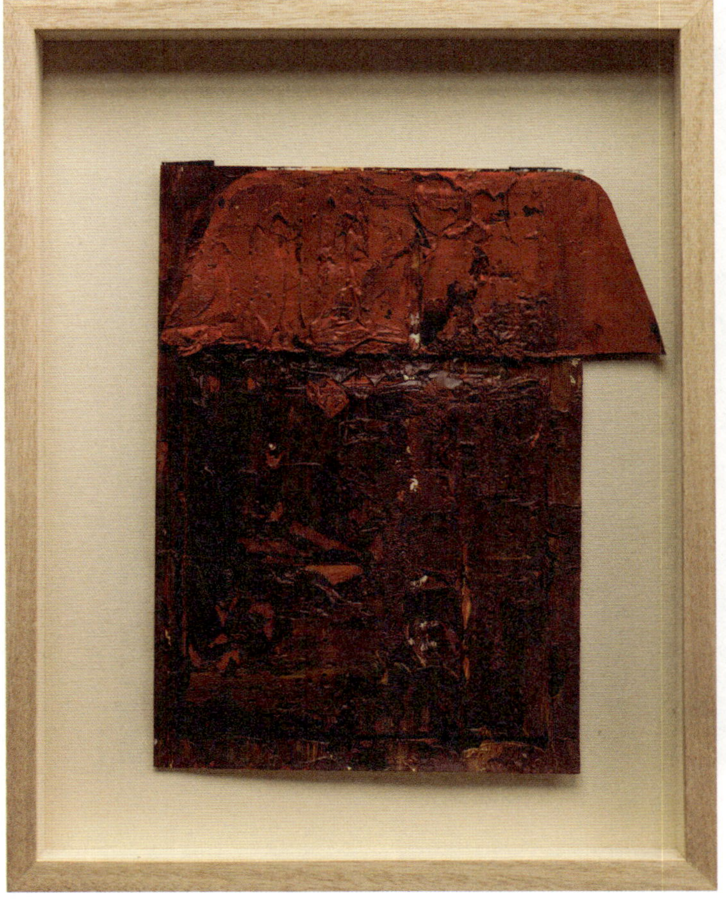

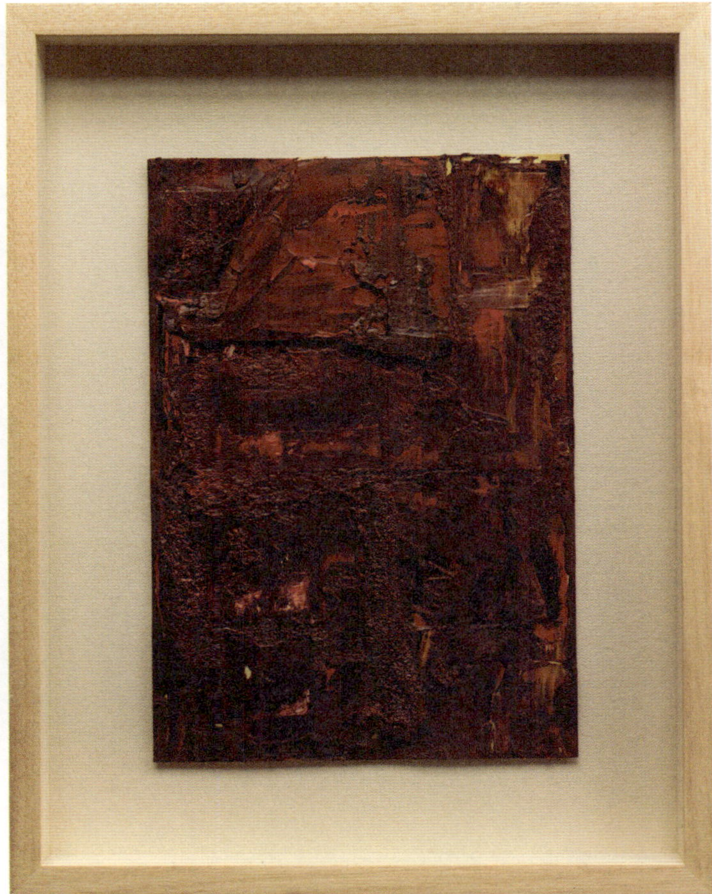

1-Beta Chain 14, 2020, oil on cut cardboard, 30 × 21 cm

1-Beta Chain 15, 2020, oil on cut cardboard, 30 × 21 cm

Strata of Thought 01, 2022, mixed media on canvas, 152.4 × 122 cm

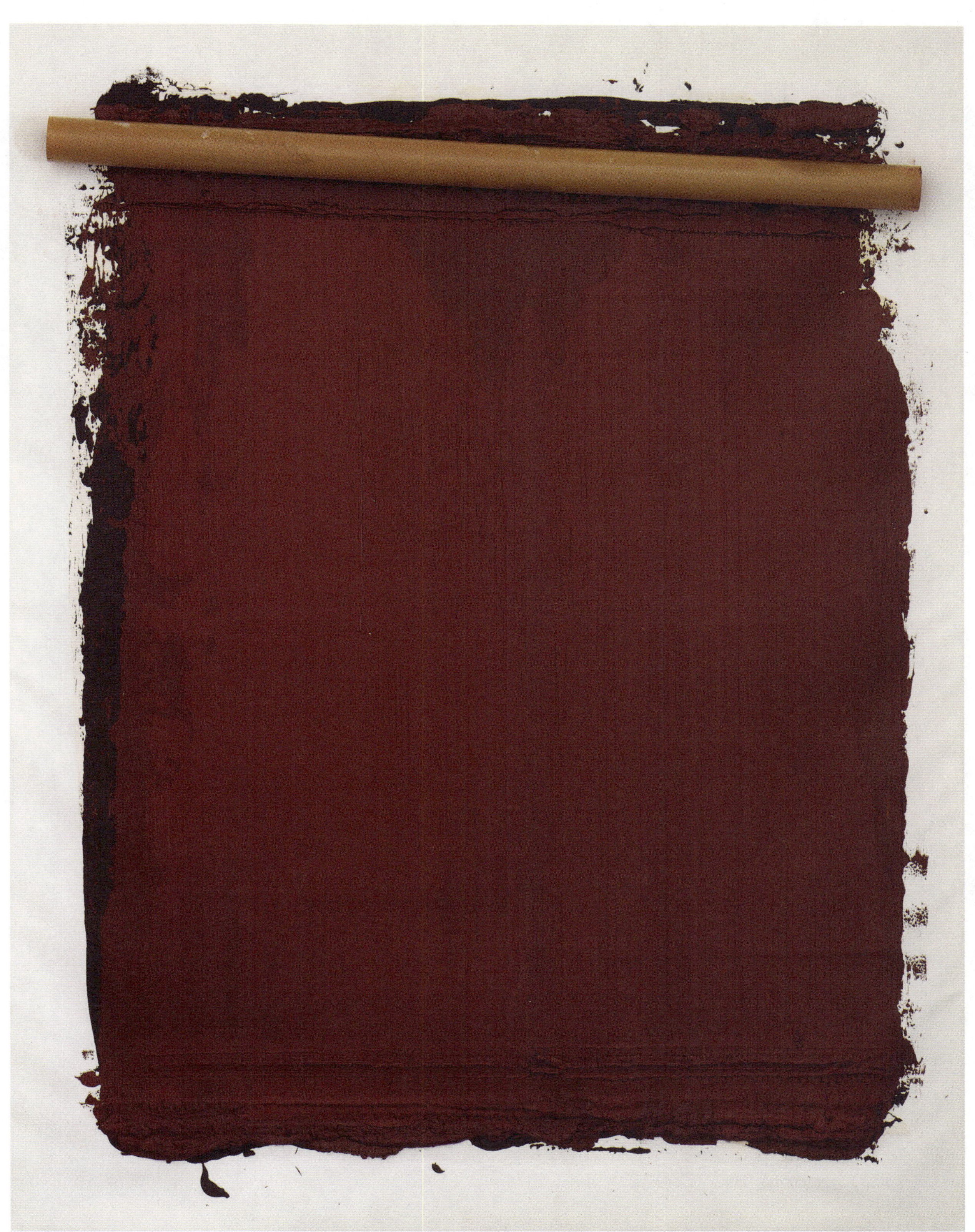

Strata of Thought 04, 2022, mixed media on canvas, 152.4 × 122 cm

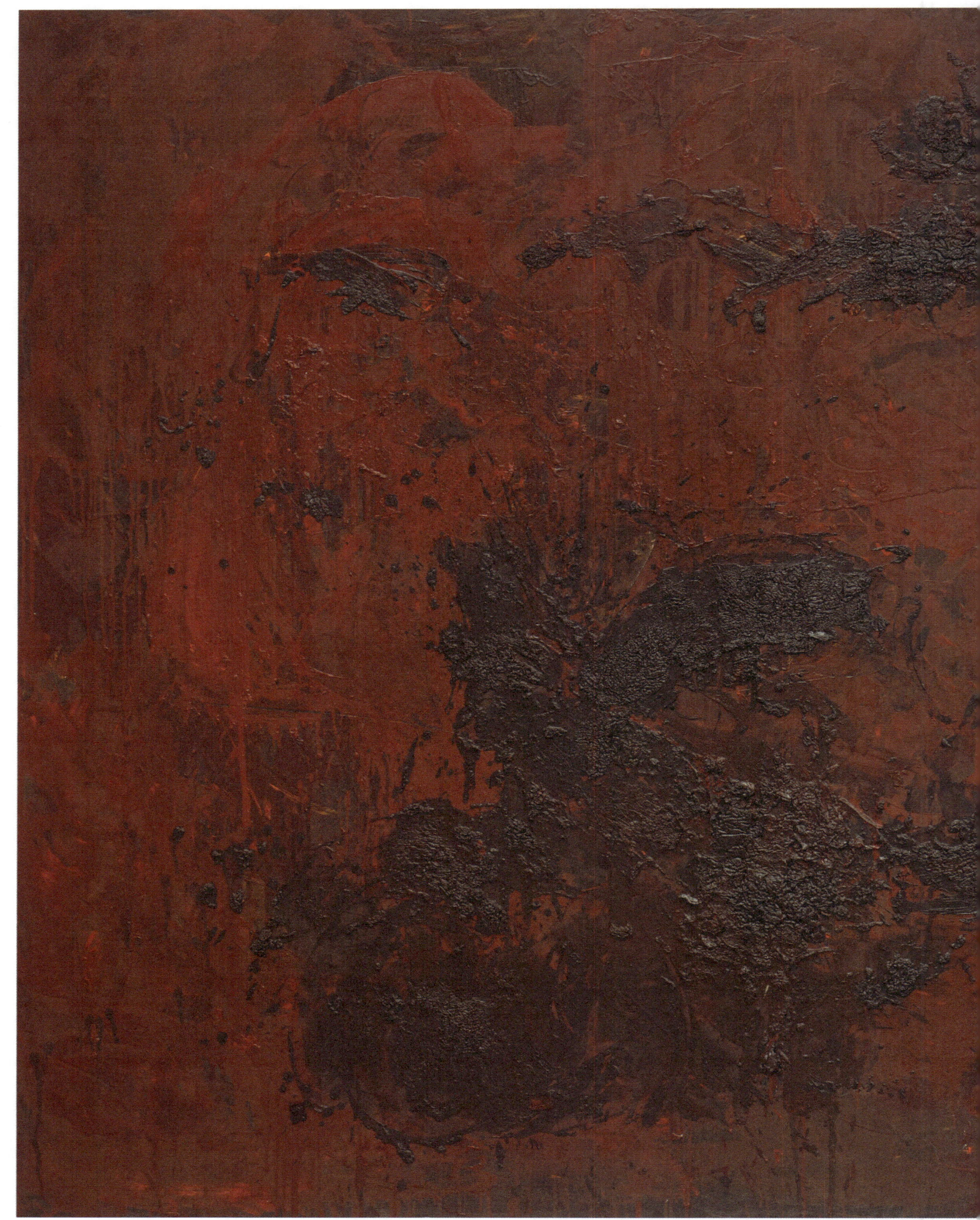

Red Object #04, 2021, oil on canvas, 182.9 × 304.8 cm

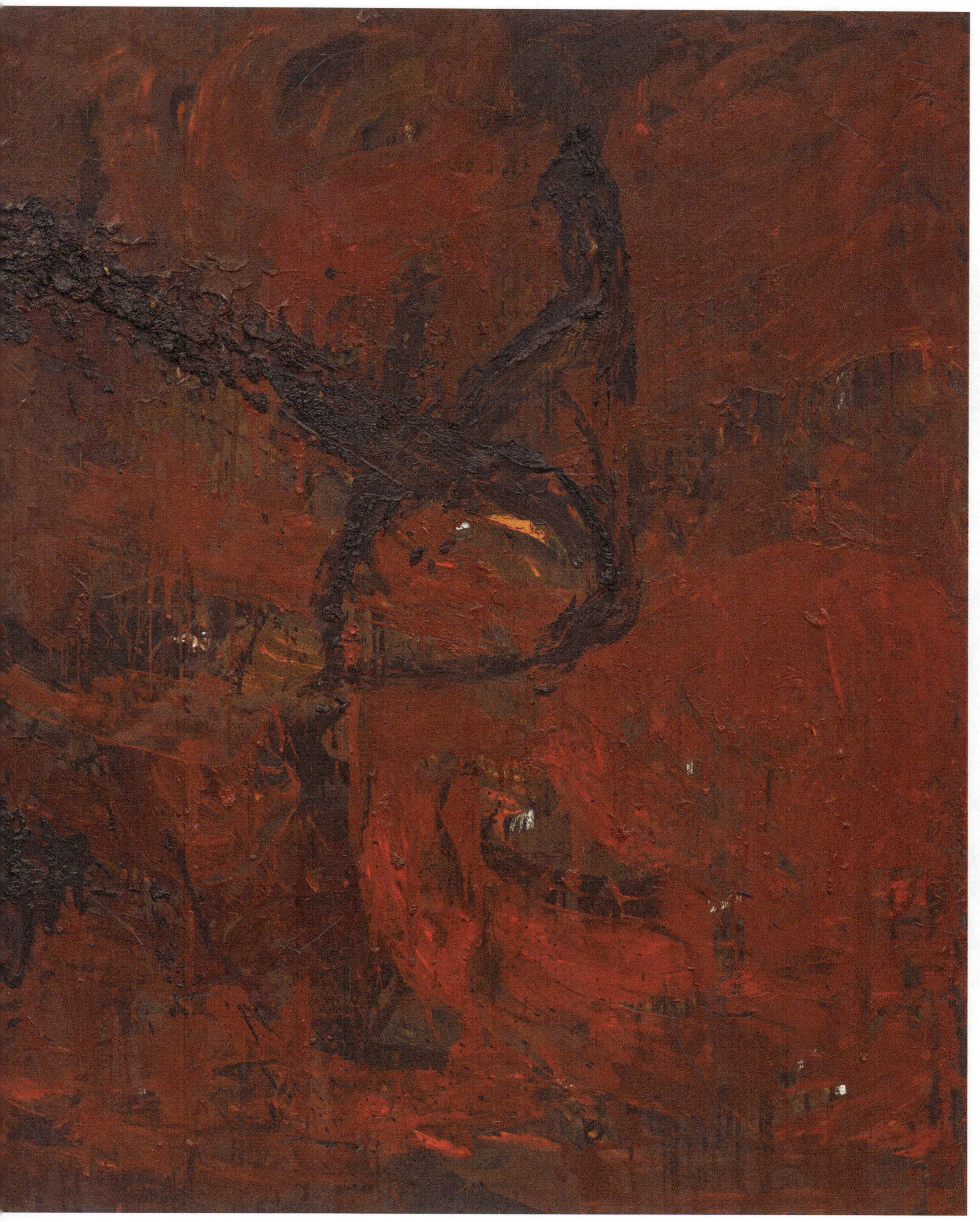

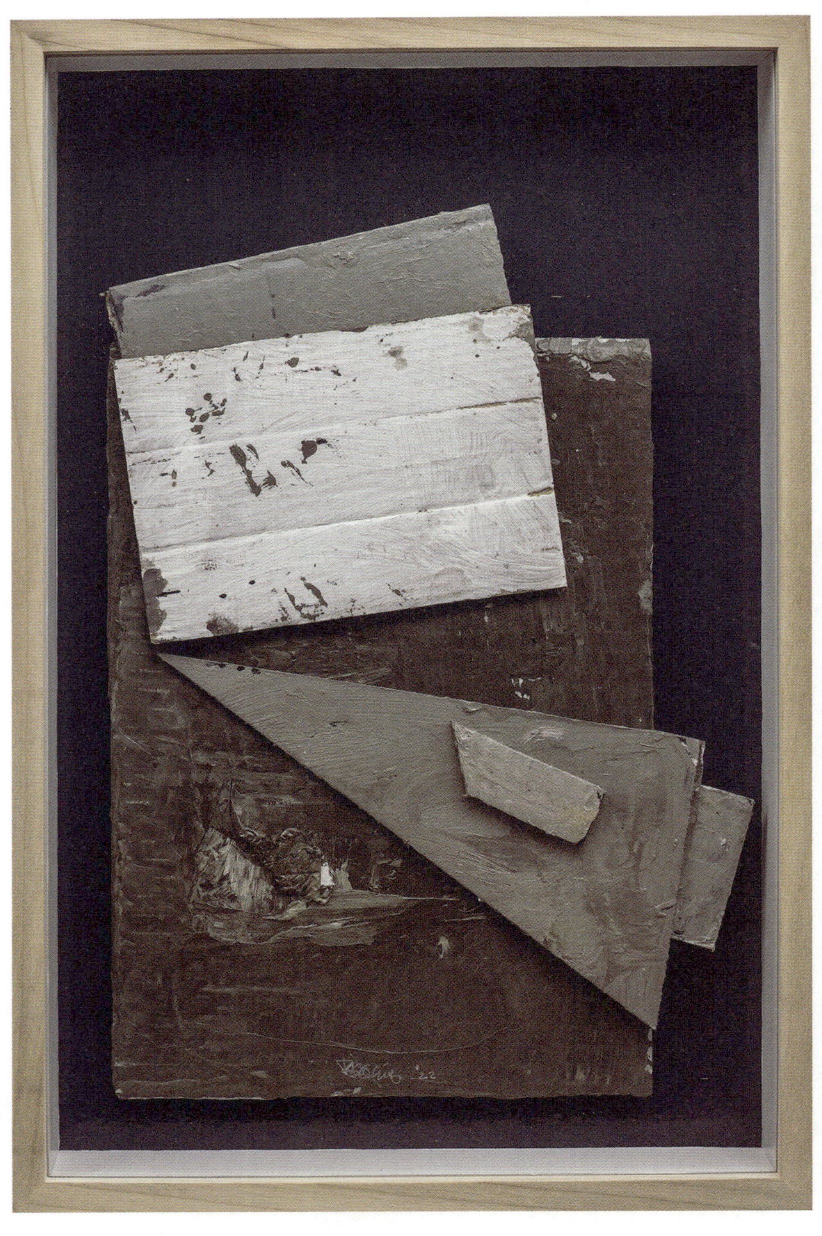

Untitled, 2022, cardboard, 45.7 × 30.5 × 5.1 cm

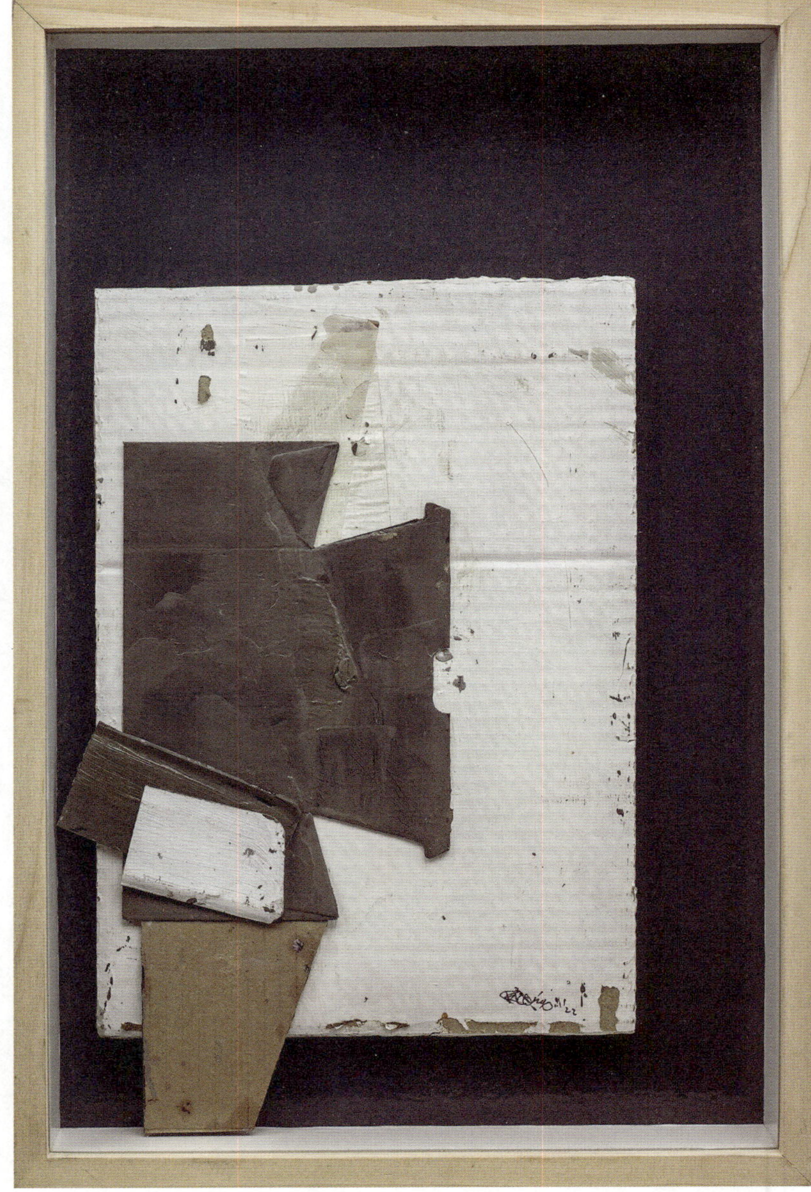

Untitled, 2022, cardboard, 45.7 × 30.5 × 5.1 cm

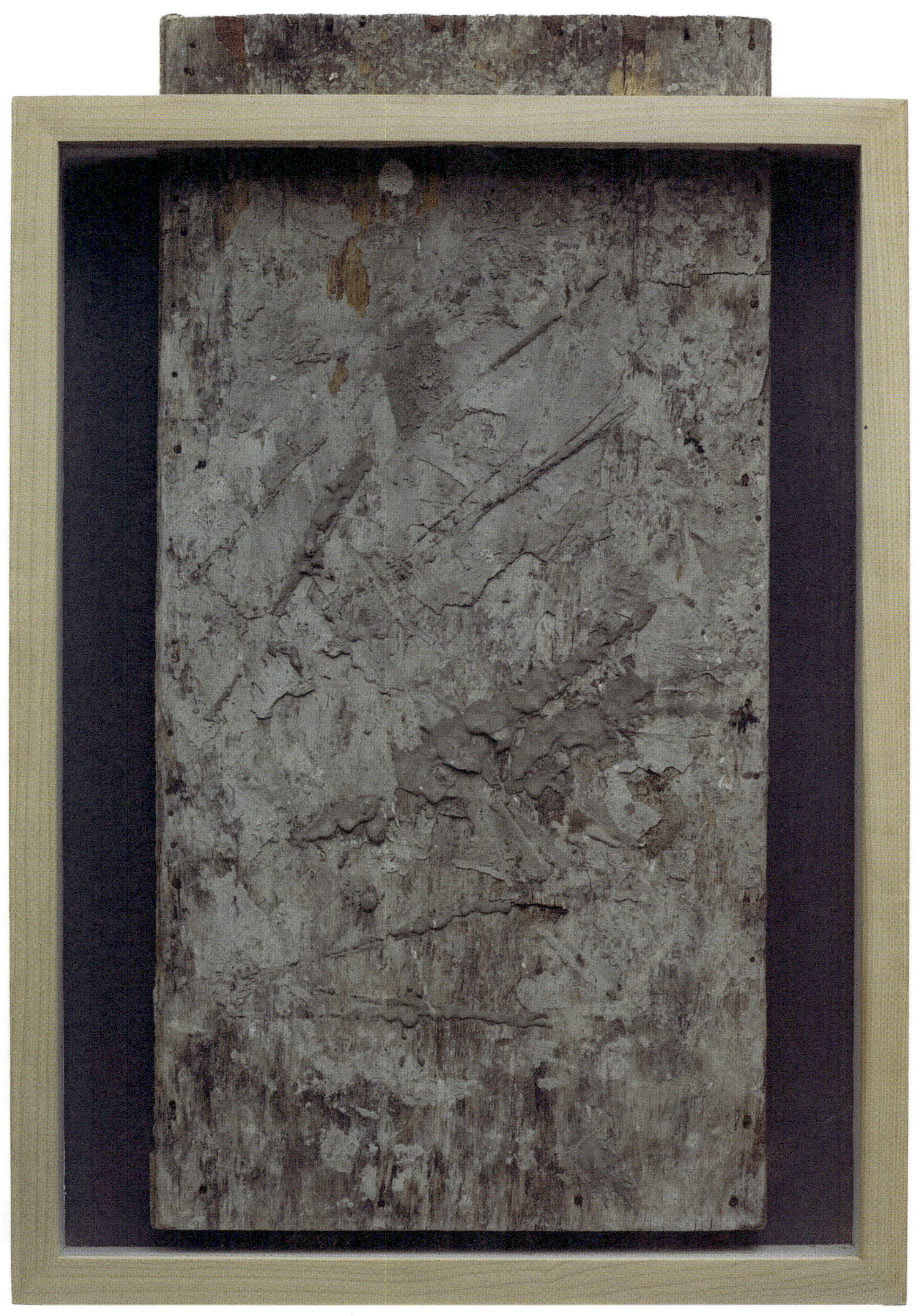

Untitled, 2022, found object, 66 × 45.7 cm

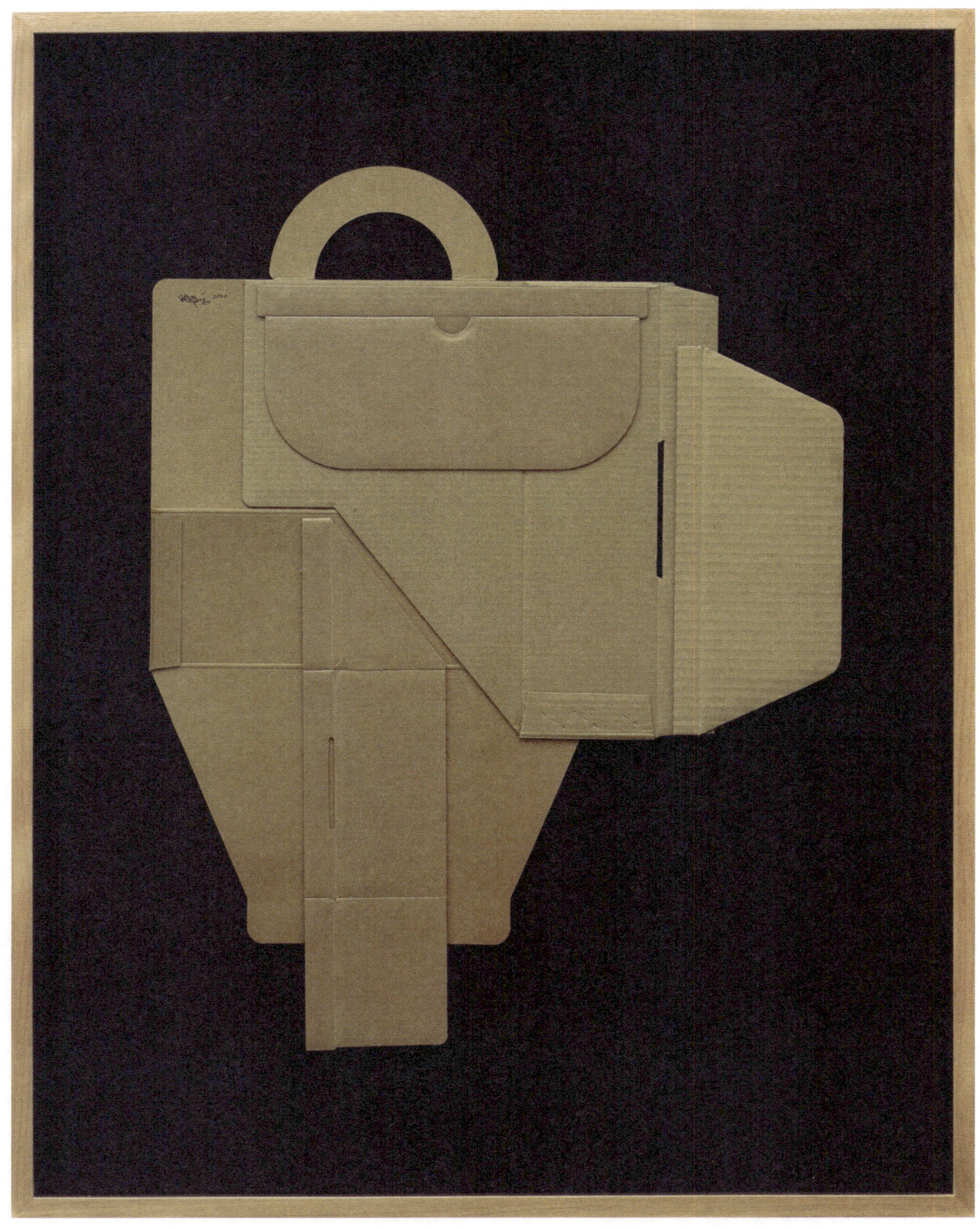

Brown Study #03, 2022, cardboard, 78.1 × 62.9 cm

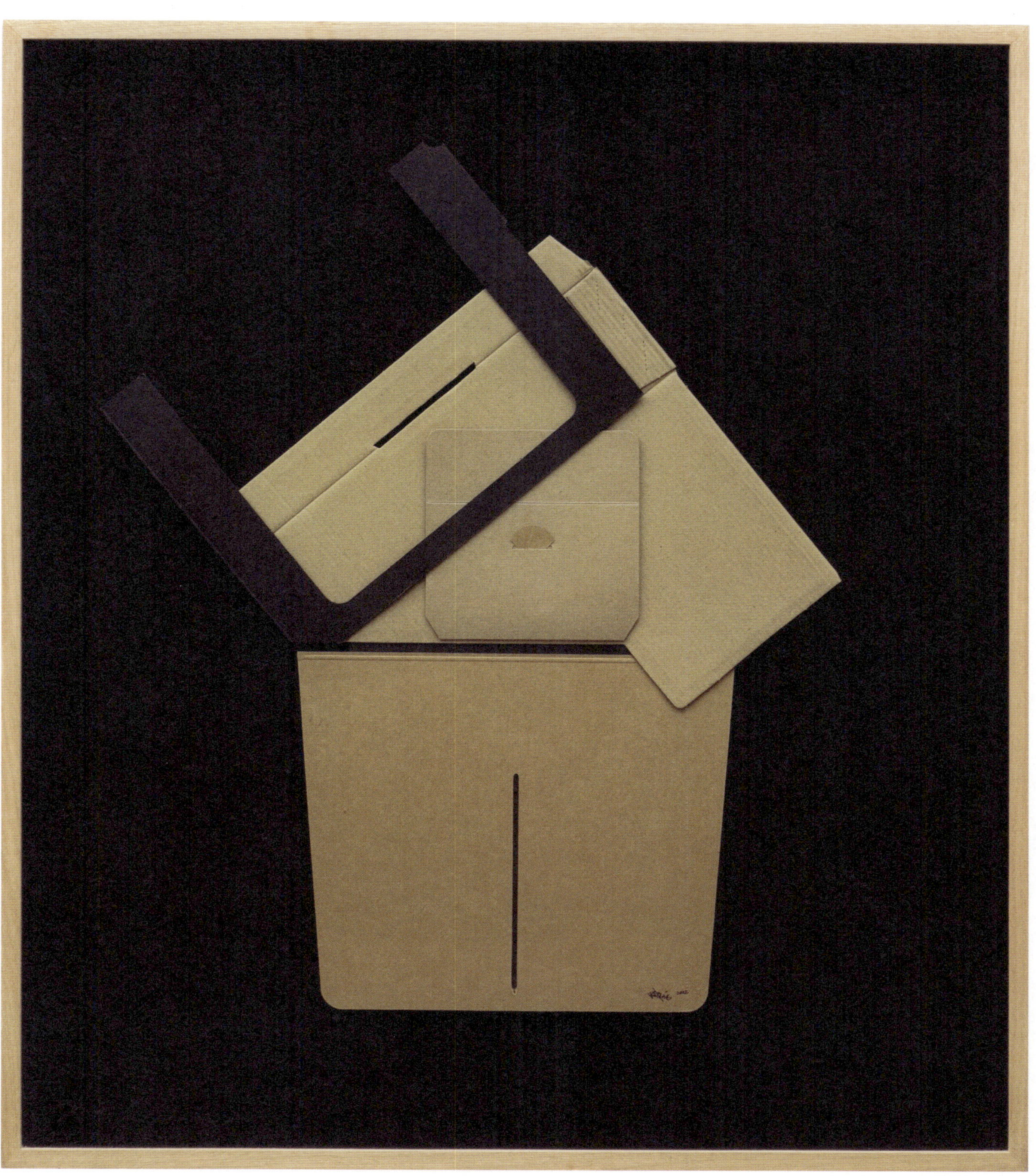

Brown Study #01, 2022, cardboard, 78.1 × 70.5 cm

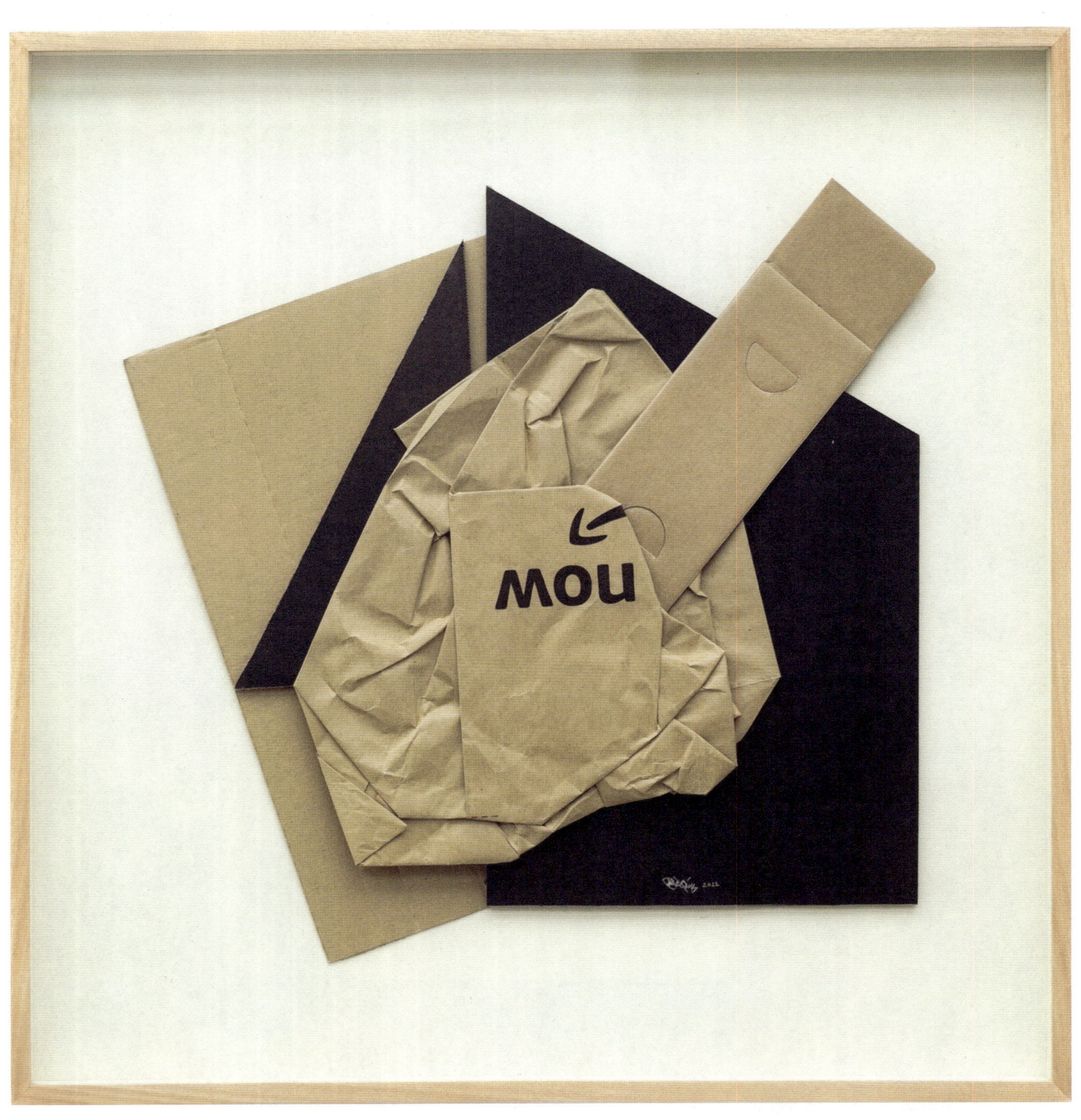

Brown Study #02, 2022, cardboard, 73 × 73 cm

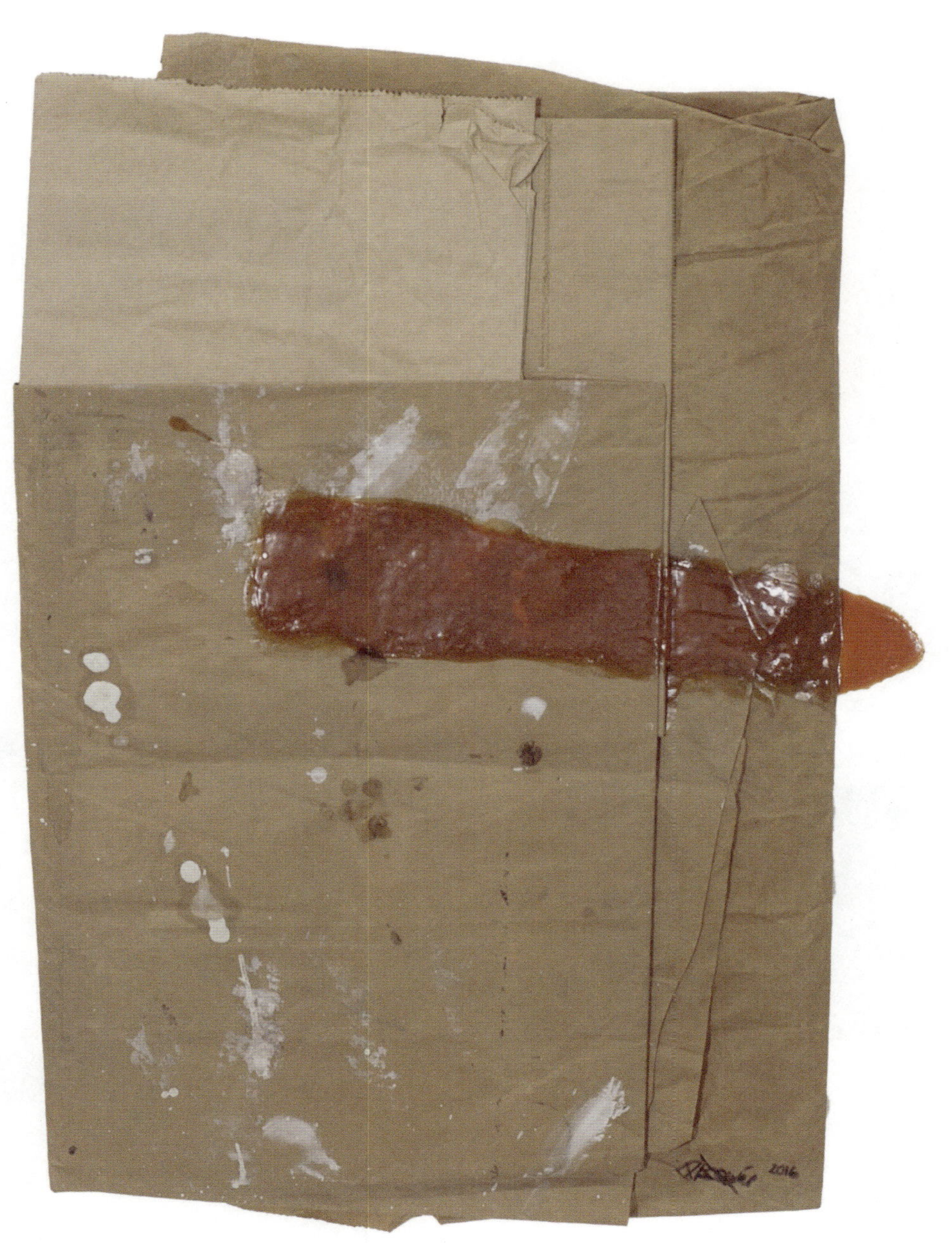

Untitled, 2016, collage, 66 × 48.3 cm

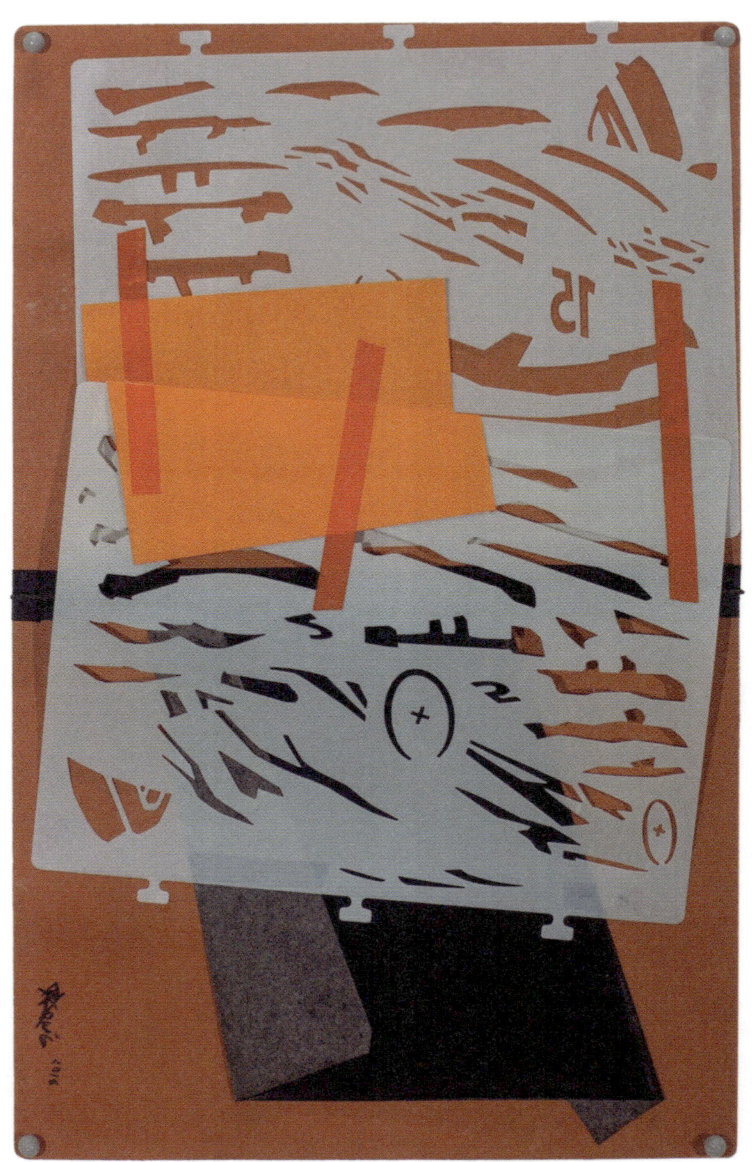

Untitled, 2016, collage, 66 × 48.3 cm

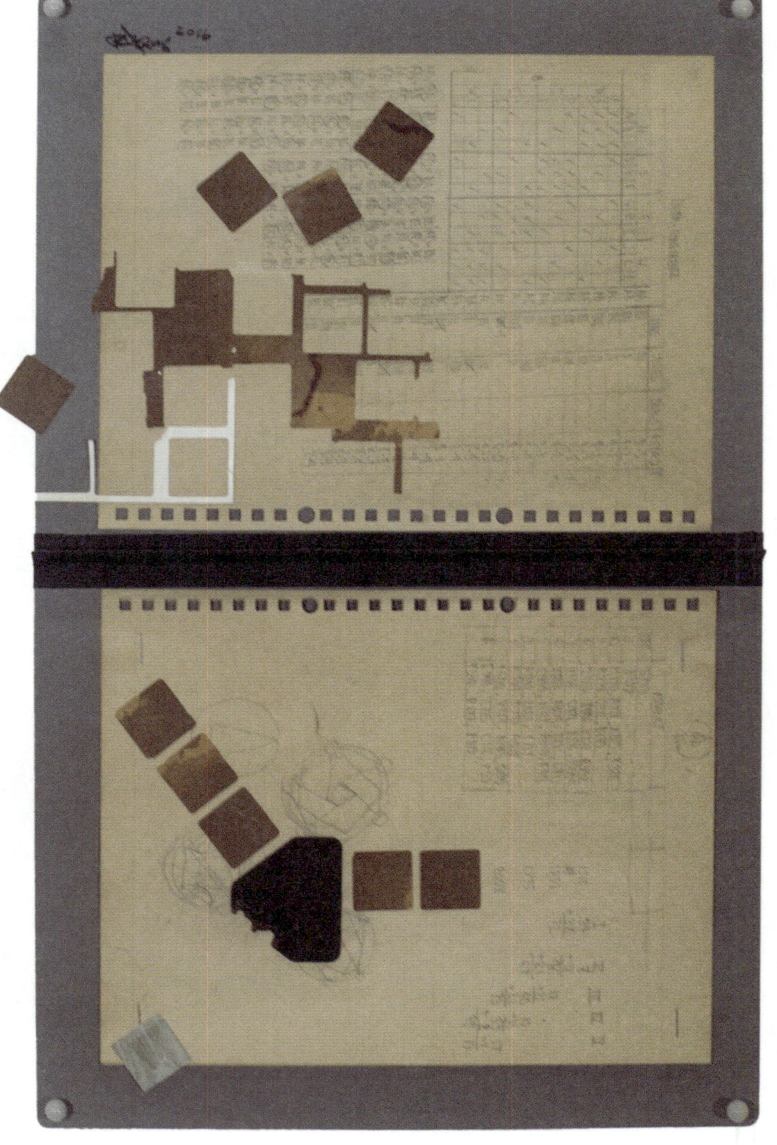

Untitled, 2016, collage, 66 × 48.3 cm

Untitled, 2016, collage, 48.3 × 66 cm

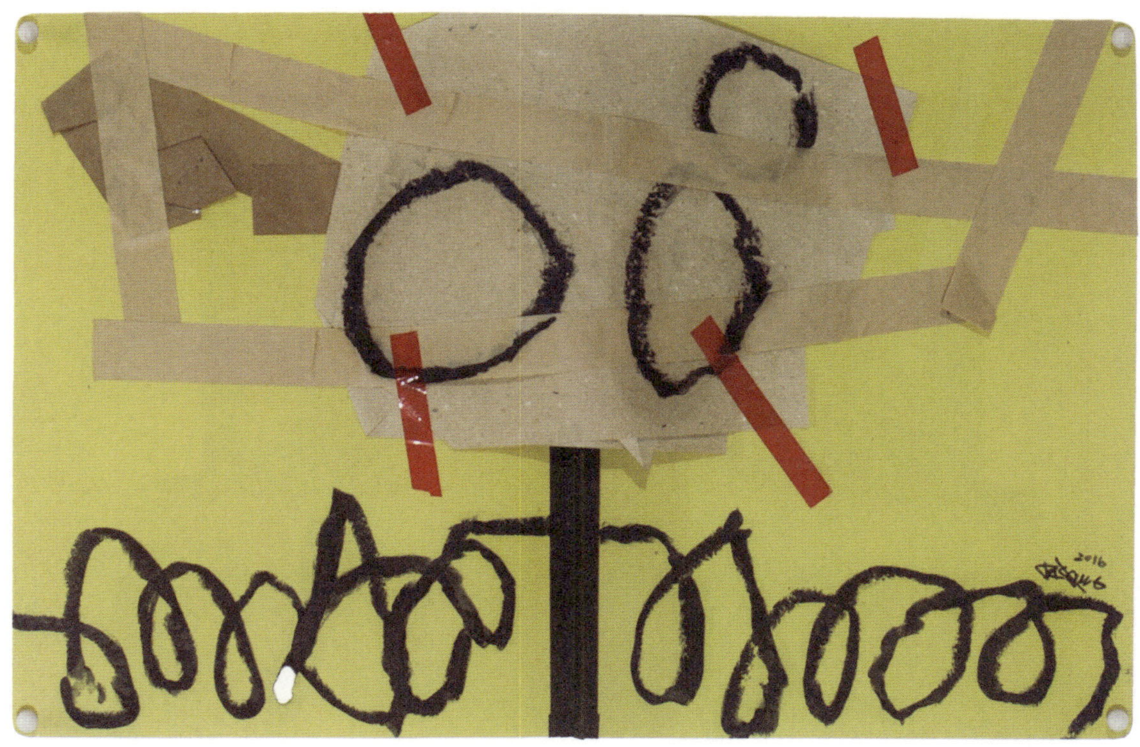

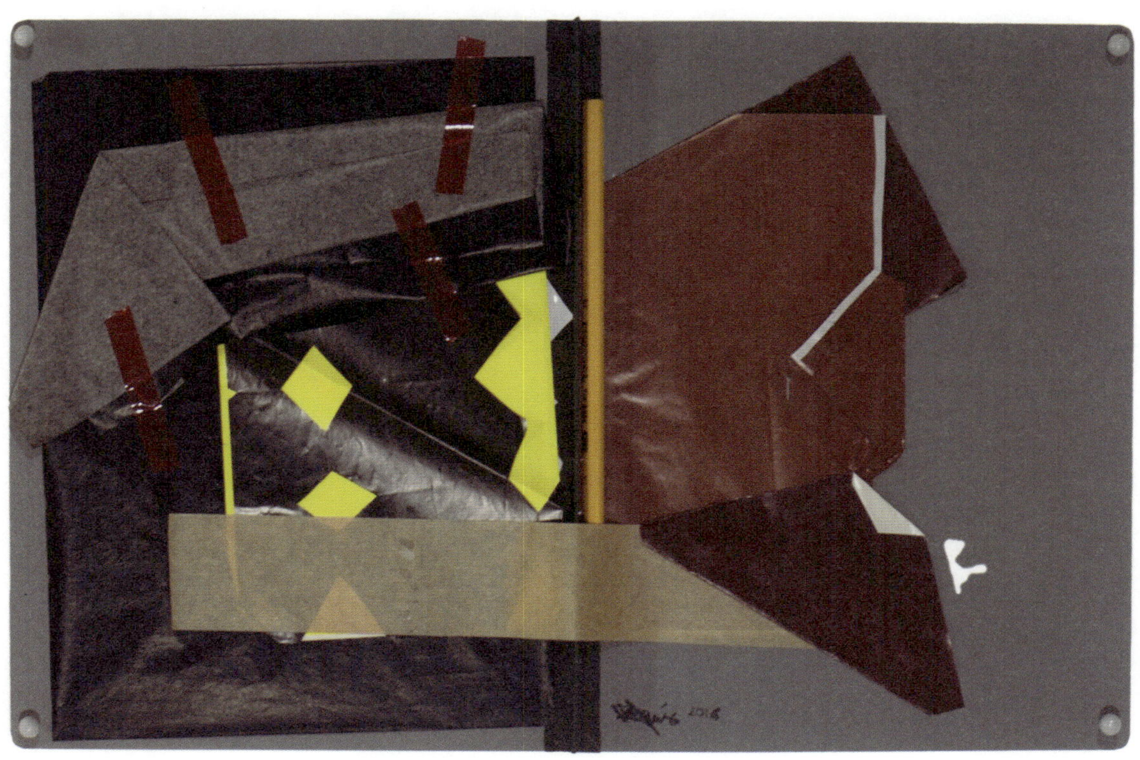

Untitled, 2016, collage, 48.3 × 66 cm

Untitled, 2016, collage, 66 × 48.3 cm

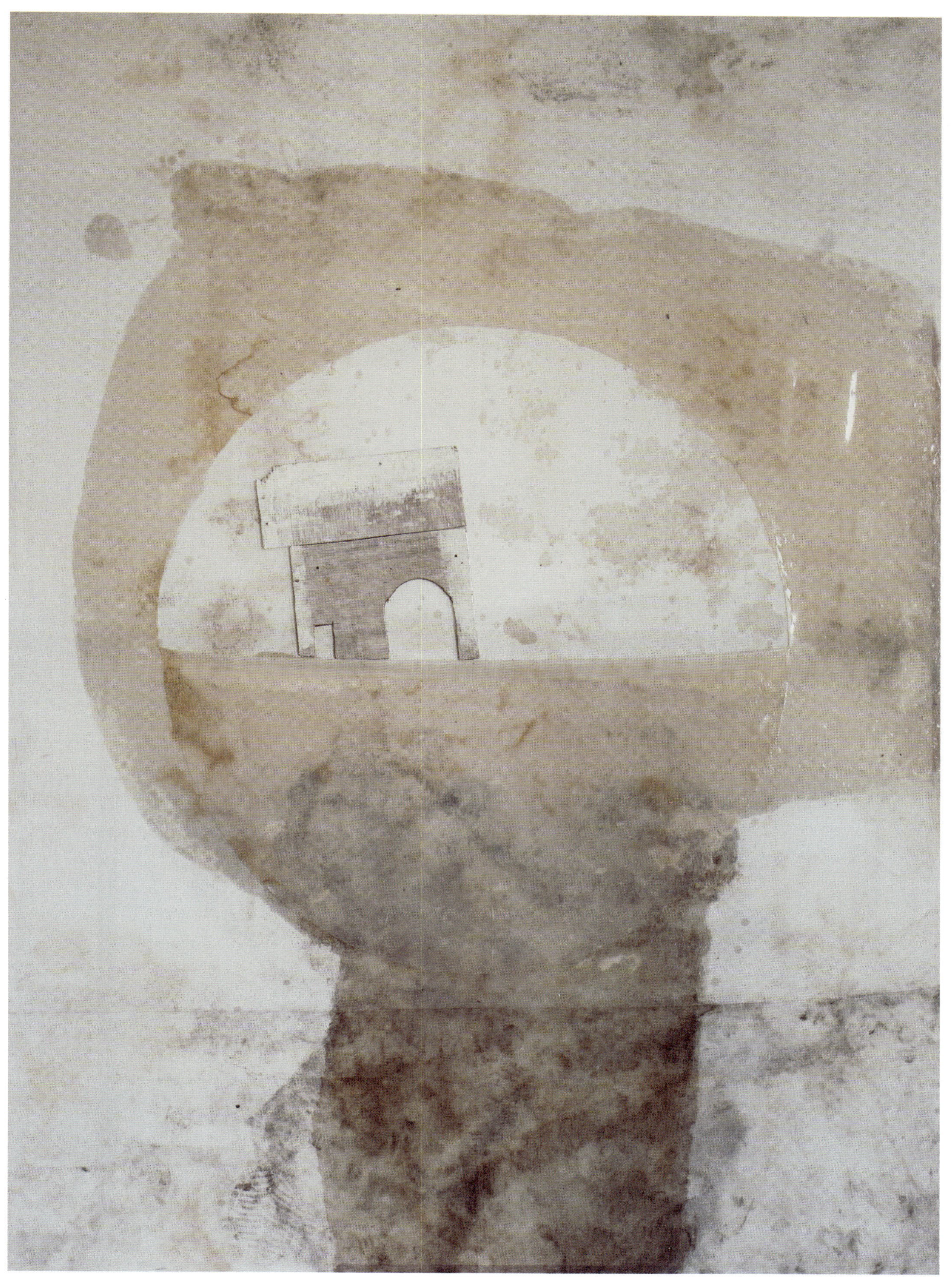

Focus Pocus, 2014, oil on canvas, 182.9 × 137.2 cm

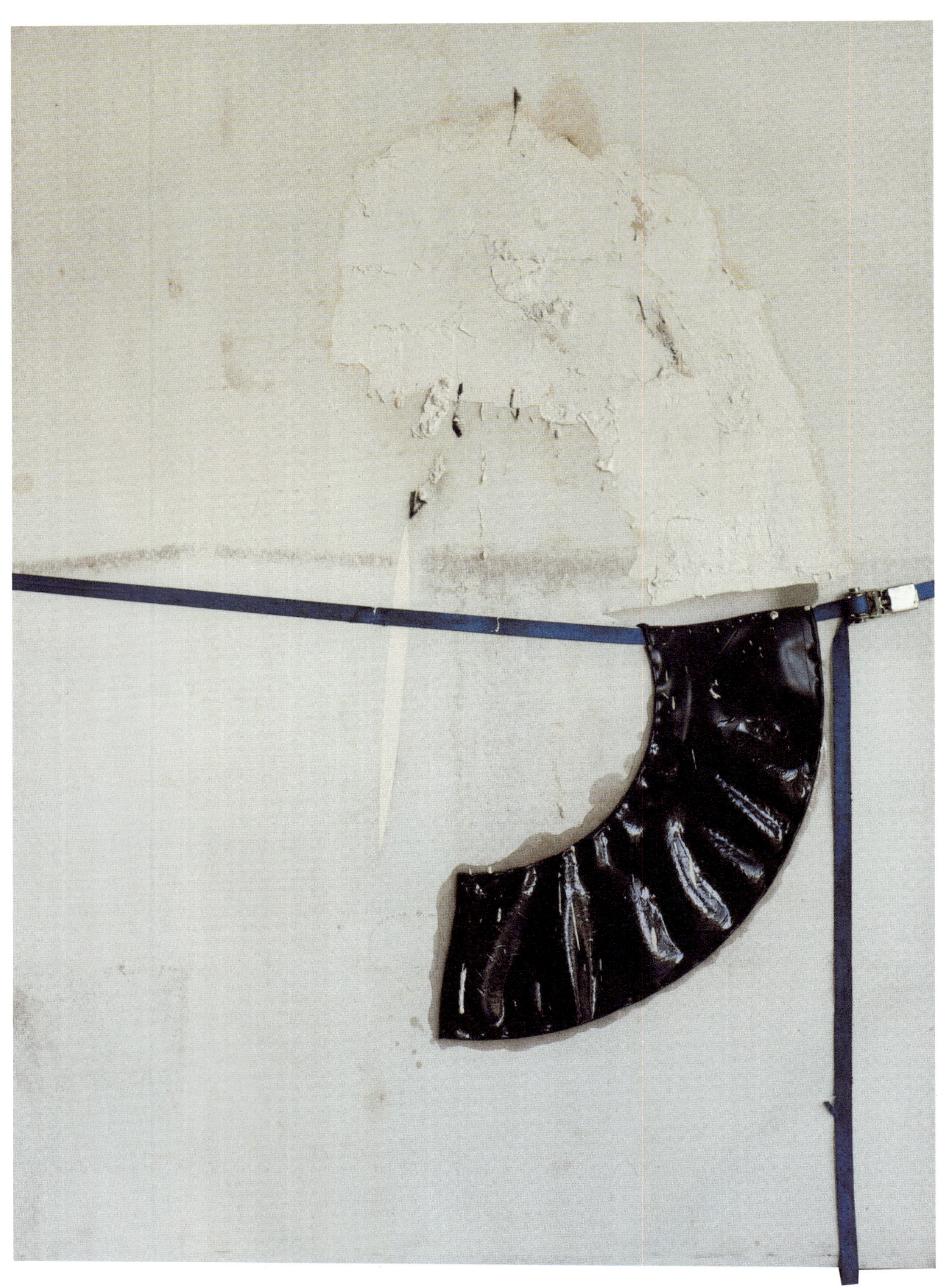

Drill Press, 2014, tire tube, ratchet, resin, oil on canvas, 182.9 × 137.2 cm

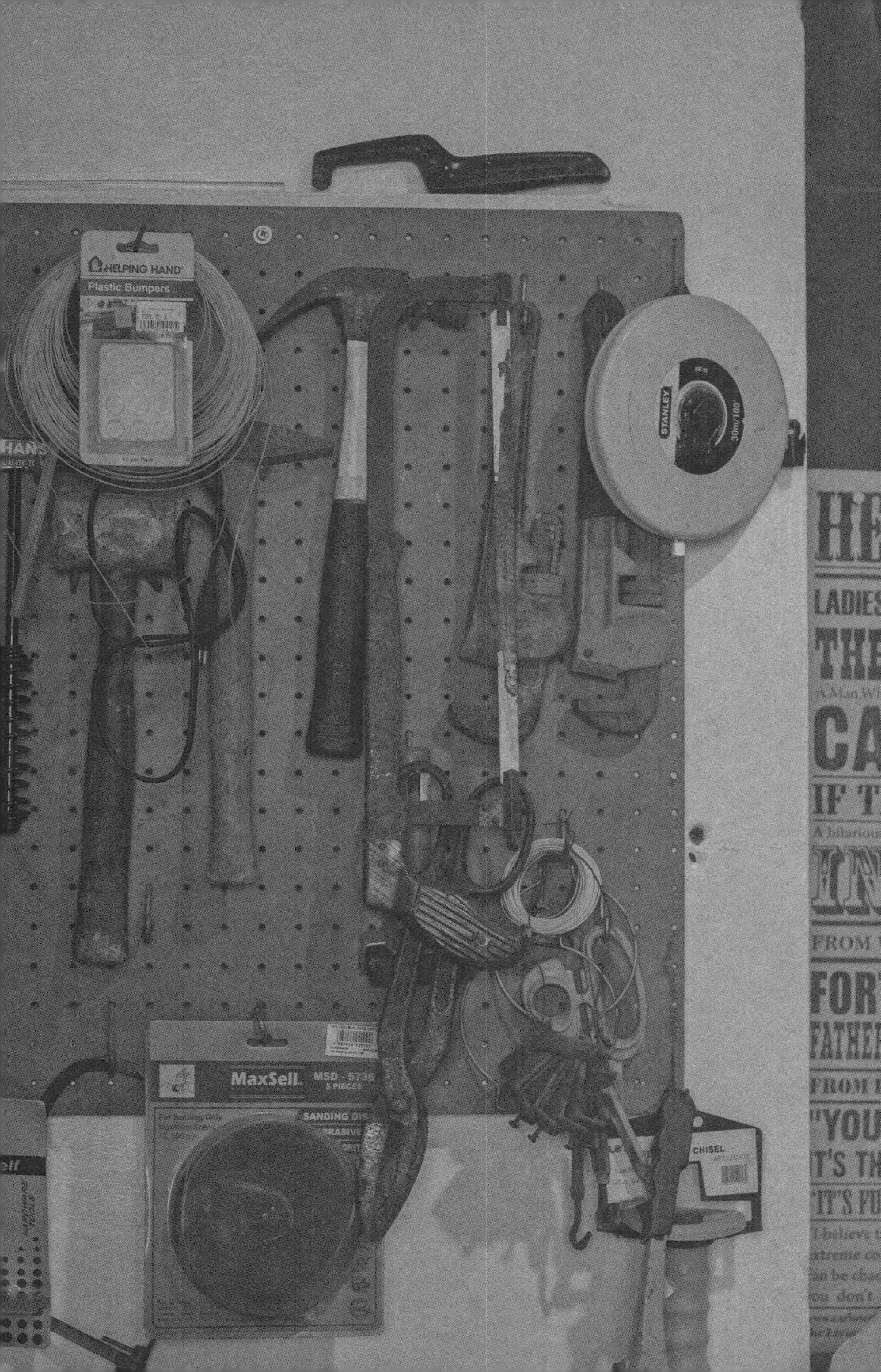
HELPING HAND
Plastic Bumpers
12 per Pack
STANLEY
30m/100'
MaxSell
MSD - 5736
5 PIECES
CHISEL
HARDWARE TOOLS
HEAR YE!
LADIES & GENTLEMEN,
THE PIED
A Man Who Is Trying To Change The Way
CARLOS
IF THESE
A hilarious irreverent educational
FROM WITHIN ITS WALLS
FORT SANTIAGO
FATHER BLANCO'S GARDEN
FROM PRE-HISPANIC
"YOU WILL LAUGH!
IT'S FUN! IT'S EXCITING!
I believe that Manila can be a reflection
extreme contrasts it can easily become an
spiritual, dirty and

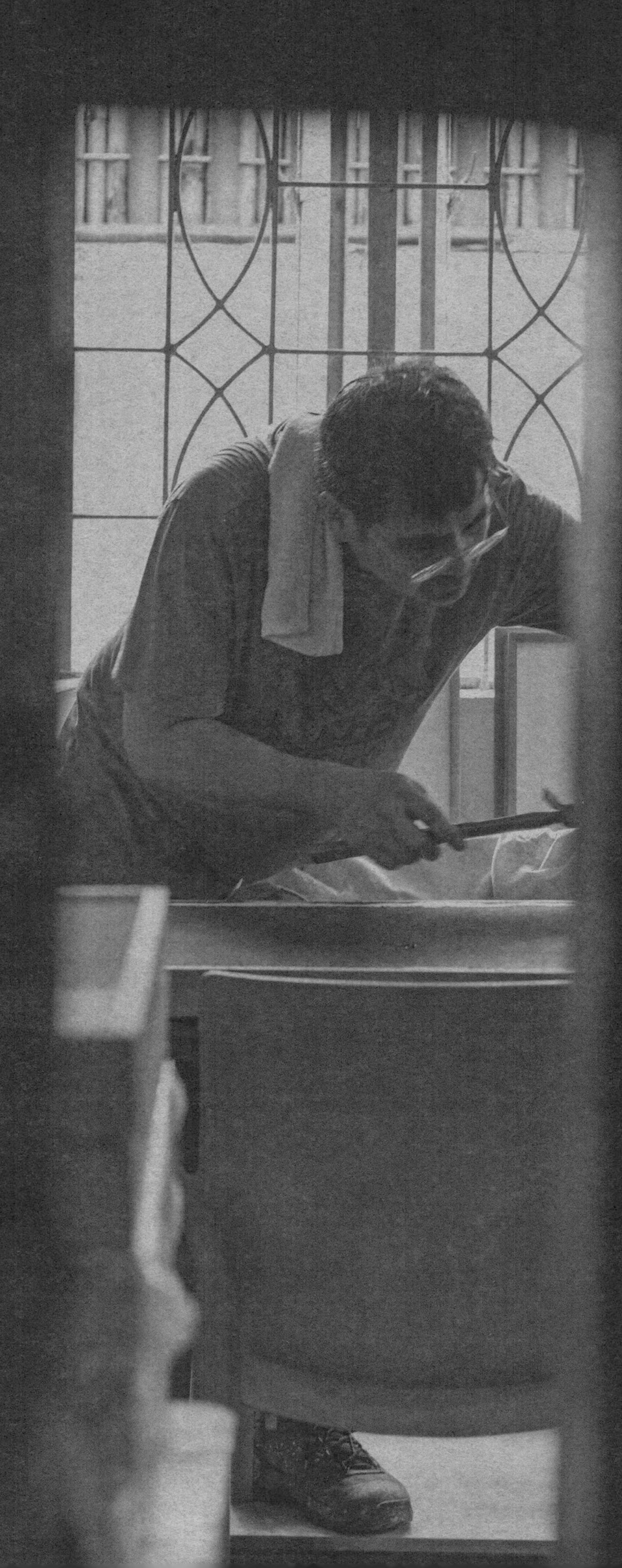

Bernardo Pacquing (b. 1967, Tarlac, Philippines; lives and works in Parañaque City, Philippines, and Singapore) is an artist broadening the expressive possibilities of abstraction in painting and sculpture. Incorporating diverse found objects that challenge conventional perceptions of aesthetic representation, form, and value, his work displaces the idea of unequivocal forms, introducing possibilities for the coexistence of affirmations and denials.

He was twice awarded the Grand Prize for the Art Association of the Philippines Open Art Competition (Painting, Non-Representation), in 1992 and 1999. He is also a recipient of the Cultural Center of the Philippines Thirteen Artists Award in 2000, an award given to exemplary artists in the field of contemporary visual art. Pacquing received a Freeman Fellowship Grant for a residency at the Vermont Studio Center in the United States.

Josephine V. Roque

Josephine V. Roque is a writer from Manila. She is the recipient of the Purita Kalaw-Ledesma Prize in Art Criticism and the Carlos Palanca Memorial Award for her essays. She graduated with an MFA in Creative Writing from De La Salle University, where she teaches art appreciation and literature. Her first book, *How to Ride a Train to Ulaanbaatar and Other Essays*, was published in 2021 by Penguin Random House SEA.

David Elliott

David Elliott is a British art historian, curator, writer, and teacher who has directed museums in Oxford (MoMA, 1976–96), Stockholm (Moderna Museet, 1996–2001), Tokyo (Mori Art Museum, founding director, 2001–06), Istanbul (Istanbul Modern, 2007) and in Guangzhou (Redtory Museum of Contemporary Art, vice director, senior curator, 2015–19). He has been the artistic director of major biennales in Sydney (2010), Kyiv (2012), Moscow (2014), and Belgrade (2016) and has taught Art History / Museum Studies at the University of Oxford (1986–96), National University of the Arts, Tokyo (2002–06), Humboldt University, Berlin (Rudolf Arnheim Professor in the History of Art, 2008), and the Chinese University of Hong Kong (2008–16). A specialist in Soviet and Russian avant-garde, as well as in modern and contemporary Asian art, he has published widely in these fields as well as on many other aspects of contemporary art. *Art and Trousers: Tradition and Modernity in Contemporary Asian Art*, was published by ArtAsiaPacific Foundation, Hong Kong, in 2020.

Russell Storer

Russell Storer is Senior Curator and Head of Curatorial Affairs at M+, Hong Kong. He was formerly Head Curator, International Art, at the National Gallery of Australia, Canberra (2022–24) where he co-curated the exhibitions "Jordan Wolfson: Body Sculpture" and "Haegue Yang: Changing From From To From." He has held curatorial positions at National Gallery Singapore (2014–22), co-curating exhibitions including "Minimalism: Space. Light. Object.," "Yayoi Kusama: Life is the Heart of a Rainbow," and "Between Worlds: Raden Saleh & Juan Luna"; at the Queensland Art Gallery | Gallery of Modern Art in Brisbane (2008–14), where he co-curated the 6th, 7th, and 8th Asia Pacific Triennials; and the Museum of Contemporary Art, Sydney (2001–08), where he developed exhibitions with artists including Simryn Gill, Matthew Ngui, Ugo Rondinone, and Juan Davila. He was a co-curator of the 3rd Singapore Biennale in 2011 and has written widely on Asian and Australian contemporary art.

Gary-Ross Pastrana

Gary-Ross Pastrana (b. 1977, Manila, Philippines; lives and works in Manila) is an artist deeply immersed in the philosophies surrounding concepts, objects, and art. His highly conceptual pieces, rich with poetic intensity, maintain an unobtrusive subtlety. Incorporating dynamic and nonsequential images along with other modes of study such as music and science, his creations form a new textual narrative. In 2004, he co-founded Future Prospects art space and in 2006, Pastrana received the Cultural Center of the Philippines' Thirteen Artists Award. Since then, he has shown at the Singapore Art Museum, Metropolitan Museum of the Philippines, the Jorge B. Vargas Museum, and was part of the 2019 The Art Encounters Biennial in Romania, 2019 Singapore Biennale, 2012 New Museum Triennale in New York, 2010 Aichi Triennale, and 2008 Busan Biennale. Other exhibitions include "Erstwhile Maps," CASE Space Revolution, Bangkok, Thailand (2020); "Every Step in the Right Direction," Singapore Biennale, Singapore (2019); "The Art Encounters Biennial," Romania (2019); "An Opera for Animals," Para Site, Hong Kong (2019), Rockbund Art Museum, Shanghai (2019); and "Utopia Hasn't Failed Me Yet," Silverlens, Manila (2018).

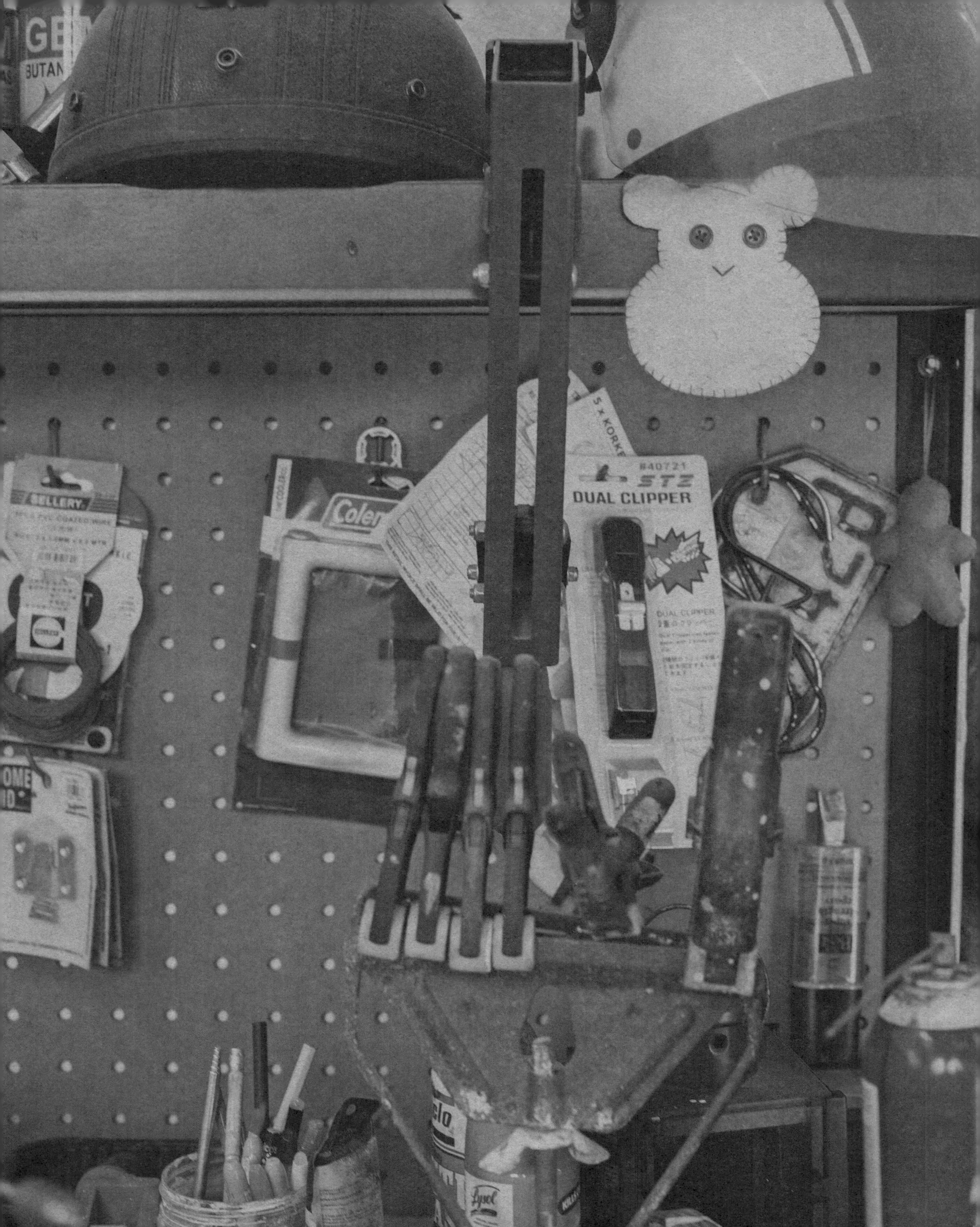
#40721
STZ
DUAL CLIPPER

Acknowledgments

The artist would like to thank:

His family
Peachy
Miguel
Sancho
Paloma

Silverlens Galleries
Moji Gonzales
Isa Lorenzo
Kach Pelayo
Rachel Rillo
Randell Tiongco

Essay contributors
David Elliott
Gary-Ross Pastrana
Josephine V. Roque
Russell Storer

ArtAsiaPacific
Elaine W. Ng

Fraser Muggeridge studio
Alexander Conway
Fraser Muggeridge

Everyday Materials: Bernardo Pacquing

First published 2024

Published by ArtAsiaPacific Foundation, Hong Kong

artasiapacific
foundation

ISBN: 978-988-70593-0-1

Printed in Hong Kong

Editors: Josephine V. Roque, Elaine W. Ng, and HG Masters
Texts: David Elliott, Gary Ross Pastrana, Russell Storer, Josephine V. Roque
Copyeditors: Isabelle Frank, Eti Bonn-Muller
Proofreader: Oliver Clasper
Designed by Fraser Muggeridge studio

Front cover: *"Untitled #3" After J.S. Bach's Partita No. 2 "Chaconne"*, 2019, assemblage, 100.3 × 152.4 × 81.3 cm

Inside front cover: *J.S. Bach's Double Violin Concerto*, 2008, two broken violins, leather, wall putty, house paint, tin can, 41.5 × 41.5 × 30 cm

p. 2: *1-Beta Chain series II no. 5* (detail), 2020, charcoal pencil on paper, 29.7 × 21 cm

p. 3: *1-Beta Chain series II no. 10* (detail), 2020 charcoal pencil on paper, 29.7 × 21 cm

pp. 118–19: Bernardo's Manila studio, 2022

p. 137: The artist's tools

p. 138: Bernardo in his Manila studio

p. 142: The artist's studio

p. 145: Bernardo's Manila studio, 2024

pp. 146–53: Bernardo's Manila studio, 2022

Inside back cover: *Wood work 05* (detail), 2019, assemblage on wood, 28 × 26 × 4.9 cm

Back cover: *Wood work 06*, 2019, assemblage on wood, 45.5 × 25 × 15.4 cm

Images on pp. 70–71 courtesy of West Gallery.
Fig. 2 on p. 76 courtesy of Galeria Duemila.
Fig. 9b on p. 82 courtesy Mark Saquing.
All other images © courtesy the artist and Silverlens.

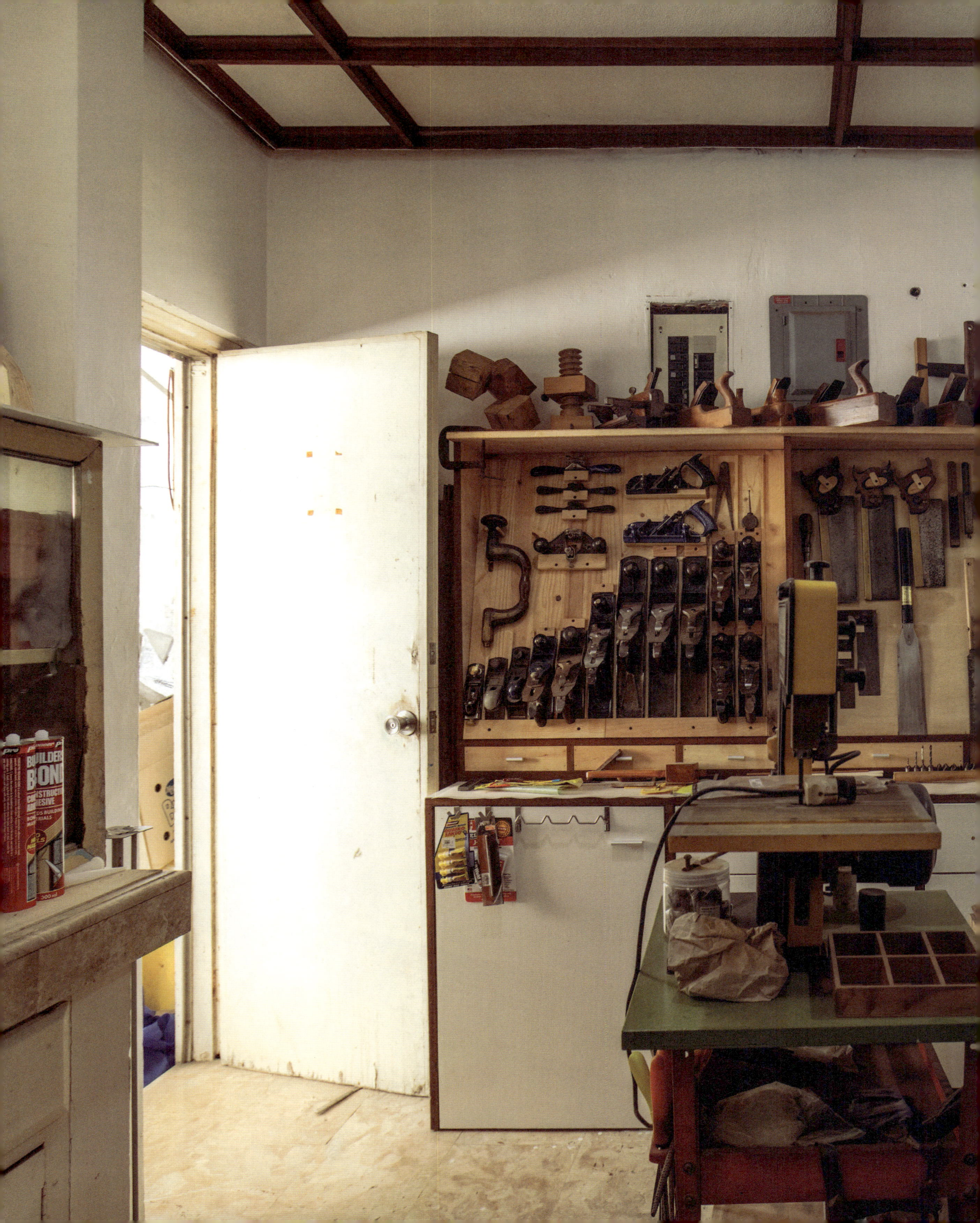
pro
300 ml

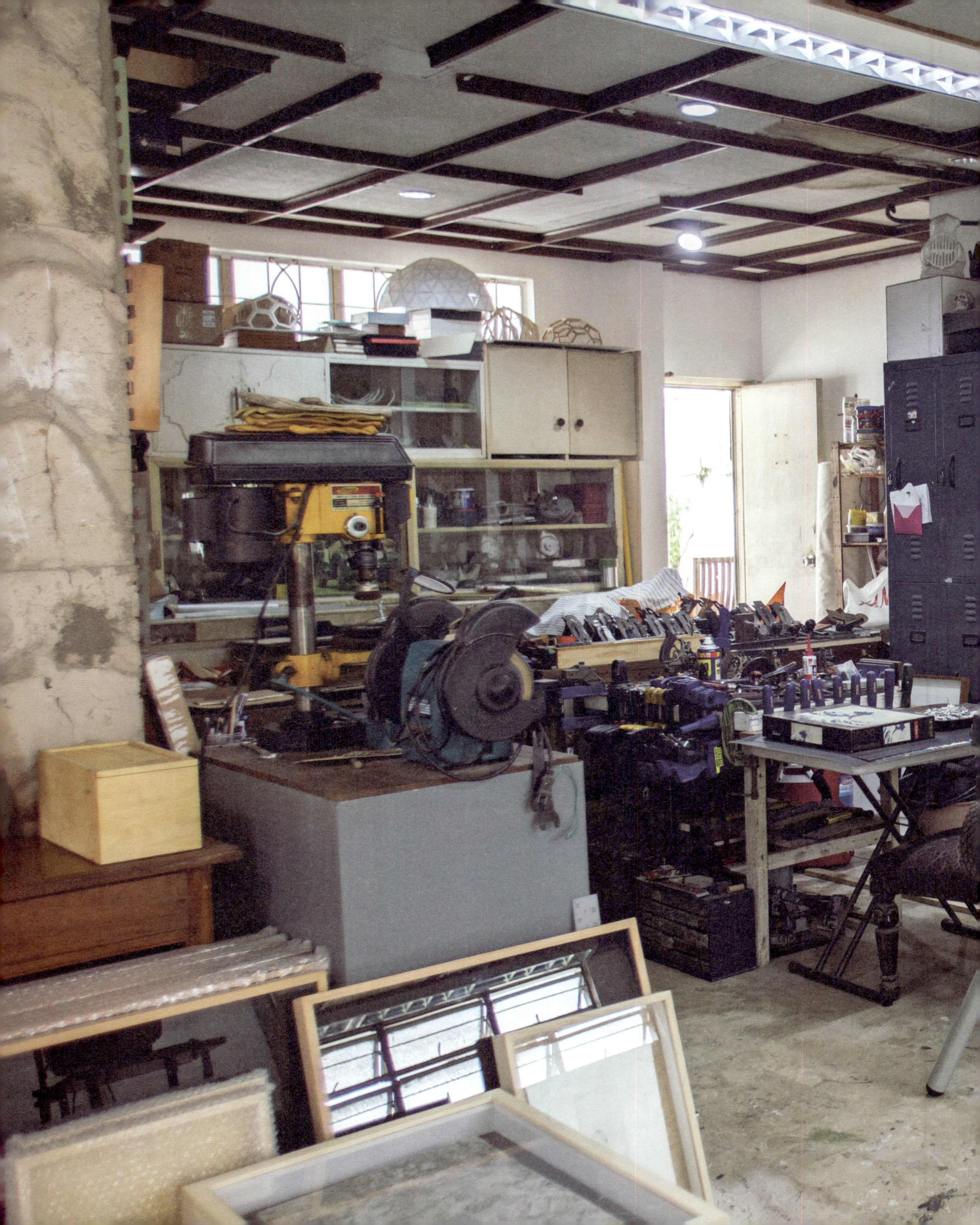

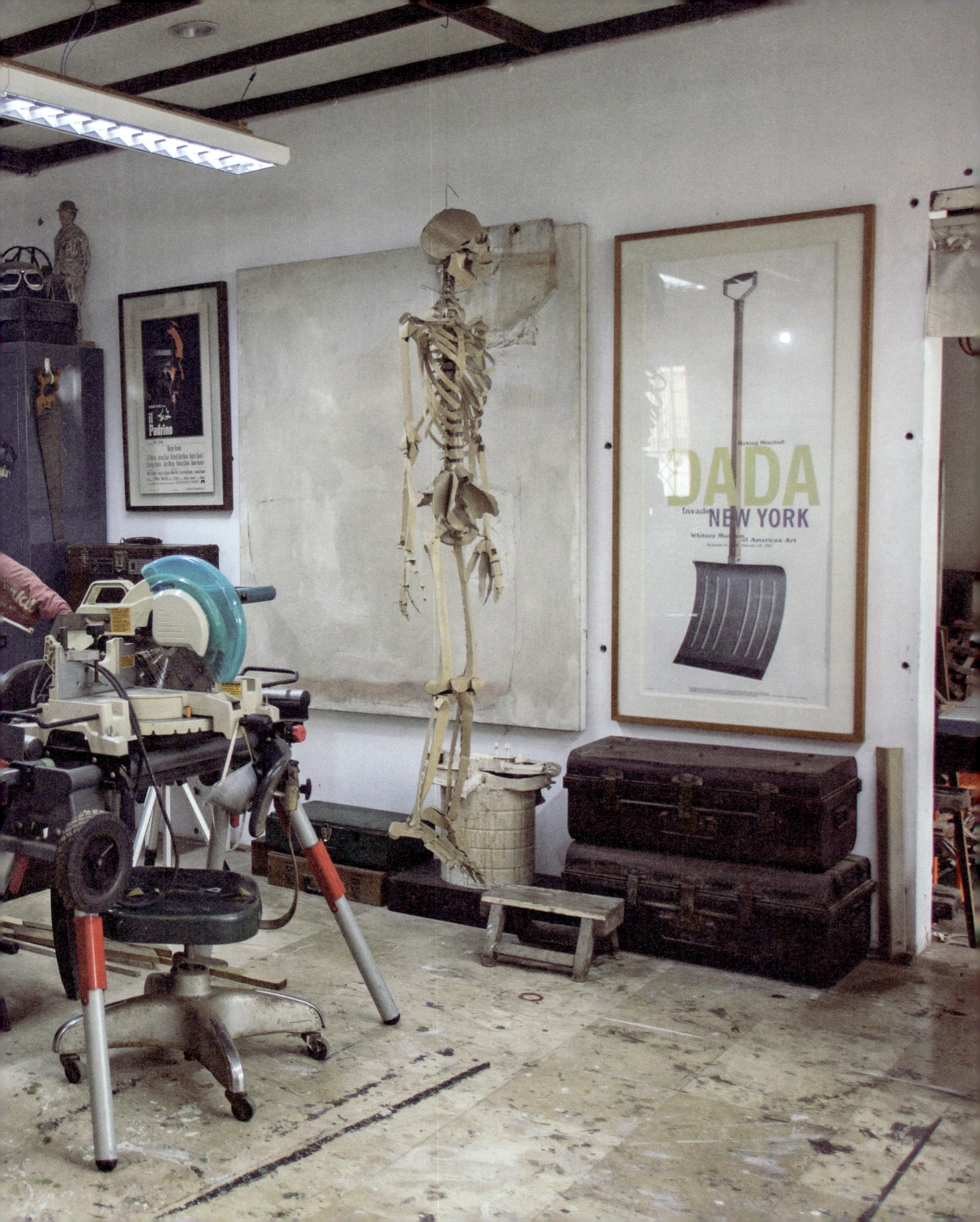
il Padrino
DADA
NEW YORK

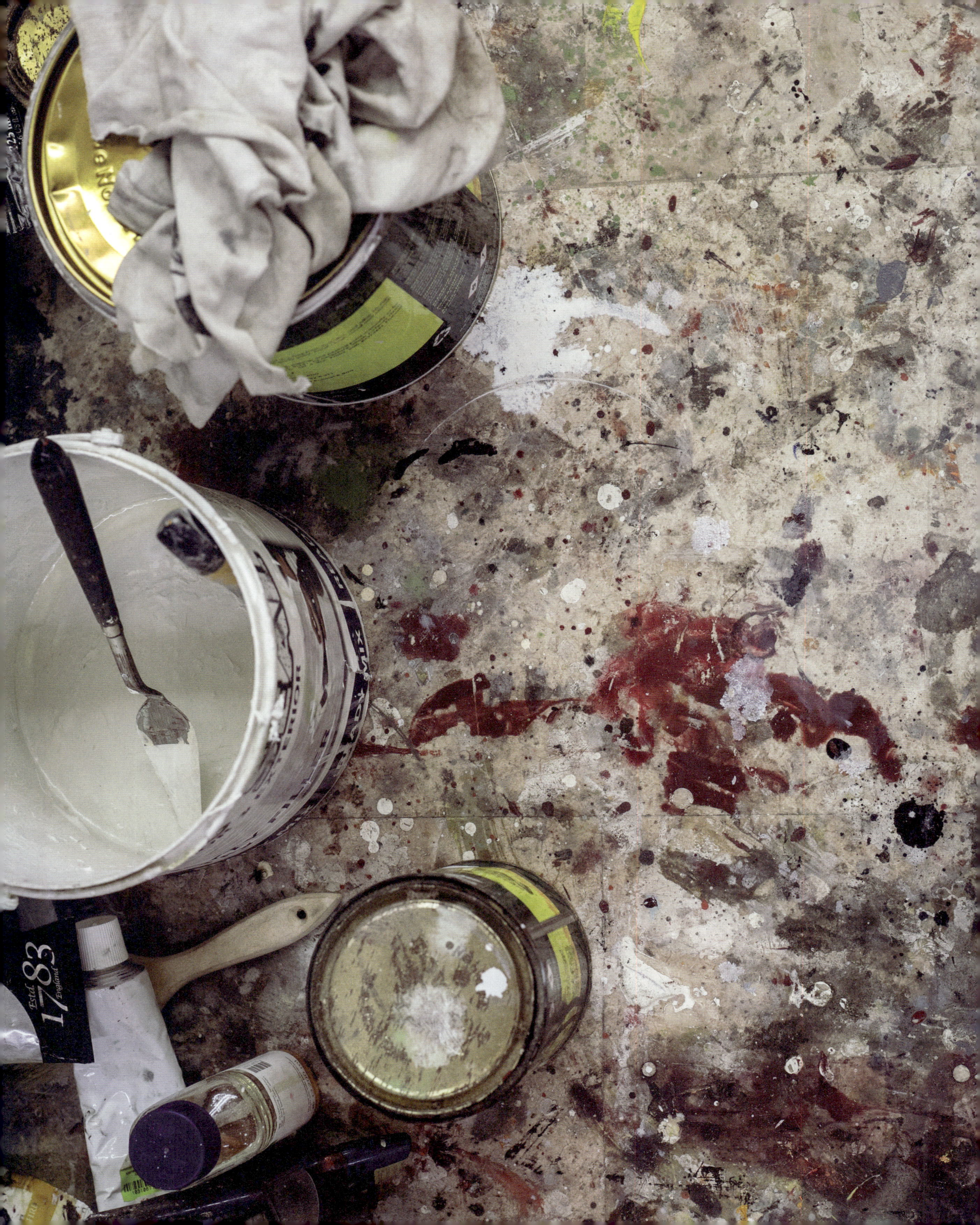
Estd
1783
England

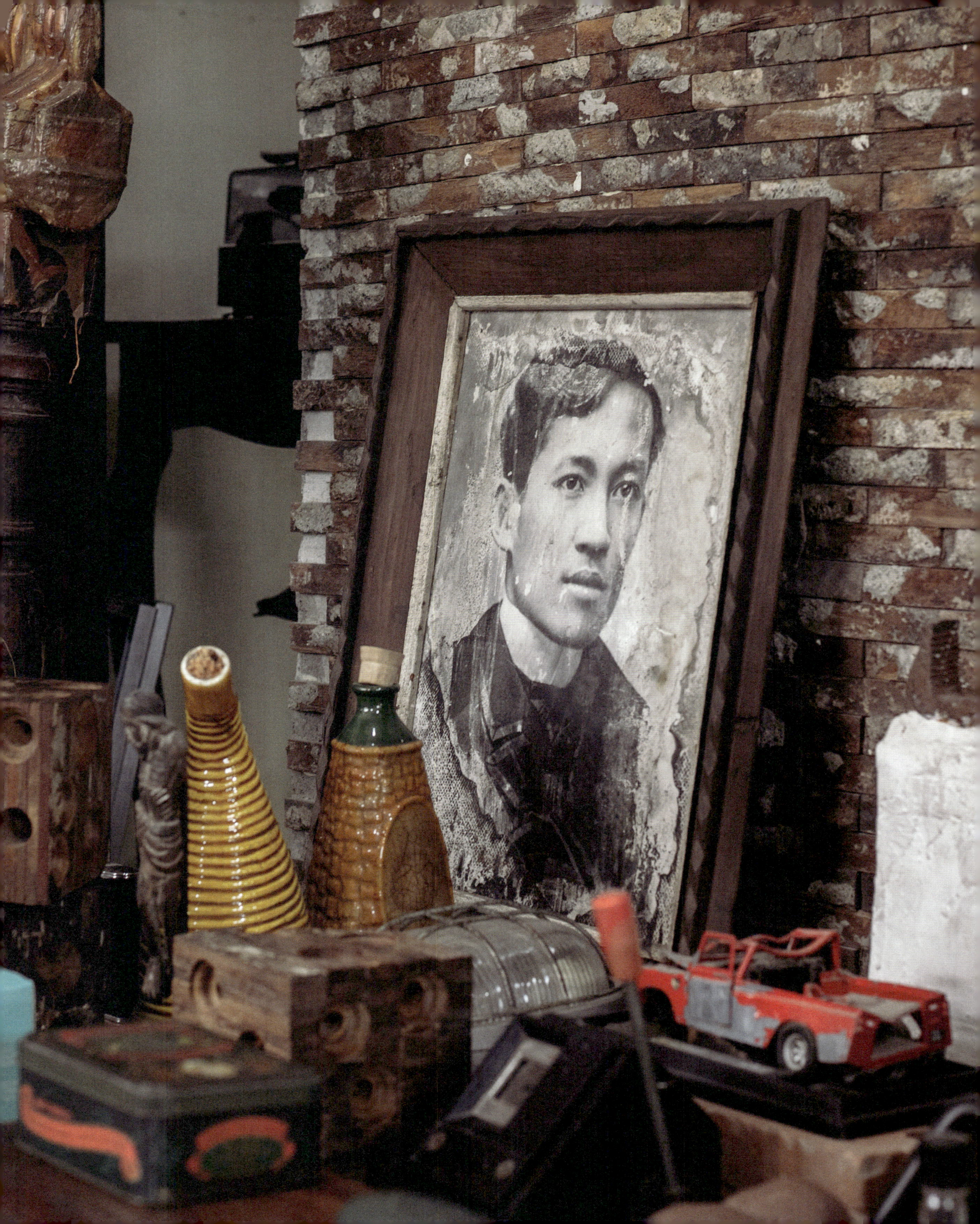

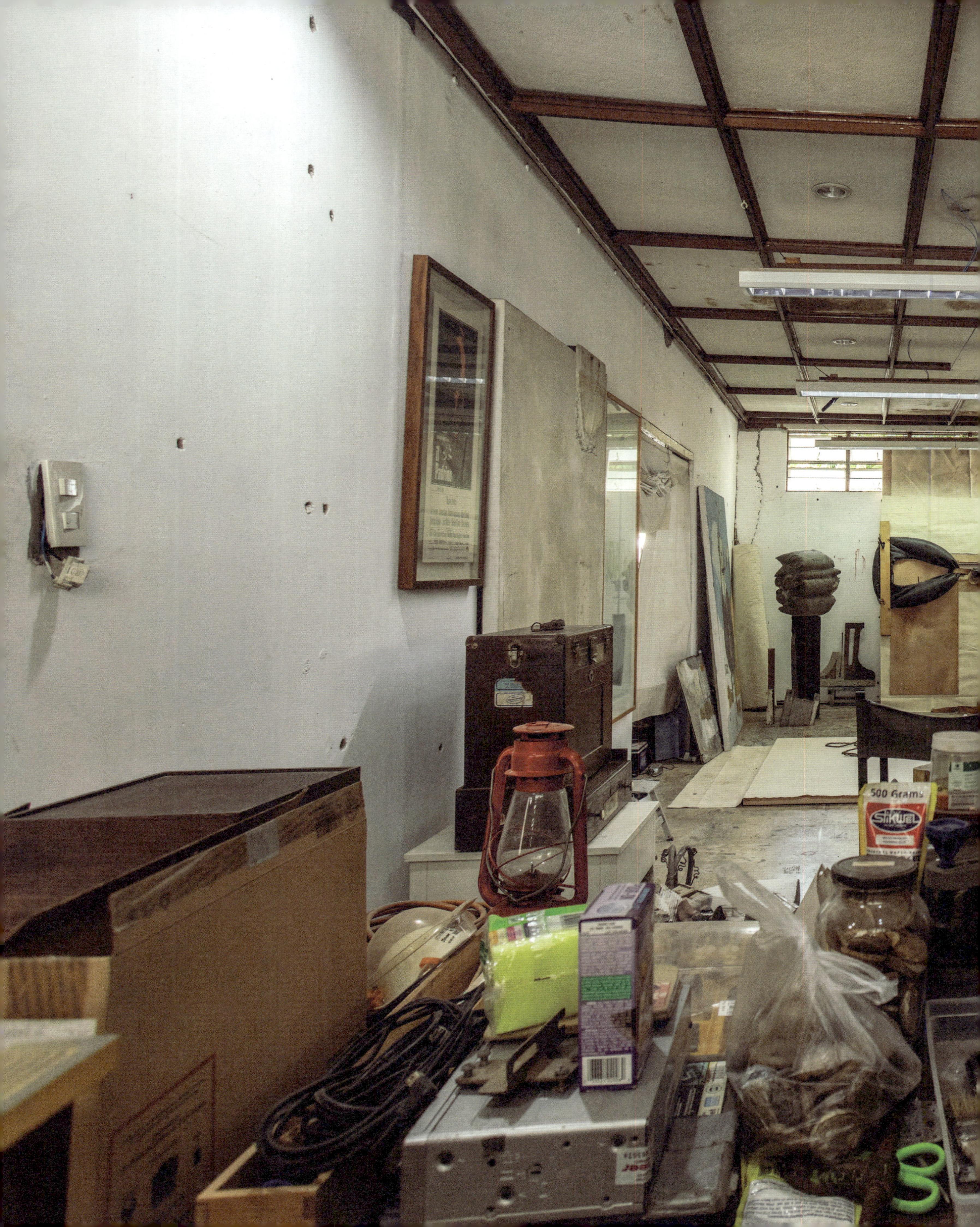
500 Grams
SIKWEL

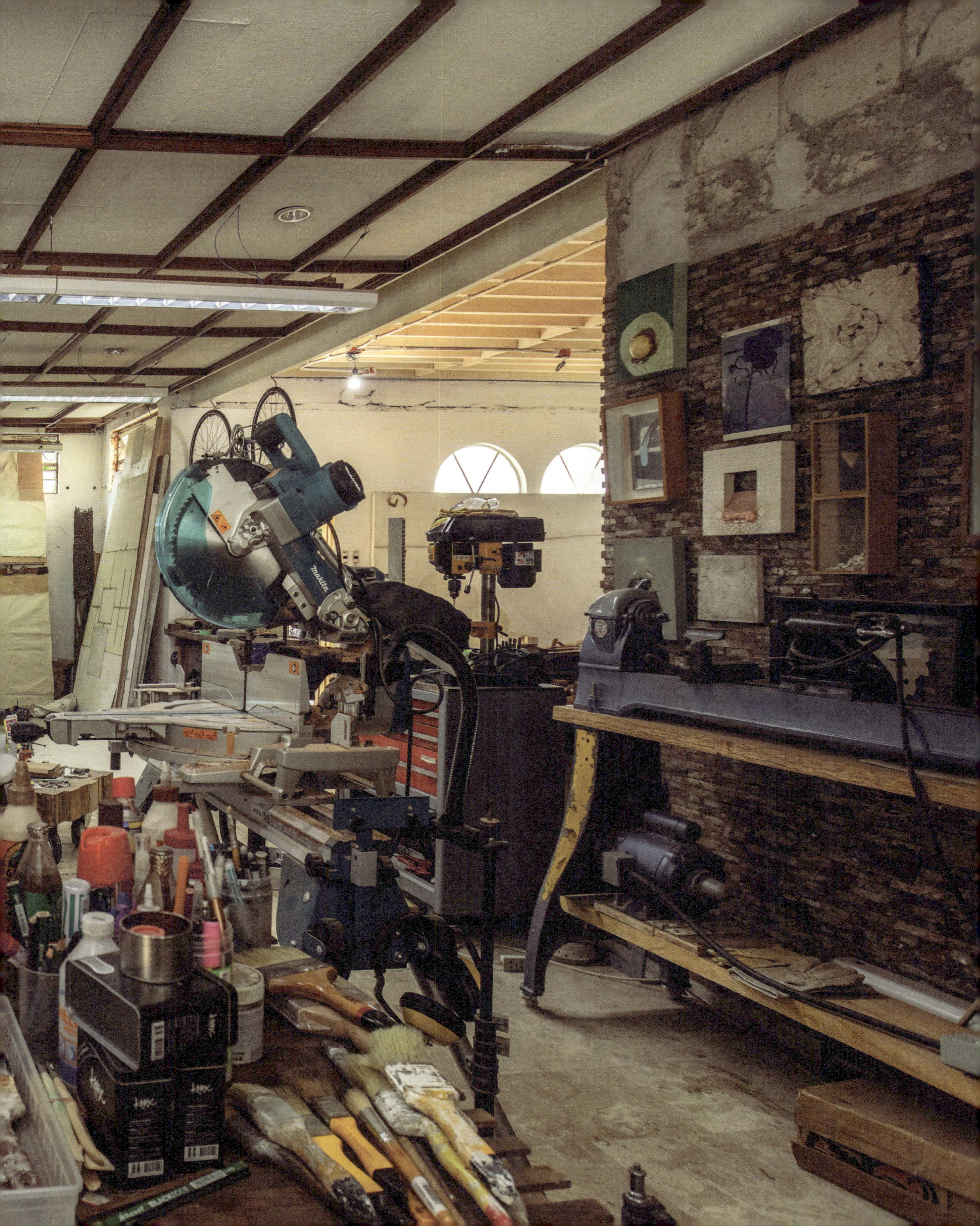
makita

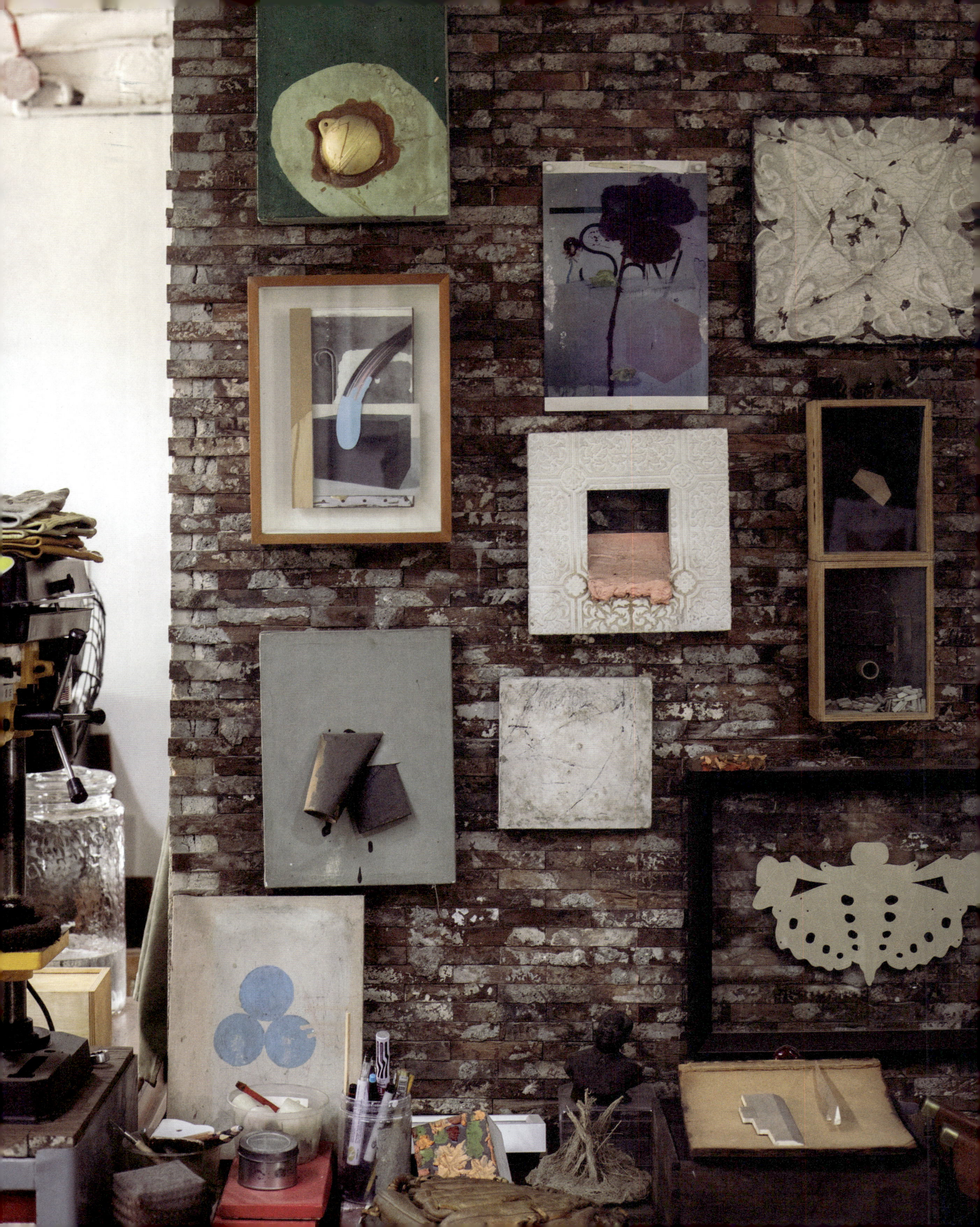